Download You...
Ebook T...

Your print purchase of *Social Work Leaders Through History,* **includes an ebook download** to the device of your choice—increasing accessibility, portability, and searchability!

Download your ebook today at:
http://spubonline.com/swleaders
and enter the access code below:

15XH46NU3

SPRINGER PUBLISHING COMPANY

springerpub.com

Jessica Lyn Gladden, PhD, LMSW, is a social worker in Grand Rapids, Michigan. She obtained her MSW from Grand Valley State University in 2003. After several years of providing therapy to survivors of sexual abuse and domestic violence she moved to Hawaii. While in Hawaii, Jessica had the opportunity to work in many areas, including with kids diagnosed on the autism spectrum, in crisis work, and in leading an Assertive Community Treatment Team. She returned to Michigan and completed her PhD at Michigan State University in 2012. Jessica pursued her interest in refugee work, completing her dissertation on the coping strategies of refugee women living in Kenya after visiting the Kakuma Refugee Camp, then opening a nonprofit support program for refugees in Grand Rapids. She has taught at several universities in Michigan since 2008, with her primary areas of focus being in policy, diversity, and foundational clinical skills. Jessica is currently training to be a yoga therapist to assist individuals with trauma histories.

Source: Photo by Matt Jarrells.

Social Work Leaders Through History

Lives and Lessons

Jessica Lyn Gladden, PhD, LMSW

SPRINGER PUBLISHING COMPANY

Springer Publishing Company, LLC
11 West 42nd Street
New York, NY 10036
www.springerpub.com

Acquisitions Editor: Kate Dimock
Compositor: Exeter Premedia Services Private Ltd.

ISBN: 978-0-8261-4644-1
ebook ISBN: 978-0-8261-4645-8

Instructor's Materials: Qualified instructors may request supplements by emailing textbook@springerpub.com:
Instructor's PowerPoints: 978-0-8261-4646-5
Sample Syllabus: 978-0-8261-4647-2

The author and the publisher of this Work have made every effort to use sources believed to be reliable to provide information that is accurate and compatible with the standards generally accepted at the time of publication. The author and publisher shall not be liable for any special, consequential, or exemplary damages resulting, in whole or in part, from the readers' use of, or reliance on, the information contained in this book. The publisher has no responsibility for the persistence or accuracy of URLs for external or third-party Internet websites referred to in this publication and does not guarantee that any content on such websites is, or will remain, accurate or appropriate.

Library of Congress Cataloging-in-Publication Data

Names: Gladden, Jessica Lyn, author.
Title: Social work leaders through history: lives and lessons / Jessica Lyn Gladden, PhD, LMSW.
Description: New York, NY: Springer Publishing Company, LLC, [2018] | Includes bibliographical references and index.
Identifiers: LCCN 2017060769| ISBN 9780826146441 | ISBN 9780826146458 (ebook)
Subjects: LCSH: Social workers—Biography. | Social service—History.
Classification: LCC HV40.3 .G53 2018 | DDC 361.3092/2—dc23
LC record available at https://lccn.loc.gov/2017060769

Contact us to receive discount rates on bulk purchases.
We can also customize our books to meet your needs.
For more information please contact: sales@springerpub.com

Printed in the United States of America.

Contents

Preface

I have been teaching foundational policy classes to graduate and undergraduate social work students for some time. To me, the most intriguing part of the class was often minimalized—the history of social work and the people who created a whole new profession. While I tried to find supplemental materials to bring into the classroom about the people behind the profession, I could never find what I was looking for. Several texts, such as Jansson's *The Reluctant Welfare State* and the edited text by Wichers DuMez entitled *Celebrating Social Work: Faces and Voices of the Formative Years* provided brief snapshots of many of the leaders and creators of social work. However, this was not as in-depth as I wanted. I wanted to find a book that would present much more than just an overview of the person's work. I wanted to learn about the individuals, their families, their personalities—to see the real people behind the work.

Several years ago I attended a Council on Social Work Education's Annual Conference and began to ask various publishers if there was a book available that covered our social work leaders in greater detail. The answer I always received was no, but that other educators had also asked for something along these lines. I (perhaps foolishly) decided that if nothing had been written, I should just write it and make it available to others. This started the 2-year journey of researching and writing this book. As many authors probably say when writing their first book, had I known what was ahead of me in this project, I might not have done it. I had not expected some of the challenges that came up along the way. I did not expect that I would be traveling to multiple states to read through archived collections at other universities. I didn't expect to meet the relatives and descendants of these fine people. I had not planned on needing to interview people to have enough material to be able to write about them. All of this took place anyway.

Each time I approached someone about being included as either a person featured in this book or about his or her relatives, I did so with trepidation. Who was I to talk to them and ask them to be in a book? I'm just a young professor from a small university in Michigan who has never written a book. I'm not a social work historian. Yet each time, I was met with warmth and a genuine interest in the project. People seemed to feel honored to be included in my little project. I will be forever grateful to the people who I have interviewed for their responses. Tomlin Coggeshell, the grandson of Frances Perkins, was even kind enough to buy me lunch and take me on a tour of Perkins's home when I turned up in Maine. Without such positive encouragement, I likely would not have had the courage to continue contacting other people when needed.

Selecting the leaders to be represented in this book was not an easy task. There are so many more individuals who made enormous contributions to social work than are included in these few pages. I wanted a text that would flow with the timeline of the course I was teaching, something that would go through the various periods of history and provide just one example of an individual for each period during that time frame. This was extremely limiting in so many ways. So many of our early leaders should be included—individuals such as Florence Kelley, Sophonisba Breckinridge, Bertha Reynolds, and Josephine Shaw Lowell, just to name a very few. But I did not set out to write only about the early times of social work. Selecting leaders of the 21st century turned out to be a different kind of challenge. There are so many social workers out there doing amazing things and bringing the profession to a whole new level. It is also difficult to know what areas of social work in current times will become a key part of our history in future years. So how can one possibly choose who to write about? My publisher suggested including several leaders in shorter sections for the last chapter, which I thought was a brilliant idea. It was still a struggle to determine how to select individuals. I ended up choosing five areas that I personally think are important trends in social work, then selecting an individual who worked in each of these fields. My students were actually quite helpful in this. They had to do a 15-minute presentation on leaders in different eras as an assignment; their assignments gave me some excellent ideas.

Some of the individuals covered in this book have multiple books written about them already. For these chapters, simply sorting through what was available and picking out what I hoped to feature was a difficult undertaking. Others have almost nothing published on them, other than perhaps on their websites from their universities. This was a different sort of challenge: It did not seem adequate to merely reproduce what little was written about them. I attempted to provide a new perspective on these people as best as I could. I hope that beyond anything else, any student who may read this book will be able to see each of these people as having his or her own unique personality. The most enjoyable part of writing these chapters was including those little stories that made them all feel like real people, not just stuffy historical figures in old books. However, for some individuals, these stories were not easy to find. Even the changing social times caused the meanings behind situations and relationships to shift, and I could not always find the words to represent people as well as I would have liked. A good example of this is the impossibility of knowing about some of the primary relationships from people early on in the book. Historians have speculated about the sexuality and primary relationships of many of our early female leaders. Some of these women elected to keep their sexuality and intimate partners a private affair, which needs to be respected. I would love to be able to share some of the diversity of these women who today would likely identify as lesbians, especially to encourage our students who may identify as LGBTQ. This was not always possible as literature can only show us so much. I also did not want to "spread rumors" if something was not recorded and widely known about the individual. I tried to find some balance in these issues. The article "My Ever Dear" by Fredriksen-Goldsen, Lindhorst, Kemp, and Walters (2009), which is discussed in Chapter 4, provides a much better analysis of this issue.

I hope that any student who reads this book will be inspired by the greatness of these leaders. I also hope that readers will be able to see pieces of themselves reflected in these individuals and, perhaps, aspire to be like them. Current social work students are the social work leaders and educators of tomorrow and will guide the profession into the future. If, by reading this work, they are encouraged to do more and, in fact, do more, I will feel that my mission is complete.

My greatest thanks goes out to the many people who assisted in this work. Tomlin Coggeshall was a gracious host and provided me with the image of Frances Perkins as a loving grandmother. Dr. Frederic Reamer, ever the standard in ethics, surprised me with the speediness of his responses—each time I emailed him a question, he responded within a few hours. Dr. Jill Littrell took such interest in this project that she kindly gave me feedback on the first chapter, which reviews the overall history, a difficult topic to squeeze into one chapter. Dr. Doreen Elliott had great patience with me as I tried to gather information on Dr. Nazneen Mayadas, about whom much more should be published. I was incredibly impressed with the professionalism, humility, and kindness of each of the people I communicated with while attempting to put together this project.

I will end this Preface by echoing the sentiments of Mary Richmond. As social workers, we must know our history and where we come from. We can learn from the strengths and mistakes of those who came before us. By knowing our history, we ourselves are better known. We bring this knowledge into the future to guide the profession to wherever it needs to go. My best wishes to the future leaders of social work.

Jessica Lyn Gladden, PhD, LMSW

REFERENCE

Fredriksen-Goldsen, K., Lindhorst, T., Kemp, S., & Walters, K. (2009). "My ever dear:" Social work's "lesbian" foremothers—A call for scholarship. *Affilia*, 24(3), 325–336. doi:10.1177/0886109909337707

As an aid in using *Social Work Leaders Through History* in course work, qualified instructors can access the book's ancillary materials (PowerPoints and sample syllabi) by sending an e-mail to textbook@springerpub.com.

Social Work Leaders
Through History

A Social Worker at Ellis Island, 1926.

Source: From The Miriam and Ira D. Wallach Division of Art, Prints and Photographs: Photography Collection, the New York Public Library. (1905). Retrieved from http://digitalcollections.nypl.org/items/510d47d9-4e90-a3d9-e040-e00a18064a99

CHAPTER 1

The Creation and Development of the Social Work Profession

"A profession which did not know its own history, which was indifferent to the memory of the men and women responsible for its making, would still be a shambling and formless thing."

—Richmond (1923/1930, p. 556)

Social work is relatively new as a profession; however, people have been engaging in social work activities for many, many years. Popple and Leighninger (2010) give examples of what we might consider *social work* or *social welfare* from several thousand years ago, including the Babylonian ruler Hammurabi providing for the protection of widows and orphans in his code and the Islamic tradition of requiring Muslims who are able to contribute 2.5% of their wealth each year to support the needy to do so. Jewish philosophy, leading into early Christian beliefs, also stressed the need to give to others, especially older adults and those with special needs. The Old and New Testament of the Jewish and Christian religions and the Quran of Islam have numerous verses on helping other people. In Europe, monasteries began to function as early relief agencies in about the 6th century (Popple & Leighninger, 2010). Other traditions, such as the mutual aid practices of Africans, Asians, and Native Americans, resonate with what we might now consider social welfare (Reisch, 2014).

The church was seen as responsible for the physical and social needs of the poor prior to the 17th century. Early congregations incorporated regulations regarding the treatment and care of the poor into their system long before governments at any level had done so (Jansson, 2012). As the feudal system of the European nations went into decline and capitalism was on the rise, we begin to see the early formulation of social welfare as a function of the government. The Elizabethan Poor Law Act of 1601 is generally seen as the key turning point toward government intervention and away from church oversight as the primary method of caring for the poor. The law required the government, through local counties, to provide for the poor when the churches were unable to do so (Jansson, 2012). This early social welfare, although not social work, provided another area in which the roots of social work can be found through the acts of those working to provide for these poor. This law included direct care such as providing food and wood for fire and referrals for services such as healthcare.

CHARITY ORGANIZATION SOCIETIES

One of the founding systems that developed into social work was known as the Charity Organization Societies (COSs). This early system had its roots much farther back in history. In 1617, St. Vincent de Paul in France established groups that became known as the *Ladies of Charity*: "groups of leisure women whom he organized to visit the poor in their homes" (Watson, 1922, p. 16). These groups were somewhat unorganized in their practices, so in 1633 he formed a more structured organization he named the "Sisters of Charity," which worked with families after they had been screened and placed at a certain level of poverty based on their ability to support themselves. St. Vincent de Paul created both a system of friendly visitation to the poor and a format to keep from indiscriminately giving to those who may be able to at least partially care for themselves.

The city of Hamburg, Germany, also set precedence for a system of organized care for the poor. After a severe plague hit the city, the wealthier districts set up a sanitary association. One of the first challenges was the need to manage poor relief (Watson, 1922). This took the care of the poor away from the hands of the church, which had proved inadequate. In 1725, the city limited the number of people in poverty in each district to 25 to keep it manageable. The visitation of those who were ill and impoverished was also renewed in this system, and included the investigation and recording of the condition of those visited. In 1786, a professor researched the lessons from this system and wrote them into a popularly read weekly pamphlet of the time. The city of Hamburg was grouped into 60 districts with 18 visitors in each, including a system for reporting and supervision. The results of this system were extremely positive, including the elimination of begging, work being found for many, and the lowering of the number of "pauper" children to 400 by 1801, all of whom were cared for in homes, hospitals, or schools (Watson, 1922).

These and other examples of organized visiting of people in poverty wereeventually carried over to England, the home of the first formal COS. Several movements in and around London, such as The Strangers' Friend Society (founded in 1785) and The Metropolitan Visiting and Relief Association (in 1843), set precedents for this work. However, they were not able to deal with the increased poverty rates in London in the 1860s, which wereat least partially due to the American Civil War and the impact of industrialization. On April 22, 1869, the London Society for Organizing Charitable Relief and Repressing Mendicancy was founded. They became commonly known as the COS (Watson, 1922). A large degree of the success of these societies was due to the involvement of the local universities and the interest and dedication of the faculty and students. Octavia Hill, who had worked with those in poverty in London, read a paper on the "Importance of Aiding the Poor Without Alms-Giving" in the same year the COS was founded, reinforcing the philosophy of spending time with the poor (Watson, 1922, p. 57).

The first COS in a large city in the United States was in Buffalo, New York. It was a direct transplant of relief work in England. The writings by Octavia Hill and her peer, Edward Denison, were highly influential (Watson, 1922). A number of societies for different nationalities were already present in the United States. In 1817, a group called the Prevention of Pauperism was formed in New York specifically to deal with the issues relating to poverty, in addition to the works provided by many of the local churches. In 1837 and 1838, during an extremely bitter winter, those in poverty required so much assistance that all of the hastily thrown together relief agencies failed to meet the need. This sparked an aspiration for a more systematic and cooperative format for providing relief to people living in poverty. One of the main components of this new system was the desire to investigate individual needs before handing out relief (Watson, 1922). Many forms of societies were structured, some to help specific segments of the population, such as children, or to provide specific items, such as fuel to heat homes. Few of these societies, however, made use of the "friendly visitor" as investigator until 1877, when the Buffalo COS was formed under the English clergyman Reverend S. H. Gurteen, who had previously worked with the COS of London (Watson, 1922). After viewing its success, New Haven, Connecticut, soon organized its own COS, followed by the Philadelphia Society for Organizing Charity and others. By the 1870s, many cities in the United States had their own COSs, and the beginnings of social work as a profession came into existence (Wenocur & Reisch, 2001).

One of the key beliefs of the COS was that society can be made whole by using scientific principles in a relationship of love and kindness (Specht & Courtney, 1994). The relationship of the friendly visitor to the poor was central to these workings. As Watson (1922) stated, "the need for friendship and neighborliness is so great . . . that charity organization societies develop friendly visiting as a fundamental part of the personal service they render to many of their families" (p. 149). In theory this was to provide a supportive relationship for the individual. However, there was a fundamental contradiction within this method. The visitors were expected to be both the person investigating the family to see if they would receive assistance and a friend at the same time (Katz, 1996). The idea of individual responsibility was strongly represented in the COS. The organizations sought to find ways for the friendly visitor to encourage those in need of assistance to become independent of assistance, which unfortunately continued the stigma of those in poverty (Wenocur & Reisch, 2001). Mary Richmond (see Chapter 4), who began working with the COS of Baltimore in 1888, took the system of friendly visiting and turned it into a method that could be used by others to learn about or "investigate" the client's situation to better assist him or her. This meant asking questions and looking at the person through a systems theory lens. Knowing both the individual and the situation that individual was in was a novel idea at the time. She wrote the book *Social Diagnosis* (Richmond, 1917) on this method. The book became the first major text to be utilized in teaching the future social worker (Specht & Courtney, 1994). Richmond was highly involved in teaching social work in the very beginnings of the educational system. Due to the emphasis on investigation into the specific needs of each individual or family, a case-by-case method was utilized. Records on each individual and his or her characteristics were kept (J. Littrell, personal communication, July 29, 2017). This is similar to the social work casework model that many BSW students use in their practice, otherwise thought of as micro practice.

Around the time that the COS movement was beginning, other pioneers of the work that developed into social work were moving into their labors. Many of these pioneers were involved in macro-oriented work, such as large policy reforms with educational components. Dorothea Dix was busy visiting prisons and advocating for the separation of the mentally ill from the prison system (see Chapter 2). She was engaged in a large educational campaign in the 1830s through 1860s that focused on both the general public and elected officials to make policy changes that would improve the care of the mentally ill (Jansson, 2012). This was a macro-oriented social work technique. Josephine Shaw Lowell, who helped organize and guide the New York Charity for 25 years, concluded that one of the primary reasons for poverty was low wages. She also became involved in macro or policy work, advocating for better wages and helping in the foundation of the Consumer's League of New York (which organized workers). She even wrote a book about improving wages without resorting to strike (Katz, 1996). Still others were finding different ways they could assist those in need. Some chose to live in the neighborhoods where immigrants and those in poverty lived, as seen in the settlement house movement.

HULL HOUSE AND THE SETTLEMENT HOUSE MOVEMENT

Settlement houses were on the other side of the development of social work, opposite to the friendly visitors. Settlement houses were hubs for reform. They were generally places where upper middle class workers voluntarily lived in the neighborhood as they provided services to the impoverished families around them. Services included programs such as English language lessons, citizenship classes, arts and crafts, and health services. The movement began in Europe, but was quickly adapted by reformers in the United States. In 1889, Jane Addams and Ellen Gates Starr (see Chapter 3) opened Hull House in Chicago. This became the most famous settlement house in the United States (and possibly the only one most students have heard of). One of their basic theories was that community life and culture exist even in poverty and that by supporting that community one could make it stronger and better (Specht & Courtney, 1994). As another author says, settlement houses created a method of "self-help for urban poor" (Wenocur & Reisch, 2001, p. 38). They provided for concrete needs as well as social needs in a new environment. By the early 1900s, over 100 settlement houses were established in the United States (Wenocur & Reisch, 2001).

Jane Addams and Hull House were not only involved in direct community services, but also advocated on a range of issues. They saw the main focus of Hull House as a manner of preparing individuals from other countries to participate in a democracy (J. Littrell, personal communication, July 29, 2017). Their activities included organized labor and supporting unions, outlawing child labor, and women's rights including suffrage, among others (Specht & Courtney, 1994). Not all settlement houses were involved in advocacy. Many only focused on the community around them. Additional settlement houses were opened around the country, with more than 400 of them in operation by 1910 (Jansson, 2012). The movement examined the culture and social problems of those in poverty and looked at the strengths they brought to solving their own problems (Specht & Courtney, 1994). When compared to COS, many settlement houses were highly involved in advocacy activities. Addams and others in the settlement movement had a strong association with social reform and community work (Specht & Courtney, 1994). Many of the early leaders and educators in social work had their start at Hull House, including Florence Kelley, Sophonisba Breckinridge, Edith and Grace Abbott, Julia Lathrop, and Frances Perkins (see Chapter 5).

While the popularity of the settlement house movement grew quickly in the first decade of the 20th century, the movement just as quickly lost momentum. Immigrants joined the army for World War I and came back integrated and identifying as Americans. When they returned home, they were able to find employment (J. Littrell, personal communication, July 29, 2017). The settlements shifted the focus away from social reform and failed to pursue tasks that would strengthen social work as a profession (Wenocur & Reisch, 2001). The settlement houses tended to work closely with churches, hospitals, and other agencies, which eventually replaced much of the programming that was the first part of the settlement movement. Settlement houses were generally very supportive of labor leaders, which made the business class grow to dislike them. Several leaders in the settlement house movement, including Jane Addams and Lillian Wald, were pacifists firmly against the war, which also brought some unpopularity to their movements (Wenocur & Reisch, 2001). Over time, the social justice focus of the original settlement houses became more a part of the overall social work theory than its practice, and the settlement houses closed their doors.

DEVELOPMENT OF SOCIAL WORK EDUCATION
AND THE PROFESSION

The COS and the settlement house movements were central to the development of the idea of an identified person working on social reform at both the individual and community/governmental levels. The early workers in these movements were often called philanthropists, then friendly visitors or social caseworkers. Although neither format lasted in the long run, and some considered the COS movement to be a failure (Katz, 1996), the foundation for social work at both the individual level and the community or macro level had been formed. There was a recognized need to develop into something new, something with specifically trained and educated workers. In the first decade of the 20th century, many COS agencies were leaving behind the voluntary friendly visitors and instead were hiring paid workers (Wenocur & Reisch, 2001). By the early 1900s, the settlements and COS began to merge into the new field of social work (Trattner, 1999). The term *social work* itself—coined around the turn of the century—developed from the term *social works*, as in good works (Specht & Courtney, 1994). Events outside of social work often brought the necessity of the work to the forefront. World War I, with the number of families left behind and later returning soldiers with a variety of needs, was a time of growth in social work (Agnew, 2003), as the need to assist these families became apparent. In 1917, Mary Richmond helped form the Home Service Division of the American Red Cross, reaching these individuals and families nationwide (Agnew, 2003). By June 1918 there were 3,400 offices and 40,000 workers in these programs (Specht & Courtney, 1994). Unfortunately, the program was dissolved in 1921. The impact of previous reforms and industrialization gave strength to the need for social welfare beyond the churches, and social work was seen as an occupation that could be an organized part of meeting those needs through scientific expertise (Wenocur & Reisch, 2001).

In 1897, Mary Richmond gave one of the first speeches calling for the development of a training and educational program for the new social workers. She, among other leaders in the field, acknowledged that the many different forms of trainings, lectures, and apprenticeships that were being utilized were not enough to provide common ground and a systematic acquisition of scientific knowledge to provide support for those new to the field (Leighninger, 2000). Soon after Richmond's speech, in 1898, the first summer course for social workers was developed and provided by the New York COS, drawing 24 students (Jansson, 2012; Leighninger, 2000). In the first 3 years of the school, 70 students from 17 states were trained (Wenocur & Reisch, 2001). By 1904, this program had expanded to an 8-month program (Leighninger, 2000). Starting in 1910, the time frame of these training courses was expanded to a full 2-year program. Two of the leading faculty members, Sophonisba Breckinridge and Edith Abbott, created the first school of social work that was connected to a major research university, the University of Chicago's School of Social Service Administration. Many of the social workers trained under Breckinridge and Abbott at this school later worked with the Russell Sage Foundation (where Mary Richmond led the program) or at the Children's Bureau (Sealander, 1997). In 1919, Richmond founded the first graduate school for social work at Columbia University (J. Littrell, personal communication, July 29, 2017).

In 1919, there were 15 schools of social work in operation. In general, these programs were focused on the casework models, such as those Richmond discussed in her book *Social Diagnosis* (Richmond, 1917). The Russell Sage Foundation, with whom Richmond worked, was highly involved in the shaping of early education, partially through funding and the involvement of its staff (Wenocur & Reisch, 2001). The foundation subsidized some of the schools by establishing fellowships (Bruno, 1944). As the Russell Sage Foundation was primarily involved in the COSs, their interest and much of the foundation of social work education tended to focus on the casework angle more than the settlement homes or advocacy perspectives. Opportunities for social work moved into other areas as well, such as public recreation, juvenile and adult probation, public health, immigrant aid, and social legislation, although social casework was the main focus (Wenocur & Reisch, 2001). Flexner's paper "Is Social Work a Profession?" became a turning point in which social work argued for its consideration as a profession. Flexner (1915) argued that social work did not have enough theory unique to social work or an educational format to transmit technique, and thus was not a profession. This outraged many social workers and encouraged further formation of formal education, especially at the graduate level. Social workers argued that their generalist social work model was able to be adapted to the various problems and tasks that social workers encountered (J. Littrell, personal communication, July 29, 2017).

By the 1920s, social work and social work education were firmly established. Many training schools were now graduate programs associated with universities (Jansson, 2012). There were more than 40 schools by 1930 (Wenocur & Reisch, 2001). In 1932, a curriculum committee adopted a minimum curriculum to ensure that social workers had a basic education in 13 different subjects covering four categories (Bruno, 1944). The role of a social worker had expanded out to include much more than just people living in poverty. It now dealt with family issues, mental health issues, medical problems, problems with children and school, and more. The association for COSs officially changed its mission from relief to casework in the 1920s (Jansson, 2012). In 1921, the first large professional organization was formed, the American Association of Social Workers (Jansson, 2012). The primary focus remained on social casework, with the person in the environment as a key element.

During the 1920s a new idea was rising—that of psychiatric social work. This new area grew out of the ideas of Freud, with the central concepts of intrapsychic matter and the relationships within the family. Social workers adopted the Freudian concepts and methods quickly and decisively, bringing a stronger focus to the inner workings of the mind and away from the focus on the environment around the individual (Bruno, 1944; Jansson, 2012). Psychiatric social work worked closely with the medical profession (Specht & Courtney, 1994). The shift in focus to the emotional needs strengthened the focus on the psychotherapeutic role of a social worker. Private practice was seen as a potential role for a social worker after the Home Service department was dissolved in 1921. However, the Great Depression made the cost of private service unobtainable for the average worker. Without payment, it was not an ideal area of practice for social workers who needed the income (Specht & Courtney, 1994).

Clinical social work, with a focus on diagnosis and psychiatric theories, also continued to grow during the 1930s (Kendall, 1982). Another shift was taking place within social work from the evolving COS agencies. During the 1930s, COS began to consider, and in some cases provide, financial support in addition to friendly visiting. These agencies had a difficult time meeting the many needs of the people during the time of the Depression. The needs of the large number of people impacted by the Great Depression were beyond the capabilities of existing agencies' available services. The time for government intervention to provide for individual needs had arrived.

THE NEW DEAL

Social work and social welfare are extremely difficult to separate (Wenocur & Reisch, 2001). A major shift in the way Americans thought about social welfare took place when the Great Depression hit the country. Instead of poverty being explained as due to the fault of an individual, the Great Depression showed that the real cause of poverty is at the societal level (J. Littrell, personal communication, July 29, 2017). The Supreme Court had previously ruled that the Constitution did not cover the care of the poor or needy. It was not until President Roosevelt's New Deal legislation was passed in the 1930s to assist with the impact of the Great Depression that the U.S. federal government became involved in social welfare (Jansson, 2012). The Social Security Act of 1935, spearheaded by Frances Perkins (see Chapter 5) and directed by social worker Harry Hopkins, was the first nationwide legislation that provided for the welfare needs of the average person. As this alleviated the need to provide basic income support through the gatekeeper of the COS, social workers were now able to provide social services as caseworkers or in a psychotherapeutic role (Specht & Courtney, 1994). Some social workers were also practicing group work or community development. Before this time, most social workers worked in private agencies. Now, thousands of jobs for social workers were formed in the New Deal's government agencies. The number of social workers rose from 40,000 in 1930 to 70,000 in 1940 (Jansson, 2012). Social workers also filled key positions on the newly formed Social Security Board and even in government roles. The nature of these positions was slightly different, as Harry Hopkins hired many people who did not have degrees to provide food and income for individuals. The land grant colleges began to offer BSW programs, which were accredited by the National Association of Social Administration, a different accrediting body from the graduate programs (J. Littrell, personal communication, July 29, 2017).

By the end of the Great Depression, social work had evolved to require a bachelor's degree, and the master's degree was a 2-year program. There was a continued emphasis on casework or work at the individual level, with only a secondary focus on macro or policy work (Jansson, 2012). The growth seen during the New Deal time period continued and expanded during World War II, when social workers were once again needed to assist returning veterans and their families. Services included practical issues and also the need to assist in the area of coping with emotional trauma for those involved in the Second World War (Kendall, 1982). By the time the Great Depression and World War II were over, social work had shifted from a small number of people practicing in many different areas to a much larger industry with the thousands of social workers in the new public service agencies practicing a more standardized service. This new social welfare system transformed the profession of social work, making the public sector the primary area of service. Unfortunately, this new market was somewhat difficult to manage, as it came with a new set of restrictions and the government as the sponsor (Wenocur & Reisch, 2001). Clinical or psychotherapeutic social work became an option, with some social workers beginning to move into private practice or other therapeutic settings. A competing profession of clinical psychology was also developed to address mental health issues (J. Littrell, personal communication, July 29, 2017). Social workers in the psychotherapeutic role gained important new methods in 1951 when Carl Rogers introduced client-centered therapy. This was a break from the previously popular Freudian system of psychoanalysis (Specht & Courtney, 1994).

GROWTH AND DEVELOPMENT IN THE 20TH CENTURY

Social work professional and educational associations began to form and then come together during the 1940s and 1950s. In 1946, the precursor to the current Council on Social Work Education (CSWE) was formed, eventually being renamed to the current organization in 1952 (Wenocur & Reisch, 2001). CSWE organizes what is required for social work programs to be accredited, which allows for consistency between programs. There were multiple professional organizations for social work individuals, all focused on different specialties. However, in 1955 the seven associations joined to become the National Association of Social Workers (NASW). They started with 18,000 members and a requirement of 2 years of graduate study (Jansson, 2012). The 1973 classification of the BSW degree as an entry level professional social work degree is considered by some to be the most significant change to the structure of social work during this time (Wenocur & Reisch, 2001). The NASW continues to be a uniting body today, paying little attention to the differing schools of thought in the field and focusing on how the needs of the profession and society can best be served (J. Littrell, personal communication, July 29, 2017).

The debate between casework and social justice/macro work sides continued through this time. Perhaps due to difficulties defining macro work and lack of funding for positions in this area, casework continued as the primary method, with psychiatric casework continuing almost on the side as a popular format of psychotherapy. In the 1960s, the NASW encouraged lobbying and advocacy (Jansson, 2012), although the training in these areas was still not as strong. The 1960s and 1970s were also a time when there were many movements to change the structure of society, such as the civil rights movement, the women's movement, the antiwar movement, the deinstitutionalization movement, and the welfare rights movement (J. Littrell, personal communication, July 29, 2017). Some of the leaders in the civil rights movement included social workers, such as Whitney Young (see Chapter 6), who brought the National Urban League into the movement and became an advisor to Presidents Kennedy, Johnson, and Nixon (Jansson, 2012). In 1969, the NASW made a controversial decision to allow social workers with only a bachelor's level degree to join the association.

The social work profession grew quickly between the 1950s and 1980s due to the increased government spending on social welfare (Wenocur & Reisch, 2001). The United States moved into a more conservative era during the 1970s and 1980s. Social welfare programs were shrinking or being defunded, especially during the Reagan era. Some social workers, such as Senator Barbara Mikulski (see Chapter 9), protested the many spending cuts Reagan proposed (Jansson, 2012). Social work had a new concern and focus on minority populations, as well as outreach to and advocacy for the disadvantaged (Kendall, 1982). Social work overall continued its growth. By the mid-1980s, there were 100,000 members of the NASW. About 40% of them worked in nonprofit organizations, and another 45% were in public or governmental programs (Jansson, 2012). Most social workers were direct care providers, but some worked in either administration or macro positions. States began to require licensure, which often allowed for reimbursement for services by insurance companies. A growing trend in the profession was the movement of more social workers toward private practice. Many social workers worried that this would bring services only toward those who were able to fund it themselves, leaving out those in poverty or in vulnerable populations. This could be considered to make private practice more of another form of psychotherapy than social work (Wenocur & Reisch, 2001). This continues to be a debate in the profession even today.

Specht and Courtney (1994) argue that this growing trend toward private practice shows how far social work has strayed from its roots. For some social workers, this move toward private practice is led by the dissatisfaction with the low wages and poor working conditions of individuals with the MSW degree in the public sector (Wenocur & Reisch, 2001). The core of the debate comes down to the same issues that were discussed between the COS and settlement house movements: When looking for the cause of an individual's problems, is the root cause within the individual (based on genetics, brain chemistry, or personal history), or is the problem in the overall structure of our current society?

NEW FIELDS AND CHALLENGES IN THE 21ST CENTURY

It seems clear that social work in the 21st century will see a continuation of focus on the clinical side of the practice, especially with the steady interest in private practice. Other trends in social work have a view on vulnerable populations. This includes the CSWE practice competencies regarding understanding diversity (CSWE, 2015) and the evidence-based practices that continue to incorporate trauma practice into social work. Schools of social work now often have two tracks, clinical and macro, to ensure that social workers are well trained in their area of interest and specialization. With a continuously challenging political climate, it is not surprising that many social workers tend to be more interested in clinical or individual-based work, especially since that is where most employment can be found for social workers (Ginsberg, 2005). However, some social workers are finding their way into political positions, such as Senator Barbara Mikulski (see Chapter 9) in order to have greater influence over legislation. Some social workers argue that due to the dependency of the field on government funding of social services, the well-being of social work for both clients and social workers will require us to be more involved in political action (Reisch, 1997).

Collaboration with other professional fields has contributed to social work's ability to expand into new areas. Advances in science, particularly in neuroscience, has allowed greater understanding of how the brain works. Social workers work with those in the medical field to use this knowledge and provide better treatment for clients (Garland & Howard, 2009). A greater understanding and focus on trauma has also developed, partially due to a greater understanding of the impact of trauma on the body and the brain (van der Kolk, 2014). Social workers are adding new formats for treatment by specializing in areas of treatment such as play therapy for children or yoga therapy for individuals with somatic or trauma-related issues. Some of these newer areas of social work are discussed in Chapter 10.

Recent years have brought new (or reoccurring) challenges to the social work field. Dominelli (2017) discussed how racism and structural inequality have continued to be areas where society, and social workers, struggle. Trends toward an increase in acceptable racism, especially Islamophobia, can be seen in the United States as well as in European nations. Global development and the large movements of migrants due to political crises have brought greater attention to the Global South and issues around increased worldwide and intercountry inequities, as well as issues such as female empowerment and human trafficking (Dominelli & Hackett, 2012; Polack, 2004). The political climate in the United States has recently become less willing to provide services for those in poverty or with special needs, especially if some form of government assistance is needed. However, increased communication and facilitation of international social work, particularly in areas of social development, has seen some key examples of partnership between the West and the Global South, such as with small business loan programs in countries such as Bangladesh and El Salvador (Mayadas & Elliott, 1997).

Social work has become the largest mental health profession (Specht & Courtney, 1994). According to the Bureau of Labor Statistics (2016–2017), there are currently about 650,000 jobs in social work. With more social workers than ever before, and increased collaboration within and outside of the profession bringing a greater expertise into existence, hopefully social work will rise to the challenges of a new and ever changing field to continue to make the world a better place (U.S. Department of Labor, Bureau of Labor Statistics, 2016). There is a challenge before us to stay true to the original mission of social work provided by the COS, settlement house movement, and those who helped organize Social Security and modern social welfare (Specht & Courtney, 1994). Can we stay true to the ideas of social justice and eliminating oppression while moving into a world based on private practice and managed care? Or will our profession formulate a new mission, one that fits our rapidly changing 21st century society? How will you, as a social worker in this newest era, balance your needs as a worker with the greater mission of social work?

CLASSROOM ACTIVITIES

1. Watch the video "Legacies of Social Change: 100 Years of Professional Social Work," available through the NASW (www.social-workers.org). As a small group or class, discuss the progression of social work through the individuals highlighted through the film. What important aspects of social work do you see exemplified in these individuals? What do you think is important to social work today that is not discussed?

2. Discuss the types of work found in government-funded programs, nonprofit organizations, and in private practice. Which populations tend to be served in each format? What are some of the pros and cons for working in these different environments? Which do you think fits more closely with the *Code of Ethics* and the overall mission of social work? From a social justice standpoint, is one more closely aligned than the other?

REFERENCES

Agnew, E. N. (2003). Shaping a civic profession: Mary Richmond, the social gospel, and social work. In W. J. Deichmann Edwards & C. De Swarte Gifford (Eds.), *Gender and the social gospel* (pp. 116–135). Chicago: University of Illinois Press.

Bruno, F. (1944). Twenty-five years of schools of social work. *The Social Service Review, 43*(2), 152–164. doi:10.1086/634854

Council on Social Work Education. (2015). *2015 educational policy and accreditation standards for baccalaureate and master's social work programs*. Alexandria, VA: Author.

Dominelli, L. (2017). Social work challenges in the second decade of the 21st century: Against the bias. *Affilia, 32*(1), 105–107. doi:10.1177/0886109916681390

Dominelli, L., & Hackett, S. (2012). Social work responses to the challenges for practice in the 21st century. *International Social Work, 55*(4), 449–453. doi:10.1177/0020872812440784

Flexner, A. (1915). Is social work a profession? In National Conference of Charities and Corrections, *Proceedings of the National Conference of Charities and Corrections at the forty-second annual session held in Baltimore, Maryland, May 12-19, 1915* (pp.576–590). Chicago, IL: Hildmann. Retrieved from http://socialwelfare.library.vcu.edu/social-work/is-social-work-a-profession-1915

Garland, E., & Howard, M. (2009). Neuroplasticity, psychosocial genomics, and the biopsychosocial paradigm in the 21st century. *Health and Social Work, 34*(3), 191–199. doi:10.1093/hsw/34.3.191

Ginsberg, L. (2005). The future of social work as a profession. *Advances in Social Work, 6*(1), 7–16. Retrieved from http://journals.iupui.edu/index.php/advancesin-socialwork/article/view/71/62

Jansson, B. (2012). *The reluctant welfare state: Engaging history to advance social work practice in contemporary society.* Belmont, CA: Brooks/Cole.

Katz, M. (1996). *In the shadow of the poorhouse: A social history of welfare in America.* New York, NY: Basic Books.

Kendall, K. (1982). A sixty-year perspective of social work. *Social Casework: The Journal of Contemporary Social Work, 63* (7), 424–428.

Leighninger, L. (2000). *Creating a new profession: The beginnings of social work education in the United States.* Alexandria, VA: Council on Social Work Education.

Mayadas, N., & Elliott, D. (1997). Lessons from international social work: Policy and practices. In M. Reisch & E. Gambrill (Eds.), *Social work in the 21st century* (pp. 175–185). Thousand Oaks, CA: Pine Forge Press.

The Miriam and Ira D. Wallach Division of Art, Prints and Photographs: Photography Collection, the New York Public Library. (1905). *A social worker at Ellis Island, 1926.* Retrieved from http://digitalcollections.nypl.org/items/510d47d9-4e90-a3d9-e040 -e00a18064a99

Polack, R. (2004). Social justice and the global economy: New challenges for social work in the 21st century. *Social Work, 49*(2), 281–290. doi:10.1093/sw/49.2.281

Popple, R., & Leighninger, L. (2010). *The policy based profession: An introduction to social welfare policy analysis for social workers* (5th ed.). New York, NY: Pearson.

Reisch, M. (1997). The political context of social work. In M. Reisch & E. Gambrill (Eds.), *Social work in the 21st century* (pp. 80–92). Thousand Oaks, CA: Pine Forge Press.

Reisch, M. (2014). U.S. social policy and social welfare: A historical overview. In M. Reisch (Ed.), *Social policy and social justice* (pp. 5–42). Thousand Oaks, CA: Sage.

Richmond, M. E. (1917). *Social diagnosis.* New York, NY: The Free Press.

Richmond, M. E. (1930). The biography of a social worker. In J. C. Colcord & R. Z. S. Mann (Eds.), *The long view: Papers and addresses by Mary E. Richmond* (pp.539–546). New York, NY: Russell Sage Foundation. (Original work published 1923)

Sealander, J. (1997). *Public wealth & private life: Foundation philanthropy and the reshaping of American social policy from the Progressive Era to the New Deal.* Baltimore, MD: The Johns Hopkins University Press.

Specht, H., & Courtney, M. (1994). *Unfaithful angels: How social work has abandoned its mission.* New York, NY: The Free Press.

Trattner, W. (1999). *From poor law to welfare state: A history of social welfare in America* (6th ed.). New York, NY: The Free Press.

U.S. Department of Labor, Bureau of Labor Statistics. (2016). *Occupational outlook handbook: 2016–2017.* Washington, DC: Author. Retrieved from https://www.bls .gov/ooh/community-and-social-service/social-workers.htm

van der Kolk, B. (2014). *The body keeps the score: Brain, mind, and body in the healing of trauma.* New York, NY: Viking Penguin.

Watson, F. D. (1922). *The charity organization movement in the United States: A study in American philanthropy.* New York, NY: Macmillan.

Wenocur, S., & Reisch, M. (2001). *From charity to enterprise: The development of American social work in a market economy.* Chicago: University of Illinois Press.

Dorothea Dix.
Source: United States Library of Congress.

CHAPTER 2

Dorothea Dix: Bringing Individuals With Mental Illness Out of Prisons

April 4, 1802—July 18, 1887

"I come as an advocate of helpless, forgotten, insane and idiotic men and women; of beings, sunk to a condition from which the most unconcerned would start with real horror; of beings wretched in our Prisons, and more wretched in our Alms-Houses."
—Dix (1843, p. 2)

Dorothea Dix's advocacy role began long before formal social work existed in this country. During the mid-1800s, mental health was not viewed in the same way that it is today. Just as poverty was often considered to be due to a moral failing (Trattner, 1999), most people also believed that what was then called insanity was due to a moral defect in the person who was experiencing mental health issues. In many cases, the family would choose to care for those affected who were not considered dangerous. However, in cases where the individual exhibited violent behaviors, family members often had no other choice than to allow the person to be restrained in a prison setting. Dix was not aware of this situation any more than most people in the general public. She learned of the containment of the mentally ill when she was in her 30s and visited a prison to give Sunday school lessons to a group of female prisoners. After this turning point in her life, she worked tirelessly to change the system and provide separate hospitals where the mentally ill could receive treatment for the majority of their remaining lives.

While reading about Dorothea Dix's work and her journey in helping the mentally ill, you should keep in mind the Council on Social Work Education (CSWE) Educational Policy and Accreditation Standard's Competency 1: Demonstrate Ethical and Professional Behavior. Although Dorothea Dix lived long before these competencies were in place, you will notice many times where her professional behavior was key to her success. Dix lived in a time when most women worked at home, on the farm, or in factories. Women were not expected to take on a leadership role, and certainly not expected to confront large systems; the men were usually in charge of these systems. You may also notice the persistence that Dix needed to have in order to obtain the changes to the prison and hospitalization system that worked with the mentally ill. Persistence is still needed to make changes in the social work world today—perhaps even more than in Dix's time. In our highly bureaucratic system, nothing seems to happen quickly. This is especially true when policy changes or funding is needed—and Dorothea Dix needed both. Take note that even a person who we highly regard as a leader in the social work community had failures. The president once personally vetoed a bill that Dix had proposed and Congress had approved! Yet she continued with her mission; throughout the course of her career she played a part in the opening of 32 new mental hospitals in the United States and several in Europe (Marshall, 1937).

CONTEXT OF THE TIMES

Dix practiced during a very different era than the one we are in today. This was the period of the settlement of the frontier, the Civil War, and the development of the industrial age. During the 1830s to 1850s, the United States was at the height of the Sunday School movement, as it was thought that it was the people who stopped going to church who would become "alcoholics and then delinquent or insane" (Jansson, 2012, p. 99). There was little compassion for "paupers," as land was so abundant that it was thought that any individuals could obtain it and take care of themselves. However, looking at the trends for the 100 years leading up to 1850, we see the rise of factory labor, with the number of people working in a wage labor position rising from 6% to 27% (Katz, 1996). More and more people were moving away from being landowners and becoming wage workers in urban environments.

Treatment, especially inpatient treatment, for those with mental illness was fairly rare in the mid-1800s. It was thought that a moral defect caused the condition, and hence mental illness was the fault of the individual. In the thinking of that time, many of these "paupers" or those who were "insane" were "undeserving" (Wenocur & Reisch, 2001), that category reserved for people who had a hand in their own impoverished fate. Consider that in the beginning of the 19th century there were only four "insane asylums" in the entire country (Tiffany, 1890). It was not a priority in this country to care for those who might suffer from mental illness; most thought it could not be cured, so the method of approach more closely resembled how to shelter them away from society instead of how to treat them. This is the context in which Dix discovered the many mentally ill being isolated in prisons and other poor conditions.

CHILDHOOD AND TEACHING CAREER

Dorothea Dix did not have an easy childhood. Although her grandparents had a substantial amount of money, her father was estranged from them due to his choice of Dorothea Dix's mother as his wife. As Harvard did not allow married men to attend the university, his marriage also ended his education. Joseph and Mary Dix were sent by his father to oversee the family's land holdings in Hampden, Massachusetts—then considered the frontier (Stroup, 1986). Joseph was able to use his personality and education to forge a career as a Methodist minister, but he also dabbled in other work as well. Over the years he had several shops selling various items, was a frontier evangelist, and sold religious pamphlets. The family, especially young Dorothea, often assisted him in these endeavors. Both Mary and Dorothea Dix were required to stitch together the pamphlets that he sold, a task that young Dix hated. Dix did enjoy the short time when her father sold books from his shop, as she loved to read. Much of the caretaking of the home often fell to Dix, as the oldest child of an often-ill mother. The home was described by one author as crude and showing evidence of neglect (Marshall, 1937). Young

Dorothea Dix's happiest times were likely when she was able to visit her grandparents, or they visited the home, as both grandparents were very fond of her. On his visits, her grandfather, a doctor and businessman, liked to show her the trinkets that his ships brought back from trading in the Indies.

Not much is known about Dix's early education. One of her parents likely taught her how to read and write, although it is possible that she had attended the village school. At 12 years old, Dix ran away from home and showed up at her grandmother's home in Boston, asking her grandmother to allow her to stay with her and go to school. This long journey was not expected of a 12-year-old girl. Her grandmother, who was 68 at the time and a widow for the past 5 years, did not seem prepared to be the guardian of such an unruly child. However, she allowed her to stay. Dix was able to attend school and made great strides in her education. After 2 years, she was sent to live with her great aunt Sarah Duncan, who was much more understanding of a young girl who had been raised without much discipline. It was at this home in Worcester, Massachusetts, that Dix brought up the idea of opening her own school, partially because she felt she should be earning an income to pay for her stay at her family's house. At this time, children had to know how to read and write before they attended school, and the opportunities for early schooling were quite limited, especially for the youngest children. Although Dix was only 14 years old, in 1816 she opened her first school. The school was first in an unused room at a local school house, and then in a vacant building found by the family (Marshall, 1937). To make herself look older, she lengthened her skirts and fashioned her hair in the manner of an adult.

Dix's school became popular and she quickly gained students. She became known for her strict discipline. One student, General William Lincoln, later stated, "I don't know that she had any special grudge against me but it was her nature to use the whip and use it, she did" (Marshall, 1937, p. 16). Young girls received a different form of discipline. A story that is often told is of a young girl who was made to walk through town with a sign around her neck proclaiming that she was a "very bad girl, indeed" (Marshall, 1937, p. 17). Although by today's standards these stories may seem harsh, it is likely that this is similar to what other schools of this type expected around this time. Dix was possibly overly aware of the need for strict discipline due to her young age.

She ran this school for 3 years. Dix then returned to her grandmother's home and soon opened a school in Orange Grove in 1821 (Stroup, 1986). It was in this year that her father died. The elder of Dorothea's younger brothers, Charles, came to live with them, while 6-year-old Joseph stayed with their mother, Mary. Teaching became a way to pay for the upkeep of the family. Dix also had private tutors and attended public lecture courses given by Harvard professors to continue her own education.

For several years, she had continued teaching both the school for private students, whose parents were able to pay, and a separate charity school for more impoverished students. In addition to continuing her studies, she wrote her first book, *Conversations on Common Things*, a textbook for children published in 1824 that became widely popular and went through 60 editions (Tiffany, 1890). Her health suffered with this overload of activity and her voice was growing weak and husky. She had never been physically strong, and often had throat and pulmonary disorders (Marshall, 1937). Her "frequent attitude, as she stood to conduct her classes, was that of supporting herself with one hand holding on to the desk, and the other pressed hard to her side as though to repress a sharp pain" (Tiffany, 1890, p. 21). Her doctor soon recommended that she give up teaching for 2 to 3 years. During this time away from teaching Dix committed her time to writing several other volumes, including a hymn book for children and a devotional. She traveled with family friends as the children's tutor and nanny. She returned to teaching after a time, but once again was forced to close her school, this time a boarding school, due to poor health. In 1836 Dix suffered a major nervous and physical collapse and was told that she should never teach again (Marshall, 1937).

DISCOVERING HER MISSION

In the late 1830s, Dix spent time traveling to help recover from her collapse. For about 18 months she lived in England. While there, she met Dr. Samuel Tike, from whom she learned of York Retreat in England, founded in 1792 to care for those with mental illness. This visit likely introduced Dix to the idea of methods for the care and treatment of those considered insane and possibly provided a foundation for her work in the future.

In 1841, Dix heard that there was a need for a woman to teach Sunday school to the women in a local jail. Although she was cautioned against going due to her health, Dix insisted, saying "I shall be there next Sunday" (Marshall, 1937, p. 60). This event changed her life's path.

Dix began teaching Sunday school at the jail, and after the class would walk around and talk with the prisoners. She was appalled to find out that there were a number of "insane" people living among the criminals, obtaining no treatment for their illnesses. When visiting their living quarters, she discovered that the area of the jail reserved for those considered insane had no heat. When Dix asked why there was no stove, she was told that they did not need it, as they did not feel the cold the way others did. Dix immediately brought the matter up to the court in East Cambridge. She enlisted the support of philanthropists and had local officials investigate the jail. Her efforts were soon satisfied, and the cells were heated (Muckenhoupt, 2003).

Dix's experience in the local jail made her wonder how the *insane* were treated in other locations. She became convinced that a survey was needed to determine the housing and treatment of the mentally ill (Stroup, 1986). In the 1840s, people with mental illness were considered to be disgraceful and something to be hidden away (Marshall, 1937). In these situations, the social welfare system, such as it was at the time, largely failed those with mental illness (Jansson, 2012). Unless the family was somewhat wealthy and could afford to pay for private care for the family member with mental illness, there were few options. Where were they to be found? "Some were in cells or cages; some in outbuildings, garrets, or cellars; some in county jails; some in almshouses, in brick cells, never warmed by fire, nor lighted by the rays of the sun" (Dix, 1848, p. 8). The variety of locations was wide and conditions could be vastly different, but overall were quite poor. In some locations, the *insane* were set up at a county auction, to go to the bidder who would charge the least for their care for the year (Abbott, 1963).

After seeing the conditions in the local jail, Dix began her survey of the facilities housing the mentally ill in Massachusetts. She discovered that many facilities provided far worse conditions than what she had found at the jail in East Cambridge (Jansson, 2012). Dix thought it would take several months to survey all the living quarters; in reality, it took her about 18 months of visits, sometimes with numerous visits to the same location. She began compiling all of her information into one report. The stories she told were often heartbreaking, and gave compelling images of the conditions that some people were kept in. Dix reported one such example of a resident of an almshouse in Danvers in her Memorial to the legislature of Massachusetts (Dix, 1843):

> Long before reaching the house, wild shouts, snatches of rude songs, imprecations and obscene language, fell upon the ear, proceeding from the occupant of a low building, rather remote from the principal building to which my course was directed. Found the mistress, and was conducted to the place which was called "the home" of the forlorn maniac, a young woman, exhibiting a condition of neglect and misery blotting out the faintest idea of comfort, and outraging every sentiment of decency. . . . There she stood with naked arms and disheveled hair, the unwashed frame invested with fragments of unclean garments, the air so extremely offensive, though ventilation was afforded on all sides save one, that it was not possible to remain beyond a few moments without retreating for recovery to the outward air. Irritation of body, produced by utter filth and exposure, incited her to the horrid process of tearing off her skin by inches. Her face, neck, and person were thus disfigured to hideousness. She held up a fragment just rent off. To my exclamation of horror, the mistress replied: "Oh, we can't help it. Half the skin is off sometimes. We can do nothing with her; and it makes no difference what she eats, for she consumes her own filth as readily as the food which is brought her." (p. 7)

This is one example of the many poor conditions that Dix found in her travels. Compiling all of the information into her Memorial, Dix submitted her report to the state government with a plea to provide adequate housing in the form of asylums for those with mental illness, thus allowing for their removal from prisons. Her report was met with a great deal of disbelief, with some calling it full of "sensational and slanderous lies" (Tiffany, 1890, p. 83). One of Dix's methods of fighting back was to have mental hospital superintendents from around New England write letters supporting the new asylum, and to attend the legislature's debates. She also used the media at the time in the form of newspaper articles sharing what was learned about the prisons and the conditions of those within. In the end, the legislature voted to enlarge the current institution by an additional 150 to 200 beds, but refused to build a new hospital (Muckenhoupt, 2003). Dix had succeeded in raising awareness of the issue and increasing the resources for this population, even though her hope for a new hospital was not met. More importantly, Dix had found the calling to her life's work.

PURSUING FUNDING FOR HOSPITALS FOR THOSE WITH MENTAL ILLNESS

These encounters in Massachusetts began nearly 25 years of advocating for persons with mental illness to receive better treatment and living conditions. From the time of Dix's first visit to the jail in 1841 to the beginning of the Civil War, Dix toured endlessly across the country documenting the conditions under which the mentally ill were living. She also began appealing to local businessmen who were known to be inclined to donate to charities. Many were uninterested and told her she would fail in her work, but by no means was she always unsuccessful. After meeting with Cyrus Butler in Providence, he asked her what she wished him to do. Her response was, "I would like you to give me fifty thousand dollars, for the enlargement of the insane asylum of this city. It will forever stand as a monument to your generosity" (Brooks, 1957, p. 31). Butler agreed to donate $40,000, with the stipulation that another $40,000 be raised from other sources, and soon the Butler Hospital was established. Dix moved from state to state, relying on multiple methods to accomplish her mission. When there were people who could be persuaded to donate to such a cause, she approached them. Other times she returned to the methods she had utilized in Massachusetts, visiting and documenting the living conditions of the mentally ill and making appeals to the state legislatures. In the 4 years from June 1843 to August 1847 it is estimated that Dix traveled about 30,000 miles, all the way from Canada to the Gulf of Mexico and from the Atlantic to the Mississippi River (Marshall, 1937). Much of this travel was by stagecoach or by steamboat—not particularly comfortable modes of transportation. In 1845, she wrote to a friend in England stating she had

> visited eighteen state penitentiaries, three hundred county jails and houses of correction, more than five hundred

almshouses . . . besides hospitals and houses of refuge. I have been so happy as to promote and secure the establishment of six hospitals for the insane, several county poorhouses, and several jails on a reformed plan. (Brooks, 1957, p. 36)

She was making progress through her persistent and steady work.

One of these establishments was the New Jersey State Hospital in Trenton, created after the passage of a bill through the state's legislature. Prior to this, New Jersey had no provision for the mentally ill. Dix systematically toured each location, detailing how many of New Jersey's mentally ill were being housed in other states. Dix strategically approached members of the legislature that might be open to her cause or who might be able to approach others on the committees and win their votes. On March 25, 1845, her bill was approved. The new State Hospital was one of the first to be established due to Dix's work (Chapin, 2014). She sometimes referred to this hospital as her "first born child" (Marshall, 1937, p. 109). It was to this establishment that Dix returned 45 years later, to live out the last years of her life in apartments given to her by the institution, when she was mostly bedbound due to severe and long-term illness (Tiffany, 1890).

While awaiting the New Jersey decision, Dix was busy assessing the state of the prisons and other locations where the mentally ill were being housed, starting with Pennsylvania. Although the mentally ill were in similar locations to those in other states, Dix was particularly appalled at the conditions she found. She described the jail in Pittsburgh as combining "all the faults and abuses of the worst country prisons in . . . the United States," where the mentally ill were forgotten (Marshall, 1937, p. 108). Her report resulted in a committee that instructed the state of Pennsylvania to build a new hospital and take other measures to prevent these conditions. The measure was approved by the legislature.

Dix compiled a volume summarizing some of what she had seen, titled *Remarks on Prisons and Prison Discipline in the United States* (published in 1845). This report summarized what she had learned in 4 years of investigating the prison system, and attempted to answer two questions: "How shall the criminal and pauper be disposed of, in order to reduce crime and reform the criminal on the one hand, and, on the other, to diminish pauperism and restore the pauper to useful citizenship?" (Dix, 1845, p. 5). She believed that the best method to work with prisoners showed that "steady, firm, and kind government of prisoners is the truest humanity and the best exercise of duty" (Dix, 1845, p. 21). After completing this work, she set off for the first of her long trips out West, heading for Kentucky and then down to New Orleans, visiting jails and institutions at every available stop along the way (Marshall, 1937). Dix was so single-minded in her work that she often neglected daily items such as clothing. Her lifelong and close friend Ann Heath would send her new dresses on occasion, as Dix would not take the time to acquire them for herself (Wilson, 1975). Ann was also the friend to whom she wrote and told of her journeys and discoveries. As there was no formal system of support for her, Dix had to make due with friends and the doctors that she came into contact with during her travels.

The decade is filled with similar patterns. Dix traveled long distances to visit institutions, gave reports, and encouraged more hospitals and services for the mentally ill, with a fair amount of success. Eleven new institutions were established, in locations such as Maryland, Jacksonville, Illinois, and "Dix Hill" in North Carolina (named after her grandfather as she would not allow it to be named after herself).

Not all of Dix's enterprises were met with success. After spending 10 years on the road advocating for services in different states, in 1850 Dix turned her attention to the federal government. Instead of asking state legislatures for sums to be set aside for new asylums ranging from about $50,000 to $200,000, Dix now asked for five million acres of land to be set aside across the country for the locations for new asylums to be built. Of the approximately 22,000 people with mental illness, there were still only about 3,700 being cared for through these institutions (Stroup, 1986). She had begun requesting land as early as 1848, but without progress. She now raised the amount requested to over 12 million acres, which is about three times the size of the state of Massachusetts (Tiffany, 1890). To accomplish this, Dix employed many of the tactics that had worked for her at the state level. She met with many of the representatives who would be voting on the bill, often in the alcove of the Capital Library that Congress had set aside for her use (Tiffany, 1890). She appealed to her friends, the superintendents of the institutions she had assisted over the years, to advocate for the bill. She wrote more letters than could be counted. Yet, in spite of her efforts, the bill was deferred time and again until it was allowed to lapse. In 1854, after several years of bringing the bill back, it was finally passed by both the House and the Senate. In the midst of the beginnings of celebration, terrible news came to her—despite passing through both branches of Congress, President Franklin Pierce had vetoed the bill. The president had decided that it was not in the power of the federal government to provide for humanitarian efforts. After 6 years of work, the result came to naught. With this resolute defeat, Dix decided to spend some time away from this work and traveled through Europe for several years. Although the intent was to take time away from her work, Dix did, of course, end up visiting prisons and institutions throughout her journey, making recommendations and advocating for improvements wherever she went.

THE CIVIL WAR: SUPERINTENDENT OF NURSES

In 1856, Dix returned home from Europe. Although many requested that she write a book on all that she had learned over the years, Dix found too many appeals for assistance from the institutions she had aided in founding to take the time to do so. From the time of her return to the United States until the outbreak of the Civil War, Dix busied herself in this work (Tiffany, 1890). She traveled extensively in the South, despite (unfounded) fears that she would be ill-received due to her Northern heritage. During Dix's journey, she unwittingly stumbled across a scheme to seize Washington and prevent Abraham Lincoln's inauguration (or end his life in the attempt). Dix went to the office of Mr. Fenton, president of the Philadelphia and Baltimore Railroads, and told him what she had learned. He promptly hired detectives to investigate and Lincoln was smuggled safely into Washington, with the plot ended. Dix thus had a small role in saving the life of the president-elect (Marshall, 1937).

In 1861, Dix's career took an abrupt shift. After the first skirmishes of the war took place, Dix promptly returned to Washington, DC, and offered her services to the Department of War (Stroup, 1986). She was given an unpaid commission as the "Superintendent of United States Army Nurses"—the first commission of its kind (Stroup, 1986). Dix was tasked with selecting and assigning the "nurses"—often untrained young women—who arrived to assist with the effort (Tiffany, 1890). Dix was particularly severe with her standards for nurses. She stated, "No woman under thirty need apply to serve in the government hospitals. All nurses are required to be plain-looking women. Their dresses must be brown or black, with no bows, no curls, no jewelry, and no hoop-skirts" (Stroup, 1986, p. 143). Dix wanted women who were dedicated to the service, and not frivolous young women seeking romance and husbands. Although her instructions sounded harsh, in reality Dix was unendingly kind to her volunteers, often housing and feeding them with her own funds, and offering places for recovery in her home when they themselves fell ill (Muckenhoupt, 2003). One of Dix's most famous charges was Louisa May Alcott, the author of *Little Women*. Alcott spent 6 weeks nursing at the Union Hotel before becoming ill with pneumonia. During Alcott's illness, Dix came by to ensure she was cared for. Alcott wrote that "Miss Dix brought a basket full of bottles of wine, tea, medicine, and cologne, besides a little blanket and pillow, a fan and a Testament. . . . She is a kind old soul, but very queer and arbitrary" (Cheney, 1889, p. 143). Alcott later wrote a very detailed short book about her experiences as a nurse titled *Civil War Hospital Sketches* (Alcott, 1863). In the book, she calls Dix their Florence Nightingale. Dix directed the nurses for several years, although often with conflict from the administration of the hospitals and the government. In 1863 she was relieved of the duty of selecting nurses, though she continued working in the office until after the war had ended.

THE END OF A LONG CAREER

With the war ended, Dix stayed to tie up loose ends. She concluded her service in this area by raising funds to erect a monument in honor of the soldiers who had died in the war (Stroup, 1986). When she was later asked what she would like in recognition of her service to the country, she almost jokingly stated, "the flag of my country" (Stroup, 1986, p. 144). She was surprised when she later received the flag with a letter of gratitude from the secretary.

In 1867, Dix returned to traveling the country, inspecting the conditions of those with mental illness and of the prisons and institutions. Although slowed in 1870 by a bout of malaria, she continued with what she was able to do until 1881, when she retired to an apartment inside her "first born child," the state hospital in Trenton, New Jersey. She spent the last years of her life restricted to these rooms. When she was able, she wrote numerous letters or read aloud to the inmates. Many friends came to visit her. For more than 5 years she continued her long and painful decline due to the ossification of the membranes of the arteries (Tiffany, 1890). On July 18, 1887, Dix died in her sleep (Muckenhoupt, 2003). Throughout her career, Dix had a hand in founding 32 asylums, from Trenton all the way to Japan. She could show 123 insane asylums and hospitals that were built due to her overall efforts (Brooks, 1957). Awareness of the need to care better for people with mental illness was greatly increased as a result of her life's work. For anyone in the 19th century, much less an unmarried woman with no official power, this was a massive undertaking and a better result than could have been hoped for.

LESSONS LEARNED

The nine new competencies of the CSWE (2015) reflect the necessary behaviors and areas of proficiency that every social worker must have. As social work students, you have likely encountered these competencies in many areas of your education, especially in your field internships and the required documentation for these courses. Each person discussed in this book exhibits these areas of expertise to some extent, although some are obviously a better fit in specific areas than others (such as Barbara Mikulski, a Congresswoman, having a great deal of experience in the area of policy—Competency 5—and discussed in Chapter 9).

There are also times when our definition of the components may have changed due to the time frame in which the individual practiced. Dorothea Dix is a great example of Competency 1, as she demonstrates ethical and professional behavior in her practice. However, Dix was practicing in the mid-1800s. At thattime, the National Association of Social Workers (NASW) *Code of Ethics* had not been written, nor was there even a formal social work occupation to give her a base for knowing how to approach her work. Especially because she did not have this foundation, Dix can be considered to have had two qualities that are important and often overlooked in social work—flexibility and creativity. Dix did not spend her time looking for a guide to show her how to do her work. Instead, she employed a strategy, and if the desired results were not found, she took a different approach. She spent a great deal of time talking to members of the community and government until she found those who supported the changes in the system that she thought necessary. Dix's use of technology was also quite different than what we see in today's world, such as her use of newspaper articles to share information with the public instead of television or the Internet. Dix spent her time traveling by stagecoach and steamboat, and handwriting letters. Issues such as confidentiality through emails would not be a consideration!

To finish this chapter, read through the following text of CSWE's Competency 1. Then you will be ready to go through the classroom exercises and discuss what you saw in Dix's practice throughout this chapter. The section reads:

Competency 1: Demonstrate Ethical and Professional Behavior

Social workers understand the value base of the profession and its ethical standards, as well as relevant laws and regulations that may impact practice at the micro, mezzo, and macro levels. Social workers understand frameworks of ethical decision making and how to apply principles of critical thinking to those frameworks in practice, research, and policy arenas. Social workers recognize personal values and the distinction between personal and professional values. They also understand how their personal experiences and affective reactions influence their professional judgment and behavior. Social workers understand the profession's history, its mission, and the roles and responsibilities of the profession. Social workers also understand the role of other professions when engaged in interprofessional teams. Social workers recognize the importance of lifelong learning and are committed to continually updating their skills to ensure they are relevant and effective. Social workers also understand emerging forms of technology and the ethical use of technology in social work practice. Social workers:

- Make ethical decisions by applying the standards of the NASW *Code of Ethics*, relevant laws and regulations, models for ethical decision making, ethical conduct of research, and additional codes of ethics as appropriate to context

- Use reflection and self-regulation to manage personal values and maintain professionalism in practice situations

- Demonstrate professional demeanor in behavior; appearance; and oral, written, and electronic communication

- Use technology ethically and appropriately to facilitate practice outcomes

- Use supervision and consultation to guide professional judgment and behavior (CSWE, 2015, p. 7).

CLASSROOM ACTIVITIES

1. Discuss how Dorothea Dix presented herself in a professional manner in a society that did not consider her to have a formalized profession. What qualities or behaviors were important? How did the way she dressed impact the way others perceived her? How do you think she attempted to make ethical decisions without the use of a guide such as the NASW *Code of Ethics*? How did she demonstrate professional behavior in her speech and writing? You have seen a small sample of her writing in this chapter—would you consider it to be professional in tone and content? Why or why not? How might she have used self-reflection and regulation in her settings, especially without a formal supervisor with whom to discuss any challenges?

2. Field Trip/Guest Speaker
   Visit a prison and speak with the officials or bring a guest speaker who works within the prison system to the classroom. If this is not possible, have students do some research on mental illness in the prison system. Review and discuss some of the following questions: How many people in the prison have some form of mental illness?

(continued)

What contributes to the number of people incarcerated who have mental illness? What other options exist for persons who have exhibited both signs of mental illness and who have also engaged in criminal behavior? How is the current system of inpatient care for those with mental illness different than in Dorothea Dix's time? In what ways might it be similar? What continuing improvements need to be made in these areas?

REFERENCES

Abbott, E. (1963). *Some American pioneers in social welfare*. New York, NY: Russell & Russell.

Alcott, L. M. (1863). *Civil War hospital sketches*. Boston, MA: James Redpath.

Brooks, G. (1957). *Three wise virgins*. New York, NY: E. P. Dutton.

Chapin, R. (2014). *Social policy for effective practice: A strengths approach* (3rd ed.). New York, NY: Routledge.

Cheney, E. (Ed.). (1889). *Louisa May Alcott, her life, letters, and journals*. Boston, MA: Roberts Brothers.

Council on Social Work Education. (2015). *2015 educational policy and accreditation standards for baccalaureate and master's social work programs*. Alexandria, VA: Author.

Dix, D. L. (1843). *Memorial to the legislature of Massachusetts*. Boston, MA: Munroe and Francis.

Dix, D. L. (1845). *Remarks on prisons and prison discipline in the United States*. Philadelphia, PA: Joseph Kite.

Dix, D. L. (1848). *Memorial of D. L. Dix praying a grant of land for the relief and support of the indigent curable and incurable insane in the United States* (as referred on June 27, 1848, to a select committee, 30th Congress, first session). Washington, DC: Tippin & Streeper.

Jansson, B. (2012). *The reluctant welfare state: Engaging history to advance social work practice in contemporary society* (7th ed.). Belmont, CA: Cengage.

Katz, M. (1996). *In the shadow of the poorhouse: A social history of welfare in America* (10th ed.). New York, NY: Basic Books.

Marshall, H. (1937). *Dorothea Dix: Forgotten Samaritan*. New York, NY: Russell & Russell.

Muckenhoupt, M. (2003). *Dorothea Dix: Advocate for mental health care*. New York, NY: Oxford University Press.

Stroup, H. (1986). *Social welfare pioneers*. Chicago, IL: Nelson-Hall.

Tiffany, F. (1890). *Life of Dorothea Dix*. Boston, MA: Mifflin.

Trattner, W. (1999). *From poor law to welfare state: A history of social welfare in America* (6th ed.). New York, NY: The Free Press.

Wilson, D. C. (1975). *Stranger and traveler: The story of Dorothea Dix, American reformer*. Boston, MA: Little, Brown.

Wenocur, S., & Reisch, M. (2001). *From charity to enterprise: The development of American social work in a market economy*. Urbana: University of Illinois Press.

Ellen Gates Starr.
Source: Jane Addams Collection, Swarthmore College Peace Collection.

CHAPTER 3

Ellen Gates Starr: The Other Founder of Hull House

March 19, 1859–February 10, 1940

"If we are to have a national art at all, it must be art of the people;
and art can only come to a free people."

—Starr (1895, p. 167)

Social work students all know the name Jane Addams, and have at least heard of Hull House. Of all the social workers and agencies discussed in social work history, these are by far the best known. Some social workers may even be able to recall a little bit about what Hull House did, and what a settlement house was. The settlement movement or settlement house movement was one of the formulating frameworks of social work, especially on the macro and advocacy side of the work. However, few students are aware of the other founders of Hull House, how they shaped the settlement movement, and thus how they formed social work overall. Several notable names can be found in this movement, and many of them worked within Hull House itself. These included Julia Lathrop, Florence Kelley, Frances Perkins, Sophonisba Breckinridge, and Grace and Edith Abbott (Deegan & Wahl, 2003). Unfortunately, we cannot discuss all of these individuals in the scope of this book.

This chapter focuses on the "other" founder of Hull House, Ellen Gates Starr. While she may not have had as much of an impact on the settlement movement as Jane Addams, she worked for 31 years within Hull House and was highly involved in advocating for workers' rights. While Jane Addams was lecturing on being a pacifist, Ellen Gates Starr was being arrested for standing with strikers in the streets. Some authors consider her one of the pioneers in the labor movement for women (Bosch, 1993). She worked closely with the artist community, bringing the British Arts and Crafts Movement to Chicago, and became a master bookbinder. She was a strong advocate of the labor movement, and an author. Starr seems to have been mostly forgotten in texts, other than a brief mention of her as the cofounder of Hull House. This chapter explores her life along with the settlement movement overall. Jane Addams is, of course, discussed, as it is impossible to have a conversation about Hull House without mentioning her. However, due to the extensive research and readings available on Jane Addams, the focus of this chapter is on the lesser known Ellen Gates Starr. Additionally, you learn about research-informed practice (Competency 4) through examples of Hull House's extensive use of research in the community.

CONTEXT OF THE TIMES: THE SETTLEMENT HOUSE MOVEMENT

The late 1800s was a time of great change. Immigration and industrialization were drastically altering the face of the country, particularly in urban environments. The time between the Civil War and the end of the First World War is generally seen as the Progressive Era. Reform movements were highly energetic and numerous, featuring many diverse areas of need. Many safety measures that we would now consider rights were not a reality of the working individual's life at the time. There were few restrictions on hours worked, safety measures in the workplace, or even ages of children who could not be employed. This resulted in dangerous working conditions, especially for women and children working in factories. There was no such thing as an 8-hour workday. Women did not have the right to vote. Basic services, even including sewer systems, were not available to those who lived in immigrant or poor neighborhoods. Cheap and safe child care was difficult for working women to find. Cultural activities and the arts were largely unavailable in schools or for any individual in impoverished areas. The residents at Hull House took on many of these issues themselves, either by providing services or advocating for changes in policy.

Hull House was founded by Jane Addams and Ellen Gates Starr 2 years after the death of Dorothea Dix, whom we read about in Chapter 2 (Muckenhoupt, 2003). It was the third settlement house to be opened in the United States, but became the most famous and long-lasting, with some of the widest varieties of services for the neighborhood in which it was located. While some settlement houses had a religious focus, only served a specific population such as African Americans or certain immigrant groups, or only had a narrow scope of services, Hull House worked to remain religiously neutral and was involved in a wide range of activities. Hull House was situated in urban Chicago, a city whose population had more than doubled in the years from 1880 and 1890. Nearly 41% of the population of Chicago was made up of immigrants (Stebner, 1997). The settlement movement was built on the idea that by living and working in communities, the resident of the settlement house would be able to bring the different classes and races together and improve the physical conditions of impoverished areas to the point of eliminating causes of distress and poverty (Trattner, 1999). They worked with three "R"s: Residence, Research, and Reform. In the minds of the settlement workers, living in the community allowed them to research the real conditions people lived under and then provide evidence to lead into action for change (Trattner, 1999).

Settlement houses in the United States were primarily the domain of women. More women than men lived in the settlement houses. In 1906, there were 262 female residents compared to 211 male, and 2,930 nonresident workers were female, compared to 977 men (Deichmann Edwards, 2003). The women were primarily more affluent and educated women. The opportunities of living and working at a settlement house were an alternative to traditional life for many women. Women were able to find a space to use their skills to help other people and to live independently from their families without the need for marriage (Stebner, 1997). Some residents in settlement houses stayed for a year or two before either getting married or moving on to a career; however, others resided and worked in the homes for decades (Brown, 1999). The settlement movement grew quickly. The first settlement was opened in New York City in 1886. By 1900, there were 103 settlements (Stebner, 1997). By 1910, there were 400 settlement houses. Hull House was generally considered to be the most successful of all of them (Brown, 1999). However, after World War I the movement began to decline, being replaced by both community centers and the beginnings of an actual social welfare system in the United States. Hull House itself lasted longer than most, closing its doors for the last time on January 27, 2012, due to a lack of continued government funds (Malekoff & Papell, 2012).

There tended to be tension between the two major movements of the early 20th century. These movements were the settlement movement and the Charity Organization Society (COS) movement (you will read more about the COS in Chapter 4). There was often a feeling of suspicion between them. While the residents of settlement houses worked and lived among the people they were attempting to help, the "friendly visitors" or charity workers of the COS movement had a more distant relationship. These workers focused more on investigating and evaluating the needs of each individual, working inside their homes instead of from a common location. Lubove notes that "charity workers reaffirmed the need for investigation in the atomized urban community where all men were strangers and stressed the primacy of gradualism over radical reform" (Lubove, 1973, pp. 10–11). Hull House, like most settlement houses, focused more on providing services for the overall community, and did not seem to have any issue with striving for radical reforms to take place. Although the debate of which method was more effective in solving social problems took place over the years, it is difficult to say which had more of an impact. In terms of social work today, we would likely think of the COS movement as the basis for individual or case management work, and the settlement movement as the basis for macro or community work and policy advocacy. Each has an important place in social work.

CHILDHOOD AND LIFE BEFORE HULL HOUSE

Ellen Gates Starr was born in Spring Park, Illinois, on March 19, 1859 (Deegan & Wahl, 2003). Although her parents came from well-established New England families, the family chose to struggle on the Western frontier, so Starr grew up on the family farm. Starr came from a fairly progressive family. Her father was supportive of both female suffrage and equal rights to education for all (Stankiewicz, 1989). Her older sister, Mary, went to Boston to live with an aunt to obtain the benefits of education on the East Coast, and eventually studied art in Europe, where she was a portrait painter before she was married (Stankiewicz, 1989). As Starr was among the youngest of the family (third of four children), she did not have the opportunities that her older siblings acquired. Starr attended a one-room schoolhouse and learned crafts from her grandmother. She graduated from high school in the nearby town of Durand (Hoy, 2010). A leading figure in Starr's life was her aunt Eliza, who was a leader in the arts in Chicago and helped to establish the famous Art Institute of Chicago (Deegan & Wahl, 2003). Eliza was a strong member of the Roman Catholic faith, and influenced her niece in this area as well. Starr also seems to have been influenced by her father's involvement in the community to better those in need, and remembered him at his memorial as being in "every movement for bettering conditions in his community" (Hoy, 2010, p. 3). Starr became involved in similar work as an adult.

Starr's family did not have an overabundance of funds. They could only afford to send her to college for 1 year. However, that 1 year had a major impact on the path of the rest of Starr's life. Starr attended Rockford Seminary in 1877. At this boarding school, Starr met her lifelong friend, Jane Addams (Deegan & Wahl, 2003). Starr and Addams remained friends after boarding school. Starr began teaching English literature and art appreciation at Miss Kirkland's School for Girls in 1879, where she continued to teach the young elite women in Chicago for a decade (Trattner, 1986). Starr also became more involved in various religious groups and read and explored the social theories of several men who figured prominently in the arts and community movements she later became involved with. Starr and Addams explored these topics in the many letters they exchanged before their eventful trips to Europe in 1888 (Deegan & Wahl, 2003).

THE DEVELOPMENT OF HULL HOUSE

In 1888, Addams and Starr went to visit Europe. The trip was primarily paid for by the more affluent Addams. The trip had an astounding impact on both individuals, in different ways. Addams returned from the trip as a pacifist after witnessing the horrors of a bullfight. Starr became more passionate about religion, labor unions, and arts and crafts. She had met Father Huntington, a priest who was highly concerned with social problems and lived in urban poverty. She learned about a dock strike in London and the British Association of Arts and Crafts (BAAC; Deegan & Wahl, 2003). Starr's newly inspired spiritual life and commitment to social justice both stemmed from this experience. Perhaps most importantly, on this trip, in June 1888, the two friends visited Toynbee Hall. This settlement house was a joint project of the Church of England and Oxford University that led "religiously inspired, radical activities in support of unionized labor" (Deegan & Wahl, 2003, p. 5). A combination of religious workers and university workers ran the newly created settlement home in an east London slum. This experience led the friends to begin planning their own version of a social settlement. They used their contacts and support in the community and local churches to raise support for the home. After they returned from Europe to Chicago, they found the house on Halsted Street and moved in on September 18, 1889 (Edwards, 2003). Although Addams had recently received $60,000, which would allow the home to be opened, many authors attribute Starr with encouraging and supporting Addams enough to leave her family's wishes behind and make the bold move of moving to Chicago to open the settlement house (Brown, 1999, in the reprint of Addams, 1999). Starr, not having a financial base from which to draw on for her work, spent her first years at Hull House trying to support herself though lectures, tutoring, and artwork (Edwards, 2003). However, this did not bring in enough income to support her through the work of Hull House. Her primary work was in the neighborhood around Hull House, union organizing, and art—not incomegenerating trades! Fortunately, a local woman from a wealthy family, Mary Wilmarth, paid her an income that supported Starr in dedicating her time to these efforts. Starr was supported through the years by several women from the Chicago elites who found her work important.

It did not take long for Hull House to attract other settlement workers to live and work in the community. For the first 3 years, all of the residents at Hull House were women, which fits in with the general trend of most settlement workers being middle- to upper-class women who were looking for an alternative way of life (compared to marriage and children, which was primarily the path most women took at the time). Hull House, at least in the earlier years, limited the number of residents to about 20 at a time (Deegan & Wahl, 2003). The work at Hull House was varied. A report written after the fifth year of the settlement discussed the many forms of work that the residents and community engaged in. These included, but were not limited to, college extension courses, summer school, a reading room, art exhibitions, music clubs, work with the labor movement, a club of women dedicated to work toward a policy for an 8-hour work day, a monthly German reception, a bank, cooking classes, child care, and the famous playground (Deegan & Wahl, 2003). One of the early areas they focused on was assisting immigrants in the neighborhood around Hull House to improve their conditions, both through these various programs and with advocacy and support of labor activities, including hosting union at the house (Bosch, 1993). It was estimated that about 2,000 people participated in events at Hull House during any given week. At its peak, Hull House had 13 buildings and was staffed by up to 65 people at one time (Jansson, 2012). In 1895, the residents at Hull House wrote a report that showed much of the information on the community gathered in their research and described the methods and activities of the settlement home. The report, written by Starr, Addams, and other residents, offered the idea that for a settlement to be effective it must:

> contain an element of permanency, so that the neighborhood may feel that the interest and fortunes of the residents are identical with their own. The Settlement must have an enthusiasm for the possibilities of its locality, and an ability to bring into it and develop from it those lines of thought and action which make for the "higher life." (in Deegan & Wahl, 2003, p. 43, but originally printed as an Appendix to *Hull-House Maps and Papers*, 1895)

The activities and involvement of the community show that the community and residents were able to connect with each other on multiple levels and with great passion. The large number of highly invested volunteers kept Hull House from needing to be connected with a college or university, as other settlement homes often did (Deegan & Wahl, 2003). In writing about the settlement movement, Starr (2003) stated:

> What is coming to be known as "the settlement movement" had its origin, in America certainly, in a very real impulse to eliminate, by disregarding them, the unreal and artificial barriers of class and station . . . and to seek to work together for mutual good, as one community, on the basis that the real good for the individual and of society must be at one. (p. 149)

The settlement house attracted many who held this belief that all needed to work together for the greater good of the community. This included many anarchists, Marxists, socialists, and sociologists who lived, attended events, lectured, and taught at Hull House, especially in the earlier years. John Dewey was supportive of bringing arts into the classroom and was a part of bringing the Labor Museum at Hull House into existence (Deegan & Wahl, 2003). Both Starr and Addams were considered to be leading sociologists of the time, although their belief systems could be quite different.

THE ARTS AND CRAFTS MOVEMENT

Starr and Addams had both been impressed by the BAAC during their trip to England and involved their new home in the arts and crafts movement, both by bringing speakers from England to Hull House and by leading a movement for arts and crafts in Chicago. They were impacted by the ideas of the need for "a unitary life of meaningful work that was aesthetically expressive and in harmony with nature and the community" (Deegan & Wahl, 2003, p. 6). Starr was particularly involved in bringing art to the people of the United States and Chicago. She worried that many people lived in ugly surroundings with no beauty to draw from. As such, she was involved in what some authors have thought of as the "redistribution of aesthetic" (Duran, 2014). She strove to bring items that were colorful and inspired by nature to the people in her community, especially children. One project was as simple as bringing color to the walls in the schools and other public places. She also searched for donations of pictures, especially those of the natural world, to adorn the walls in the schools in Chicago, along with a group of interested community members that she gathered. Starr eventually became the founder and president of the Chicago Public School Art Society (Stebner, 1997). In 1999, a Chicago newspaper noted the discovery of $20 million worth of art lying forgotten in the public schools—much of it possibly donated by this organization (Deegan & Wahl, 2003).

Starr also worked to bring art to Hull House with the exhibition of pictures in the small gallery, the Butler Art Gallery, which opened in 1891 (Addams, 1999). The gallery featured exhibits of art made by Hull House residents and friends, connecting art to the people in the neighborhood and making it a friendlier and more open place for those with little exposure to more formal art galleries. In 1897, Starr cofounded the Chicago Arts and Crafts Society (CACS; Deegan & Wahl, 2003). Frank Lloyd Wright participated in this organization for a time, speaking at Hull House in 1901 on "Art and the Machine," and his mother was a volunteer at Hull House (Stankiewicz, 1989). The CACS influenced American art through the creation and promotion of beautiful artwork, including Starr's own bookbinding. Music was also a form of art that Hull House encouraged. Residents taught music lessons and a band was formed. Benny Goodman, the Big Band era leader, took his first clarinet lessons at Hull House (Brown, 1999). Literature, as another form of art, was a focus of many of the classes and speeches at Hull House. Several residents had literature clubs or weekly discussion groups. Starr herself led classes on the works of Dante and Browning for many years—the classes were evidently quite popular (Addams, 1999). She also taught large classes in art history. Some students attended these classes regularly for 4 years (Hoy, 2010). Starr was described as having an "ardor for beauty [that] stirred many a young person to zeal" (Hoy, 2010, p. 4). Starr's passion for art in its many forms was evident in many areas of her life.

Starr wished to pursue her own desire to become a master of an art form. She returned to England in 1898 to study with the master bookbinder, T. J. Cobden-Sanderson. Starr stated that she did not wish to only lecture about art, but that "it would be a great deal better to make something myself, ever so little, thoroughly well, and beautiful of its kind" (Hoy, 2010, p. 5). Upon her return to Hull House, she opened a bookbindery. She wished to teach the skill to the local residents; however, she found this to be a challenge. Bookbinding was highly demanding and required an intense time commitment that the working community was not able to participate in. Starr chose to take on three apprentices at a time to teach the skill (Deegan & Wahl, 2003). Starr was also one of the leading authors on the topic, publishing highly technical and precise descriptions of how to participate in the work.

Starr was definitely one to follow her own path, in her beliefs, her artistic expression, and even her dress. She was described by her niece as "petite, graceful, brilliant, even to sparkling" (Hoy, 2010, p. 4). Many noted her eccentric style of clothing. For one period of time, she only wore lavender, the color that was associated with the women's movement (although we do not really know if that is *why* she chose to dress in lavender). An elderly bachelor left his possessions and $3,000 to Starr when he died in gratitude for her assistance in finding chess partners for him, and for a time she wore his raincoat as she went about town. Diliberto, as quoted by Deegan and Wahl (2003), stated that Starr wore this raincoat "and a small hat with a purple veil streaming out behind her, [as] she strode purposefully through the neighborhood, shocking many with her outspokenness" (p. 10). Starr was definitely not one who felt the need to conform to the values of everyday society!

Starr and the other Hull House residents and volunteers connected art to the labor movement through the opening of the Labor Museum at Hull House in 1900. This is an example of Starr's statement that "if we are to have a national art at all, it must be art of the people; and art can only come to a free people" (Starr, 1895, p. 167). The Labor Museum featured the traditional crafts of those in the community around Hull House. According to Addams, the museum began when she observed an Italian woman weaving in the streets of Chicago. The museum was hands on, offering demonstrations of crafts by the residents of the neighborhood. Starr's bookbinding was a part of the museum, although it was difficult to show the craft in progress, as it was a lengthy and complicated process (Deegan & Wahl, 2003).

Hull House became known as a center for research. The Labor Museum is one example of how the residents at Hull House took the time to investigate the many layers of work within the different immigrant communities around Hull House, finding the crafts and artwork of these communities for display. Perhaps the most often acknowledged research from Hull House was *Hull House Maps and Papers,* a publication that came out of the residents' surveys of the immigrant communities, their populations, and the conditions of their workplace and tenement houses (White, 2008). This publication included a color map of where different immigrant national populations could be found, which unfortunately cost so much to print that the publisher refused to print a second edition after the first one sold out. However, this research put Hull House and its residents at the forefront of sociology and the research in this field at the time. Some authors suggest this book and its contribution to sociology was the start of the Chicago school of sociology (Stebner, 1997).

The combined effort that became *Hull House Maps and Papers* was possibly the most thorough and systematic research in the era. This survey found that there were 26 different ethnic groups that lived around Hull House. There werequite a variety of people groups! A large color-coded map showed where the different ethnicities lived. At the time, this included Italians, Russian Jewish people, Irish, German, Polish, and French, among others. This survey found out many specific facts that showed how the people were living. For example, only one-fourth of the residents in this area had access to a bathroom that had running water (Brown, 1999). Once this information was known, Hull House residents could use the data in advocating for changes in the neighborhood. Starr's writing, *Art and Labor,* can be found in this publication.

THE LABOR MOVEMENT

Hull House was involved with the Labor Movement almost from its opening, with a discussion on the work in this area showing up in the report written by Starr and Addams in 1895 in the Appendix of *Hull House Maps and Papers*. The location of Hull House made it central to these issues, as most residents nearby worked in factory settings. The house itself was in the middle of the "sweat shop" district of Chicago. Several women's unions met at Hull House, and at least one strike was successfully arbitrated there. Hull House residents were also involved in introducing relevant legislation and calling for inspections (Deegan & Wahl, 2003).

Starr's first known involvement in the labor movement was during the garment workers' strike in 1896 (Bosch, 1993). Starr and other residents took up collections to help feed the families of the workers on strike. In 1904, Starr became a member of the Women's Trade Union League (Bosch, 1993). Starting around 1910, Starr's socialism and militancy increased as she became more involved with local picket lines.

Starr became more involved in working with unions, especially with those who were on strike. Starr was arrested numerous times for standing with strikers on picket lines and not leaving when being asked. In a brief description of Starr's testimony upon being arrested in 1915, she stated:

> This whole affair is grotesque; the opera bouffe is not to be compared with it. . . . They arrest us over and over again. Our cases come up and would probably be dismissed, but we insist on a jury trial that our friends may have a chance to find from our evidence what the real state of things is. Our cases have piled up until there are over a thousand of them. It is an absurd and laughable circle—arrest, bail out, return to picketing the next morning; arrest, bail out—and so it goes. Every time I am arrested, I ask the officer by whose authority he is acting. He usually replies "The boss." I tell him always that his boss is not my boss —that there is no law or ordinance to prevent my walking quietly past a building, that the public highway is mine as well as his. (*Chicago Daily News* of November 7, 1915, as quoted in Starr, 2003, p. 127)

Starr's work brought attention to the strikers, often bringing public sympathy in their direction. Her presence on picket lines sometimes made it safer for the workers who were striking, as she was well known and well connected. She eventually became known as the "Angel of the Strikers" (Deegan & Wahl, 2003). Some Hull House residents found this more militant version of Starr's personality challenging. One individual noted that "Miss Starr is so difficult when she is striking" (Deegan & Wahl, 2003, p. 27). One of the labor activists who worked closely with her said that she was never "afraid to tell me just what she thought" but that she also had "a sense of humor unequaled by anyone I had ever known" (Hoy, 2010, p. 5). Even serious labor supporters such as Starr need to have a sense of humor.

Many of the individuals who lived at Hull House ascribed to a more pacifist way of life, as advocated by Addams. They were sometime unhappy at Starr's more outspoken and militant stance. Starr testified for the workers and signed a petition to the mayor (along with Sophonisba Breckinridge) on behalf of the garment workers. In 1916, Starr had her one failed campaign for office, running to be alderman, but not winning. She ran the campaign knowing that it was unlikely that she, a female and socialist, would win, but more in order to bring attention to the issues she felt passionately about. These activities established Starr as one of the "leading advocates of unionized activities in the first two decades of the twentieth century" (Trattner, 1986, p. 687). In her work with the unions, Starr advocated against child labor, for the 8-hour workday, and alongside garment workers and other strikers. She worked as an organizer, collecting food and money, as a fund-raiser, and even as a publicist, working to bring greater awareness to the issues through speeches and the press (Trattner, 1986).

THE IMPORTANCE OF FAITH: LATER YEARS

Religion was always an important aspect of Starr's life. She even attributed her socialist beliefs to her Christianity, stating:

> I became a Socialist because I was a Christian. The Christian religion teaches that all men are to be regarded as brothers, that no one should wish to profit by the loss or disadvantage of others . . . that none should enjoy "two coats" while others are coatless; that, in effect, "none should take cake till all have bread." (Starr, 2003, p. 145)

Starr was one of the more religious of the women living at Hull House. Unfortunately, over time, her passionate religious beliefs caused the other residents to view her as fanatical, and they had difficulty accommodating this. Eventually, Starr became an active Roman Catholic (Edwards, 2003). One might think that with Hull House's and social work's focus on inclusion and diversity now that this would be an easy accommodation. However, it appears that only a more general sense of spirituality, based in Christianity but somewhat void of theological specifics, was welcome in this setting. The more intense religious beliefs were not in step with the "cool professionalism" of the other workers there (Edwards, 2003, p. 157). Indeed, it seems that many of the women at Hull House were more motivated by political goals, and that their Christianity was seeking practical results through their actions.

In March 1920, after her conversion to Catholicism at the age of 60, Starr shifted some of her activities at Hull House. Some authors state that at this time she became a Catholic nun, but a more in-depth analysis of her later years shows that her route was not so simple. While living part-time at Hull House, Starr held a Catholic poetry reading circle starting in 1923 that brought together people from multiple religious backgrounds. Her writing turned to liturgy and attempts to explain her "pilgrimage" to the Catholic faith (Hoy, 2010). She eventually found a Catholic church in Chicago that seemed to meet her religious needs. She continued to be active with the labor movements, in particular assisting the striking West Virginia coal miners in 1922. She even housed some of the strikers in her own small apartment at Hull House. In these later years, Starr spent the summers away from Hull House, traveling to visit her many friends, former Hull House residents, students, and others. She often based her residence at her sister's home in Massachusetts. In 1924, she took a final trip to Italy. Her most memorable moment from this trip was recorded as attending a Mass and receiving communion from the Pope.

Starr's health was beginning to become a challenge for her. She had several episodes of illness, and some of possible tuberculosis. At times she was sent to warmer climates for recovery. Her small income was earned from teaching and bookbinding or as gifts from friends. She became less able to teach or work on bookbinding as she grew older. Josephine Starr, Ellen Gates Starr's niece, was a professional social worker who assumed partial care of her during her older years. Starr continued with Hull House as her primary residency until after Christmas in 1929. At the age of 70, Starr became partially paralyzed from the waist down after a spinal operation. She spent some time in hospitals and tried to recover the ability to walk while living in friends' homes. She often had a private nurse paid for by her more wealthy friends. Although frustrated by her lack of recovery in her ability to stand or walk, Starr did write that she was relieved that the "paralysis never extended to hands & arms" (Hoy, 2010, p. 43). She was engaged in reading and visiting with friends. In May 1930, Starr's niece Josephine helped her settle into life at a rest house run by a Catholic community of nuns in New York. Starr missed the 40th anniversary gathering at Hull House. A second spinal surgery and a 10-month hospital stay followed. In June 1931, Starr moved to stay with the Catholic sisters at the Academy of the Holy Child in Suffern, New York

(Hoy, 2010), with whom she had visited and even lectured for several years earlier. She brought with her a nurse maid, arranged and paid for by Jane Addams. The two friends had become closer with old age than they had been in some of their busy lives at Hull House, and visited and wrote to each other with concern for one another's well-being and health.

Around this time she became a lay or secular Benedictine oblate, deepening her commitment to the Catholic Church and her spiritual life. This position is not quite the same as a nun, but is more of a lay person dedicated to and associated with a specific order of the church. Starr continued to write many letters to friends, often advocating for those in need, and to publish again as an author, but with her focus still on religious rituals and her own conversion experience to Catholicism. She occasionally painted in watercolor, and particularly loved painting pictures of flowers. Starr did return to Chicago once in 1935 for a memorial service for Addams, which was a highly publicized event. Starr had a very different end to her life, as she died and was quietly buried in a secluded cemetery with little attention. She died on February 10, 1940, after two years of a long decline that followed a stroke on Christmas Day, 1937. An obituary headline in the *New York Times* read "Ellen Starr Dies; Hull House Aide. Co-founder With Jane Addams of the Chicago Settlement Succumbs in Convent at 81. Became a labor leader. Active in garment strikes-Had Taught the Principles of Democracy to Immigrants" (Hoy, 2010, p. xi). This brief summary of her life cannot contain the great contribution Ellen Gates Starr made to the settlement movement and to what became social work.

LESSONS LEARNED

Ellen Gates Starr contributed greatly to the creation and development of Hull House, to the labor and the arts and crafts movement, and to the research that was produced out of Hull House. Hull House, as one of the most prominent settlement houses, was a leader in producing research to show the country the conditions and needs of the urban residents of Chicago. To finish this chapter, read through the text of Council on Social Work Education (CSWE) Competency 4 regarding research. Then you will be ready to go through the classroom exercises and discuss what you saw in Starr's practice throughout this chapter. The section reads:

Competency 4: Engage in Practice-Informed Research and Research-Informed Practice

Social workers understand quantitative and qualitative research methods and their respective roles in advancing a science of social work and in evaluating their practice. Social workers know the principles of logic, scientific inquiry, and culturally informed and ethical approaches to building knowledge. Social workers understand that evidence that informs practice derives from multidisciplinary sources and multiple ways of knowing. They also understand the processes for translating research findings into effective practice. Social workers:

- Use practice experience and theory to inform scientific inquiry and research

- Apply critical thinking to engage in analysis of quantitative and qualitative research methods and research findings

- Use and translate research evidence to inform and improve practice, policy, and service delivery (CSWE, 2015, p. 8)

For many students, this is one of the more difficult areas of the competencies to understand. The idea of research can be very overwhelming. However, it often is just a way to put into words what you are already doing. If you have a new client who comes from a different religion or country, do you spend a couple of minutes researching that information online before you go to meet the client? Then, do you use what you learned in working with that client? That is research-informed practice. Does your agency ever see a similar problem coming up with several clients, then put out a survey to learn more about that problem? That is practice-informed research. Obviously, the area of research can become much more complicated, but at its core, we are simply using what we know to learn more and better serve all of our clients.

Hull House was an excellent example of how this was used in the real world. Addams and Starr "researched" a method of working with those in poverty when they visited Toynbee Hall in London. They brought that method back to Chicago and applied it to their own population. When they started Hull House, they did not know all the various activities that would take place there, or the very many different needs of the people around them. But as they learned what was needed, the residents at Hull House found ways to provide for those needs. For example, when they learned from speaking to working mothers that a safe and affordable day-care situation was difficult to find, they opened a day-care center. This was research-informed practice. At times, the residents at Hull House engaged in more systematic research, such as when they surveyed the area around them for the information that became the publication *Hull House Maps and Papers*. This systematic research allowed them to have the level of information needed to advocate for changes in policy. Hull House was highly involved in macro work such as advocating for the needs of the community, and information such as this research is what allowed them to have the background to convince those in power in the city of Chicago that these were real problems experienced by large groups of people.

CLASSROOM ACTIVITIES

1. Take a field trip to the Hull House museum, or visit online at www .hullhousemuseum.org. Discuss what you notice. List how many different kinds of programs you see mentioned. How many of these programs are still relevant in today's society?

2. Think of an area that you are passionate about. What research, formal or as informal as an Internet search, have you done in the past to be more informed in your practice? What would you like to know that you have trouble finding out? What kinds of research might you engage in to learn more about that question you have? You might even consider taking on that research project as a small group or class.

REFERENCES

Addams, J. (1999). *Twenty years at Hull House with autobiographical notes: Edited with an introduction by Victoria Bissell Brown*. New York, NY: Bedford/St. Martin's.

Bosch, J. (1993). Ellen Gates Starr: Hull House labor activist. In R. C. Kent, S. Markham, D. R. Roediger, & H. Shapiro (Eds.), *Culture, gender, race, and U.S. labor history* (pp. 77–88). Westport, CT: Greenwood Press.

Brown, V. B. (1999). *Introduction to twenty years at Hull House*. New York, NY: Bedford/St. Martin's.

Council on Social Work Education. (2015). *2015 educational policy and accreditation standards for baccalaureate and master's social work programs*. Alexandria, VA: Author.

Deegan, M. J., & Wahl, A. (2003). Introduction: Ellen Gates Starr and her journey toward social justice and beauty. In M. J. Deegan & A, Wahl (Eds), *On art, labor, and religion* (pp. 1–35). New Brunswick, NJ: Transaction Publishers.

Deichmann Edwards, W. J. (2003). Women and social betterment in the social gospel work of Josiah Strong. In W. J. Deichmann Edwards & C. De Swarte Gifford (Eds.), *Gender and the social gospel* (pp. 35–52). Chicago: University of Illinois Press.

Duran, J. (2014). Ellen Gates Starr and Julia Lathrop: Hull House and philosophy. *Pluralist, 9*(1), 1–13. doi:10.5406/pluralist.9.1.0001

Edwards, R. A. R. (2003). Jane Addams, Walter Rauschenbusch, and Dorothy Day: A comparative study of settlement theology. In W. J. Deichmann Edwards & C. De Swarte Gifford (Eds.), *Gender and the social gospel* (pp. 150–166). Chicago: University of Illinois Press.

Hoy, S. (2010). *Ellen Gates Starr: Her later years*. Chicago, IL: Chicago History Museum.

Jansson, B. (2012). *The reluctant welfare state: Engaging history to advance social work practice in contemporary society*. Belmont, CA: Brooks/Cole.

Lubove, R. (1973). *The professional altruist: The emergence of social work as a career: 1880–1930*. New York, NY: Atheneum.

Malekoff, A., & Papell, C. P. (2012). Remembering Hull House, speaking to Jane Addams, and preserving empathy. *Social Work With Groups, 35*(4), 306–231. doi:10.1080/01609513.2012.673086

Muckenhoupt, M. (2003). *Dorothea Dix: Advocate for mental health care*. New York, NY: Oxford University Press.

Stankiewicz, M. A. (1989). Art at Hull House, 1889–1901: Jane Addams and Ellen Gates Starr. *Woman's Art Journal, 10*(1), 35–39. doi:10.2307/1358128

Starr, E. G. (1895). Art and labor. In R. T. Ely (Ed.), *Hull House maps and papers: A presentation of nationalities and wages in a congested district of Chicago* (pp. 163-179). Chicago, IL: Hull-House Association.

Starr, E. G. (1896). *Settlements and the church's duty*. In *The Church Social Union* (No. 28). Boston, MA: Office of the Secretary, The Diocesan House.

Starr, E. G. (2003). *On art, labor, and religion*. New Brunswick, NJ: Transaction Publishers.

Stebner, E. (1997). *The women of Hull House: A study in spirituality, vocation, and friendship*. New York: State University of New York Press.

Trattner, W. I. (Ed.). (1986). *Biographical dictionary of social welfare in America*. New York, NY: Greenwood Press.

Trattner, W. I. (1999). *From poor law to welfare state: A history of social welfare in America* (6th ed.). New York, NY: The Free Press.

White, B. W. (Ed.). (2008). *Comprehensive handbook of social work and social welfare: The profession of social work*. Hoboken, NJ: John Wiley & Sons.

Mary Richmond.
Source: Russell Sage Foundation Collection. Courtesy of the Rockefeller Archive Center.

CHAPTER 4

Mary Richmond: The Beginning of Micro Social Work

August 5, 1861—September 12, 1928

"To take the long view, to realize that the very stars in their courses, not our small army alone, are overcoming the weakness and misery of the world."

—Richmond (1930, "Dedication")

Mary Ellen Richmond is quite possibly the most overlooked, most important figure in American social work history. Most social workers will claim Jane Addams as the "mother of social work" and believe they are following the techniques, ideas, and beliefs that she brought to light and put into practice at Hull House. However, as one researcher bluntly describes, "social workers may claim Jane Addams as their source of inspiration, but they *do* Mary Richmond" (Margolin, 1997, p. 4). Our first reaction to this may be "What? But the only person we were *really* taught about was Jane Addams!" This is a fair argument, as Jane Addams is often the only social work founder that students remember from their classes. However, "to put it in a nutshell, social workers attempt to change individuals and families, while social reformers such as Jane Addams aim to change institutions and culture" (Margolin, 1997, p. 4). Which sounds more like what you plan to do in your social work career? Will you be working with individuals, families, and small groups at the micro to mezzo level? Or are you planning to work more in the community and the macro world, attempting to change the political arena and how it impacts our clients? If you anticipate your primary focus will be more micro in nature, Mary Richmond is the person who is closer to the "mother of social work" for the work you will be doing. Lubove states, "no single figure made a greater contribution to social work theory than Miss Richmond" (Lubove, 1973, p. 45). This may or may not be true, but she certainly had a much larger role than we often give her credit for. As you read through this chapter, consider the Council on Social Work Education (CSWE) Competency 7: Assess Individuals, Families, Groups, Organizations, and Communities (CSWE, 2015). See if you can identify Richmond developing formats for assessing these areas.

CONTEXT OF THE TIMES

Richmond's life spanned a vibrant and rapidly changing period of American social welfare history. She grew up in the wake of the American Civil War, the Depression of the 1890s shaped her early adulthood, and World War I and the following Progressive Period were the backdrop to her later career. There was a huge shift into industrial development at the end of the 1800s and the beginning of the 20th century. Urban poverty and labor unrest became common. She died just 1 year before the stock market crash and the Great Depression that followed (Agnew, 2004).

Mary Richmond was active in one of the most important and progressive time periods of American history, from a social welfare standpoint. The time frame of the 1890s, when she became active in the Charity Organization Societies (COSs) of the time, until her death in 1928 coincided with the "women's organizational heyday" when women brought their perspective and resources into the political arena (Sklar, 1993, p. 77). Once the impacts of the Great Depression became great enough to allow the New Deal to move forward, "many of their achievements were incorporated into national law" (Sklar, 1993, p. 77). The women's civic culture of that time (at least for the upper–middle- and upper-class women) was part of a movement to both bridge the social classes and bring social justice to those less fortunate (Sklar, 1993). Mary Richmond was firmly in the middle of this movement, especially in her roles within COS and in encouraging the formal education of social workers.

CHILDHOOD AND TEACHING CAREER

Unlike many of her peers in the COS and settlement house movements, Mary Richmond was not born into the upper class of society. Richmond was rare in that she was the only leader in early social work history who did not come from an educated middle- to upper-class White population. She was self-taught and from a family with little monetary or social standing (Wenocur & Reisch, 2001). Richmond was born just a few months after the start of the Civil War, on August 4, 1861, in Belleville, Illinois (Richmond, 1930). Richmond's parents moved to Belleville a year before so that her father, Henry could have the opportunity for higher wages in the factories manufacturing gun carriages than he could as a blacksmith in Baltimore (Agnew, 2004). The family moved back to Baltimore several years later. However, the wartime conditions in this city made this an unfortunate move for the family. Disease spread rapidly through a city without good sanitation conditions. Richmond's mother, Lavinia, died of the rampant tuberculosis, just 2 weeks after burying one of her children from the same disease. Her mother's death occurred just 2 weeks after the assassination of Abraham Lincoln (Lederman, 2005). Mary Richmond, at three and a half years old, was the only child of four who survived past the time of her mother's death. Richmond later remembered clinging to her father's legs out of a fear that the Catholic sisters would take her from him. Instead, Henry placed her at Lavinia's mother's home. It was in the home of her grandmother, Mehitable, where Richmond spent the rest of her childhood years. Her father quickly remarried and had two more children. Richmond recalled only rare visits from him after that time (Agnew, 2004). He died only 3 years later, in 1868, also from tuberculosis. Later in life Richmond worried that she was destined to die young due to the deaths of all her siblings as young children and both of her parents at relatively young ages. Richmond likely contracted tuberculosis herself. She exhibited symptoms in high school, when she was noted to have a "lovely pink and white complexion" that possibly indicated the fever of consumption (Agnew, 2004, p. 23). As an adult, Richmond had x-rays completed that showed scars from tuberculosis as a child. At this period of time, many thought that tuberculosis was hereditary, which likely contributed to her belief that she would die young.

Richmond's grandmother, Mehitable Harris, was a widow who ran a boardinghouse in a working class area in Baltimore. The city had a great deal of diversity during the time Richmond was growing up, but it was also divided along class and race lines. Mehitable did not appear to have much in the way of extra funds. Meals were thin and Richmond wore clothing that was handed down to her and made over. There was no money to take Richmond to a doctor when she was ill as a child. Medical care was a luxury many could not afford (Agnew, 2004).

Mehitable hosted lively debates at her boardinghouse, which provided some intellectual stimulation to Richmond before she attended school. Mehitable supported both women's suffrage and the abolitionist cause (Lederman, 2005). Reading material related to both of these topics, such as the newspaper *Revolution* created by George Train, Elizabeth Cady Stanton, and Susan B. Anthony (Agnew, 2004) and the Pickwick Papers (Richmond, 1930), was available in the house. Mehitable appeared to be sympathetic to immigrant laborers, which may have formed Richmond's early impressions of socialism and labor reform. There was a countrywide depression in the early 1870s that contributed to the labor crisis in Baltimore. Richmond's aunt Ellen was involved in the animal saving and antivivisection movements (and was possibly a vegetarian, which was not very common at that time). She passed on a love of cats to Richmond. Richmond did not grow up to agree with all of the ideas that were presented to her by her family. She did not actively support the suffrage campaign, for example, and tended to think of gender norms in a more traditional manner. For most of her career, social class and poverty were her primary focus (Agnew, 2004).

Richmond did not attend school until she was 11 years old (Richmond, 1930). Her grandmother did not agree with the format utilized by public schools at that time, which focused on rote memorization. However, she was a passionate reader, and once wrote about how reading aloud helped her through long winter nights (Agnew, 2004). A family friend named Mrs. Basil contributed to Richmond's education by allowing her to borrow copies of books from her extensive library. The agreement was that Richmond would write a report on each book before borrowing another one (Richmond, 1930). As a child, Richmond particularly loved the books written by Charles Dickens. She clearly remembered crying when she learned about his death. When Richmond did enter school at the age of 11, she was very shy and could be sensitive about her clothing. Due to the lack of finances at home, she wore her aunts' old-fashioned hand-me-downs (Lederman, 2005). She did, however, appreciate the teachers she had, especially in literature. After graduation, she participated in a book club named after her teacher, who specialized in Victorian literature. Out of the 303 students who had enrolled in the new Eastern Female High School (one of only two high schools for girls in Baltimore), Richmond was in the group of 30 who passed the graduation examination. She was only 16 when she graduated.

Due to her family's financial situation, Richmond was required to begin work right away (Agnew, 2004), and she moved to New York City to live with an aunt who had found a clerical position for her (Richmond, 1930). Unfortunately, 2 years later her aunt became ill and moved back to Baltimore, leaving Richmond by herself. She had to rent a room in a nearby boarding house and often did not have enough money for food. She eventually caught malaria and returned home to her grandmother's home in 1880. After she recovered, she found work as a bookkeeper. The work was dull for her and she often became sick because of the long hours working inside, but she kept the job for 7 years. By this time she was assisting in supporting various relatives in addition to herself with her $8.00 per week salary (Agnew, 2004). Outside of work, Richmond participated in groups studying literature, and found that she was a good teacher and mentor. Richmond, along with other members of the literature club, wrote and presented papers to each other and to public audiences. Richmond became involved in the Unitarian church, which had a vision of service that fit well with her own ideas. She wrote summaries of sermons for the local newspaper (Lederman, 2005). Richmond attended concerts, went rowing and buggy riding with her close friend Betty from the literature club, and enjoyed a fairly busy social life. Even with the long working hours, Richmond found a variety of ways to be active and engage her mind in scholarly activities.

SUITORS AND RELATIONSHIPS

For decades, scholars have speculated on the sexuality of a number of the early leaders in social work, including Mary Richmond, Zilpha Smith, Jane Addams, and Ellen Gates Starr. What we do know for certain is that none of these women chose to marry, and they had very close relationships with other women. What we will never truly know is if these relationships were similar to the lesbian relationships we see in today's society. As Fredriksen-Goldsen, Lindhorst, Kemp, and Walters (2009) state, our idea of the "term *lesbian* reflects a set of understandings that have been shaped by late 20th century Western cultural values, psychosexual and identity theories, and social movements" (p. 327). We do know that the women discussed in this book, and others, had more complicated lives and sets of relationships than can be simply defined under terms such as *spinster* or *loner*.

Richmond appears to have had several suitors over the years, including a Dr. Heuser, who gave Richmond piano lessons, and Mr. Friese, a high school teacher (Agnew, 2004). However, she declined to pursue relationships with these or any other potential husbands. When Richmond was in her 20s and had been diagnosed as having tuberculosis, she told one of the men that she could not marry because tuberculosis was in the family (and thought to be potentially hereditary). This appears to have been an excuse, as there was no social thought that one needed to avoid marriage due to illness (Agnew, 2004).

Richmond did appear to have a number of very close female friends over the years, including Zilpha Smith, one of her first mentors in the COS system, and Louisa Eyre, an artist with whom she shared a summer home (Fredriksen-Goldsen et al., 2009). In some of the letters Richmond wrote to these close friends, she speaks of her love for them. In one correspondence Richmond refers to Louisa Eyre as her "partner"; however, we have no way of knowing what this term meant to her. Unfortunately, Richmond requested that all of her personal letters be destroyed upon her death, so little is known about much of her personal life (Fredriksen-Goldsen et al., 2009). During this particular historical period, women who were able to support themselves and who chose to live in long-term relationships with other women were labeled as being in "Boston marriages," and had "a degree of respectability" (Fredriksen-Goldsen et al., 2009, p. 331). It is hoped that in time more information on the relationships and sexuality of our early pioneering women will be discovered and explored.

DISCOVERING HER MISSION

After 7 years of working as a bookkeeper, Richmond was abruptly fired in 1888 (Agnew, 2004). She then worked as a hotel bookkeeper for several months, but ran across an ad for a position at the Baltimore COS. While the position was not as secure as her job at the hotel, it had the possibility of advancement and leadership. It also held the possibility of more physical movement while participating in the duties of increasing membership and knowledge of the COS in the community. All of this was sorely lacking in her $50 per month job where she was always at a tall stool near the front of the hotel (Agnew, 2004). Richmond knew little about the COS, but thought it would be worthwhile and fulfilling. She had no training in philanthropy or social work, but no one else did either. There were no training programs in those areas during the time period. Other applicants included a cigar maker, a math teacher, and a music instructor. The chair of the board, Charles Bonaparte, later stated that she "looked pathetically young and she talked like the Ancient of Days" (Agnew, 2004, p. 57). She was hired on a trial basis.

Richmond was sent to Boston to work with the COS there and learn what she would need to know for her new job (Agnew, 2004). It was here that she met Zilpha Smith, one of the leaders at the Boston Associated Charities. The two became very close friends and provided support for each other in their challenging positions as female leaders in the COS world. Richmond began her work as assistant treasurer of the Baltimore COS. She eventually moved into the role of general secretary, where she worked from 1891 to 1899. These roles entailed a great deal more than what their titles suggest to us now. Richmond was involved in administrative work, but also in teaching, writing, and public speaking to bring awareness to the community and education to the COS volunteers. At the time when Richmond began this work, the COS movement in the United States was only about 10 years old, and not very popular (Richmond, 1930). Many people did not understand what the work of the COS was. It was organized as a "protest against uncoordinated and unintelligent relief-giving" (Richmond, 1930, p. 33), providing a systematic approach to the work of providing for individuals in need. Over time Richmond defined and clarified this mission. Richmond was also involved in doing the actual work of the COS as a "friendly visitor" to those the COS served. Her first family consisted of an African American woman with four children who had been bedridden for over a year. Through this and subsequent cases Richmond learned the real work of the COS and developed the skills to both work with these families and train others in this work.

CHARITY ORGANIZATION SOCIETIES

As you read in Chapter 1, the system that became known as the Charity Organization Societies had its roots much farther back in history, particularly with the Ladies of Charity in the early 1600s and the Sisters of Charity later in that century in Europe (Watson, 1922). The first COS in a large city in the United States, Buffalo, was a direct transplant of the work in England. The Buffalo COS (1877) brought into focus the use of the *friendly visitor* as investigator, and as a way to know the needs of each individual or family. This was central to the work of Mary Richmond. Ninety-two other cities in Canada and the United States followed, opening their own COS agencies (Agnew, 2004). In 1891, Richmond became the first woman to be appointed to the chief administrator position, then called the general secretary. In this position, and taking on families as a friendly visitor herself, Richmond learned the visitor system. This was focused on the friendly visitor, or volunteer, becoming highly involved in the lives of a small number of impoverished families. The idea was that this friendship between the two classes would help to elevate those who lived in poverty into a better lifestyle. The visitor was not to offer any money or loans to the family, but to provide support and advice. As Richmond stated in her first large speech at the Baltimore COS annual meeting in 1890, it was her wish that the program would "send to each family that needs an uplifting hand, a patient, persevering, faithful friend, who, by the power of that strongest thing on earth, personal influence, will gradually teach them habits of industry and self-control" (Richmond, 1930, p. 40). The friendship from the visitor also allowed the agency to gain enough information on what was actually happening in the family to be able to support them and provide referrals and information that would fit their needs.

One of the areas that Richmond was interested in figuring out was why some charities or friendly visitors seemed to have so much more success with their families than others. She systematically assessed the cases on file, looking at each one as closely as if it were a new case.

However, after all the research was complete, the primary conclusion of what actually worked was that the feelings of particular visitors toward their clients were the most important variables; their friendliness and sympathy appeared to result in progress for the families they worked with (Margolin, 1997). The theory was that the relationships enabled these visitors to gain more information about their clients, and were thus able to better assist them. This appears to be somewhat similar to the role of the caseworker or even therapist in working with individuals long enough to understand his or her most important needs and to have the knowledge of where to direct the client for relief through individual or micro-level advocacy. Richmond advocated for visitors to only work with two or three individuals at a time so that they would be able to get to know them very well and be able to provide this in-depth support (Richmond, 1930).

Richmond eventually became convinced that concern was not enough, and she began providing training for the visitors in a series of evening classes, which became the foundation of her book *Friendly Visiting Among the Poor* (Richmond, 1903). One of the ideas discussed in this text is the need to offer support but not do everything for the family and make them feel incapable of caring for their own needs. For example, Richmond states specifically that, "It helps a man to know that some one [sic] care and will help him to find work; but it cripples him to let him feel that he can sit idle and let his friend do all the searching and worrying" (Richmond, 1903, p. 41). She continued these trainings as well as trainings for staff members when she moved to work with the Philadelphia Society for Organizing Charity (SOC) in 1900, pulling that organization out of a time of distress. Although Richmond hoped that the move to a new position in Philadelphia would allow for more time to focus on training and establishing social work standards, this did not turn out to be the case. Instead, she spent time dealing with the agency's budget deficit and working within local politics to elect a reform platform, which brought 40 women into positions on the local school boards (Lederman, 2005).

RUSSELL SAGE FOUNDATION

Richmond made a final pivotal career move in 1909, when she agreed to become the director of the Charity Organization Department of the new Russell Sage Foundation (Agnew, 2004). This new foundation had a goal of improving social welfare through "supporting social scientific research, legislation, and community initiatives" (Agnew, 2004, p. 6). This move allowed Richmond to focus on some of her areas of greatest strengths, including research, writing, teaching, and training. Part of her role at the Russell Sage Foundation was to try to bring 180 different COSs together to share information and standardize practices. This was no small task.

She led many lectures to the friendly visitors and the public, and was so popular that for one series 1,100 people purchased tickets, many more than the venue was allowed to hold (Agnew, 2004). She then had to deliver each speech three times so that all the people would be able to hear her lecture. Many of her students later expressed gratitude to her for her teachings, including Frances Perkins, who would become the first woman appointed to the U.S. Cabinet when Franklin D. Roosevelt named her as Secretary of Labor in 1933 (see Chapter 5 for an in-depth focus on Frances Perkins). Richmond developed and taught at summer institutes for COS workers until 1922. This final position was highly important to both Richmond's career and overall contribution to the field of social work. As Sealander states, Richmond used her position at the Russell Sage Foundation "not only to oversee the transformation of charity societies from the domain of voluntary 'lady bountifuls' to the province of trained professional social workers, but also to advance the foundation's position on social welfare policy" (Sealander, 1997, p. 109). Her role as in training and in policy was most fully able to be realized while she was working at the foundation.

TRAINING AND EDUCATION PROGRAMS

Mary Richmond was one of the first in the field to become convinced that training programs were a necessity. Although she did not have a college education and was one of the less educated in the circle of the COS, she advocated for training and education for the friendly visitors, "spearheading efforts to provide an educational foundation for social work" (Lederman, 2005, p. 61). As early as 1893, Richmond launched a series of educational conferences for the Baltimore workers, primarily in the hope to improve their work through a more in-depth analysis of case histories (Lubove, 1973). By 1897, she was calling for the formation of training schools, first in a paper that was read to the National Conference of Charities and Correction (Richmond, 1930). Other leaders were beginning to speak up for the need for education at the same time. She, however, wanted a formal school, something that went beyond training within the agencies in an apprenticeship model and offered a venue that would provide a broad education to prepare social workers with a wide variety of knowledge.

One year after her paper was read, the very first 6-week Summer School in Philanthropy was opened by the New York COS, with 24 students enrolled (Wenocur & Reisch, 2001). To increase their understanding of the families they would work with, about half of the students of the New York COS Summer School found places to live in the local settlement houses. After the opening of this first school, other schools soon followed, including in Boston (1902), Chicago (1903), and St. Louis in 1905 (Lederman, 2005). In 1904, the first full-year program began (Agnew, 2004). Richmond later advocated for a second year of applied training to be required, where the study would be centered around work with an approved agency for the experiential learning, much as today's social work internships take place. In 1910, Richmond became part of the faculty of the New York School (Wenocur & Reisch, 2001), and in 1911 the New York School implemented the requirement of the second year of applied training (Agnew, 2004). By 1931 (shortly after Richmond's death), more than 60% of the graduates of 2-year programs were focusing their careers on social casework (Lederman, 2005).

The importance of professional associations was also a big push, especially between 1918 and 1921 (Lubove, 1973). In 1918, Richmond formed a committee to help with the standardization of practice and a code of ethics. The committee shifted the terms of the work they were all doing away from philanthropy and to social casework and social work (Agnew, 2004). The first draft of a code of ethics was produced in 1920, with confidentiality as a core value on which to base the profession of a social worker.

SOCIAL DIAGNOSIS

Without a doubt, Richmond's most famous and most long-lasting book was the 1917 *Social Diagnosis*. This book wrote out the principles and outline for what was then being called *casework*. Richmond defines *social diagnosis* (Richmond, 1917) as:

> the attempt to make as exact a definition as possible of the situation and personality of a human being in some social need—of his situation and personality, that is, in relation to the other human beings upon whom he in any way depends or who depend upon him, and in relation also to the social institutions of his community. (p. 357)

Social casework evolved from using this meaning to find the best ways to help individuals within the systems and the factors that were impacting them. The friendly visitors attempted to focus on facts by collecting data and analyzing the situations of individuals and their households in order to best serve them. The book drew from the social medicine model formed by Richard C. Cabot. However, it was adapted to gain knowledge of the personal and the environmental factors impacting each individual seeking assistance. The primary areas of the text included work with children, families, employment, and medical issues (Toikko, 1999). Richmond believed that social diagnosis was both a science and an art form, requiring the friendly visitor to be able to both gather scientific or factual information and craft a solution for supporting the family or individual (Agnew, 2003). This book was utilized so much by the profession that it was reprinted nine times between 1917 and 1928, was translated into German and French, and was used throughout Europe in addition to the United States (Sealander, 1997).

In addition to providing a written, systematic format for assessment and investigation, this manual gave caseworkers a solid basis for the profession. As Lubove discusses, "caseworkers believed that they had at least the beginnings of a scientific knowledge base as well as a specialized skill, technique, and function which differentiated them from the layman or volunteer" (Lubove, 1973, p. 20). Because they had this model, and due to the movement toward professional paid social work instead of volunteer visitors, "casework formed the basis of a professional identity and forced upon social agencies a consideration of the roles of professional and volunteer" (Lubove, 1973, p. 20). The social worker's special skills were based on his or her ability to "base treatment upon the expert collection and interpretation of social evidence," which may include family history, personal history, medical or school records, or reports from neighbors (Lubove, 1973, p. 47). Abraham Flexner's famous paper in 1915 on social work not being a profession came out shortly before Richmond's manual was published. Interestingly, Flexner did point out how social work made up for some of what the recognized professions lacked (Flexner, 1915). Richmond formally responded to his points at the national conference in 1917. Even though she (in some ways) continued to resist moving from volunteerism to paid professionals, she did defend that social work had skills of its own to offer, one of the main items that Flexner had stated was missing and needed to have social work recognized as a profession (Agnew, 2003).

As time went on, some sections of social work began to drift more and more toward Freudian psychotherapy, as was becoming the fashion. There became an internal debate in the 1920s as to whether social work should follow the psychosocial framework that Richmond provided or they should move in the direction of psychotherapy, as some psychiatric social workers were beginning to utilize (Lubove, 1973). In the 1930s, the idea of "functional" casework emerged to "challenge Freudian concepts of therapy" (Lubove, 1973, p. 115). In this model, casework was adapted to the limitations of time and responsibility that were possible to work with in an agency setting. This helped form a balance between the psychiatric diagnosis and the impact of the environment on the client, and gave social workers a specific function.

INDIVIDUAL AND SOCIAL REFORM

Even though Richmond is most noted for her work on formalizing skills at an individual level, as is promoted through her requests for training programs for social workers and her book *Social Diagnosis*, she was also acknowledged and was active in reform movements at the regional and national levels. Through her work with individuals, she became aware of how often social realities caused the primary issues in the households she worked with. For example, she noted that many of the one-parent households became such due to health issues such as tuberculosis or industrial accidents in the workplace. This caused her to become active in calling for legislation to fund public campaigns to address both of these

issues, thus lowering the numbers of widows who were in need of assistance (Agnew, 2003).

Richmond called these two categories of service "retail" and
"wholesale." She believed that work and reform began at the individual
level, which would be a resale level. However, with the impact of the
environment in mind, wholesale measures such as education, administration, and legislation were also necessary. These two ideas were very
firmly linked. Richmond referred to this as the dual nature of social
work, saying "the healthy and well-rounded reform movement usually
begins in the retail method and returns to it again, forming in the two
curves of its upward push and downward pull a complete circle"
(Richmond, 1930, pp. 111–112). The success of the wholesale measures
depended on resale measures to have enough active participation of the
individuals impacted by certain issues to be able to make their case for
the changes at the legislative level (Agnew, 2003). While at times some
historians may consider Jane Addams to be the social reformer and
Mary Richmond to be focused only at the individual level, neither is
entirely true. Each person had her areas of influence, to be sure; however, both of these early social workers were involved with the two different levels of work—what we might now consider micro and macro
social work.

One of the areas that Richmond was involved with regarding advocacy during her time at the Russell Sage Foundation was mothers' pensions. Richmond did not agree with many of her peers in their advocacy
for the federal government to provide pensions to widows with children.
Richmond's objections to this plan were based on her research. She studied 985 widows and found that 84% of them had worked previously, primarily as maids or factory workers (Sealander, 1997). She also discovered
that pensions were not adequate to provide for a family's needs, and that
work outside the home allowed the widows to obtain more income (and
more rewarding activities relating to work) than other sources. Richmond
focused her advocacy efforts on allowing widows to work as well as on
eliminating the causes of widowhood, such as through initiatives to
eradicate tuberculosis (Sealander, 1997). Mothers' pensions eventually
dwindled and disappeared during the Great Depression. Marriage law,
with a focus on eliminating child marriage, was also an area that
Richmond was passionate about, and one of the primary topics of her
speeches near the end of her life.

LONG YEARS OF LABOR

Richmond's career varied greatly in terms of what she was involved in shaping, from areas as broad as social casework as a general format for social work, to specific areas such as helping to create the Home Service Division of the American Red Cross to assist with families who had relatives overseas in 1917, to her later work challenging child marriage laws (Agnew, 2003). As Kendall (1977) states, Richmond was both a helper of individuals as well as a systems changer. Under the guidance of Richmond and other leaders of the time, the profession, which had focused on individual casework (volunteer friendly visiting), grew into a professional, educationally based field of study and work. The Smith College School of Social Work awarded Richmond an honorary master of arts degree for her role in shaping the profession (Agnew, 2004). Social workers who now see themselves as working within the Person-in-Environment (PIE) model must also look to Richmond for her combination of casework and social reform (Agnew, 2004). As Ishibashi states, "Richmond was looking for a kind of knowledge that could be applied to specific individual people in context" (Ishibashi, 2015, p. 94). Instead of simply blaming the person, Richmond was looking at both the individual person and how the systems around each of them influenced his or her challenges and ability to provide for the individual's families.

Richmond had suffered from poor health since she was a child. She experienced recurring bouts of tuberculosis throughout periods of her life. In 1926, Richmond became ill from shingles, bronchitis, the flu, and gallstones (Agnew, 2004). She attempted to push on in her work by having a strict routine, including spending summers in the summer cottage in New Hampshire that she shared with her friend Louise Eyre. She continued writing while at the cottage. At times, her poor health forced her to "write parts of many of her books and essays struggling for breath and flat on her back in bed" (Sealander, 1997, p. 111). Richmond also continued to give speeches on her research, often in local churches, in those last years focused on reforming child marriage. She spent time writing, including studying and writing about the early reformers in what would become the social work profession, as she believed it was important to know the history of the early years of social work. In 1927, she was diagnosed with cancerous intestinal tumors and was on radiotherapy treatment. She spent weeks in the hospital. The last conference presentation she prepared, also in 1927 and in Buffalo, "Light From Hand to Hand, Life From Age to Age," was a message to encourage young social workers to join the wholesale and retail methods and work to transform society (Agnew, 2004). By 1928, Richmond was increasingly debilitated by cancer and unable to attend the national professional conference. On September 12, while in the company of several close friends and in her own home, she died at the age of 67 (Agnew, 2004).

LESSONS LEARNED

Read through CSWE (2015) Competency 7 as you finish this chapter. Then you will be ready to go through the classroom exercises or participate in discussions in the classroom regarding Mary Richmond's contribution to social work, especially to social work education and the format for working with individuals. The section reads:

Competency 7: Assess Individuals, Families, Groups, Organizations, and Communities

Social workers understand that assessment is an ongoing component of the dynamic and interactive process of social work practice with, and on behalf of, diverse individuals, families, groups, organizations, and communities. Social workers understand theories of human behavior and the social environment, and critically evaluate and apply this knowledge in the assessment of diverse clients and constituencies, including individuals, families, groups, organizations, and communities. Social workers understand methods of assessment with diverse clients and constituencies to advance practice effectiveness. Social workers recognize the implications of the larger practice context in the assessment process and value the importance of interprofessional collaboration in this process. Social workers understand how their personal experiences and affective reactions may influence their assessment and decision making. Social workers:

- Collect and organize data, and apply critical thinking to interpret information from clients and constituencies

- Apply knowledge of human behavior and the social environment, PIE, and other multidisciplinary theoretical frameworks in the analysis of assessment data from clients and constituencies

- Develop mutually agreed-on intervention goals and objectives based on the critical assessment of strengths, needs, and challenges within clients and constituencies

- Select appropriate intervention strategies based on the assessment, research knowledge, and values and preferences of clients and constituencies (CSWE, 2015, p. 7).

We can see Richmond's work moving through these main points. Although the layers of diversity may have been different in what Richmond and her contemporaries were examining, we work through many of these same issues today. Richmond's book *Social Diagnosis* was a practical manual to assist readers in collecting and assessing relevant data so that the visitor could use that knowledge to assist the individual. She looked not just at the individual, but also into his or her environmental situation, examining issues that lead to poverty. Many of her strategies for advocacy were based on this knowledge, but knowing the individuals and families in particular was highly important to Richmond throughout her career. Much of what we have seen and learned from Richmond's efforts leads into how we work with individuals as clients today.

CLASSROOM ACTIVITIES

1. Group Discussion
   Review a copy of *Social Diagnosis*. How is this book structured? What do you think of the techniques suggested? What do you think of the questions outlined for different types of families or situations found in Part III: Variations in the Process of the book? Now, take a look at the *Diagnostic and Statistical Manual of Mental Disorders* (5th ed.; DSM-5; American Psychiatric Association, 2013).

(continued)

What do you notice about the organization of this manual? How might it be similar to Richmond's manual? What is different? What might be some of the pros and cons for using these two different manuals in the field? Are there situations where you can see using the techniques of social casework as discussed in *Social Diagnosis*? If so, give some examples of when and how these techniques might be used. When might the *DSM-5* be a better manual for a social worker to use?

2. Group Discussion
   You have now read about both the settlement house and the COS models, as well as some of the leaders of these two traditions. As a small group, outline the pros and cons of both models. Which do you think contributed more to social work? Why? Can you envision either of these models working in today's society?

REFERENCES

Agnew, E. N. (2003). Shaping a civic profession: Mary Richmond, the social gospel, and social work. In W. J. Deichmann Edwards & C. De Swarte Gifford (Eds.), *Gender and the social gospel* (pp. 116–135). Chicago: University of Illinois Press.

Agnew, E. N. (2004). *From charity to social work: Mary E. Richmond and the creation of an American profession.* Chicago: University of Illinois Press.

American Psychiatric Association. (2013). *Diagnostic and statistical manual of mental disorders* (5th ed.). Washington, DC: Author.

Council on Social Work Education. (2015). *2015 educational policy and accreditation standards for baccalaureate and master's social work programs.* Alexandria, VA: Author.

Deichmann Edwards, W. J. (2003). Women and social betterment in the social gospel work of Josiah Strong. In W. J. Deichmann Edwards & C. De Swarte Gifford (Eds.), *Gender and the social gospel* (pp. 35–52). Chicago: University of Illinois Press.

Flexner, A. (1915). Is social work a profession? In National Conference of Charities and Corrections, *Proceedings of the National Conference of Charities and Corrections at the forty-second annual session held in Baltimore, Maryland, May 12-19, 1915* (pp. 576–590). Chicago, IL: Hildmann. Retrieved from http://socialwelfare.library.vcu.edu/social-work/is-social-work-a-profession-1915

Fredriksen-Goldsen, K., Lindhorst, T., Kemp, S., & Walters, K. (2009). "My ever dear": Social work's "lesbian" foremothers—A call for scholarship. *Affilia: Journal of Women and Social Work, 24*(3), 325–336. doi:10.1177/0886109909337707

Ishibashi, N. L. (2015). Mary Richmond and the causal ontological status of relatedness. *Smith College Studies in Social Work, 85*(1), 90–105. doi:10.1080/00377317.2015.985904

Kendall, K. (1977). Signals from an illustrious past. *Social Casework, 58,* 238–336.

Lederman, S. H. (2005). Philanthropy and social case work: Mary E. Richmond and the Russell Sage Foundation, 1909–1928. In A. Walton (Ed.), *Women and philanthropy in education* (pp. 60–80). Indianapolis: Indiana University Press.

Lubove, R. (1973). *The professional altruist: The emergence of social work as a career: 1880–1930.* New York, NY: Atheneum.

Margolin, L. (1997). *Under the cover of kindness: The invention of social work.* Charlottesville: University Press of Virginia.

Richmond, M. E. (1903). *Friendly visiting among the poor: A handbook for charity workers.* New York, NY: Macmillan.

Richmond, M. E. (1917). *Social diagnosis.* New York, NY: The Free Press.

Colcord, J. C., & Mann, R. Z. S. (Eds.) (1930). *The long view: Papers and addresses.* New York, NY: Russell Sage Foundation.

Sealander, J. (1997). *Public wealth & private life: Foundation philanthropy and the reshaping of American social policy from the Progressive Era to the New Deal.* Baltimore, MD: The Johns Hopkins University Press.

Sklar, K. K. (1993). The historical foundations of women's power in the creation of the American welfare state, 1830–1930. In S. Koven & S. Michel (Eds.), *Mothers of a new world: Materialistic politics and the origins of the welfare states* (pp. 43–93). New York, NY: Routledge.

Toikko, T. (1999). Sociological and psychological discourses in social casework during the 1920s. *Families in Society, 80*(4), 351–358. doi:10.1606/1044-3894.1230

Watson, F. D. (1922). *The charity organization movement in the United States: A study in American philanthropy.* New York, NY: Macmillan.

Wenocur, S., & Reisch, M. (2001). *From charity to enterprise: The development of American social work in a market economy.* Chicago: University of Illinois Press.

Frances Perkins was the only woman in the cabinet witnessing Franklin Delano Roosevelt signing the Social Security Act.

Source: United States Library of Congress.

CHAPTER 5

Frances Perkins: The First Female Cabinet Member

April 10, 1880–May 14, 1965

"I had to do something about unnecessary hazards to life, unnecessary poverty. It was sort of up to me.... The circumstances of the life of the people of my generation was my business, and I ought to do something about it."
—Martin (1976, p. 64), as quoted from the Frances Perkins Oral History at
Columbia's Oral History Research Office, Book 1

Frances Perkins is best known for her role as the first female member of a U.S. president's cabinet, holding the position secretary of labor from 1933 to 1945 under President Roosevelt during and after the Great Depression. Frances Perkins is one of the most well-known students of Mary Richmond. As we read in Chapter 4, Richmond's work influenced the entire next generation of social workers, including Perkins (Agnew, 2004). From the framework of Richmond's work, Perkins fell into the "wholesale" side of social work, focusing on legislation and change from the political side. Perkins' training also included time at Hull House and with many other leaders in early social work movements. She spent much of her life working to improve labor conditions and safety in the workplace. During the Great Depression, she worked closely with the president to develop and implement the policies of the New Deal, including the beginnings of Social Security. Much of what we now consider fair labor practices and basic government safety nets came from Perkins's work under President Roosevelt, including providing fire safety laws, 8-hour work days, the minimum wage, Social Security, and unemployment protections (Downey, 2009). As you read through these layers of work and legislation, consider Council on Social Work Education (CSWE)'s Competency 8: Intervene With Individuals, Families, Groups, Organizations, and Communities. How does Perkins intervene at various levels? Her policy work shows us how interventions at the community and organizational level, and indeed the national governmental level, can have a vast impact on many individuals. Because of her work, Perkins has been called the "heart and soul of New Deal social policy" and the "mother of the U.S. Social Security system" (Mitchell, 2011, pp. 44–45). Without Perkins, the working world would look very different today.

CONTEXT OF THE TIMES: THE GREAT DEPRESSION ERA

Perkins's work took place during some of the most difficult times in the country's history. She worked on labor reforms at a time when people, especially immigrants, were flooding the cities looking for work. It was difficult to convince factories to improve their pay and conditions when people were so desperate for work that they would take any job they could find, and there was always a line of people willing to take their job if they didn't want it or could not do it. Children often worked at factories that preferred small, quick hands. In 1920, more than one million children from the ages of 10 to 16 were reported, by the census, to be working (Martin, 1976).

At the end of the 1920s and through the early years of the 1930s, the country suffered from the worst depression in its history, the Great Depression. When Perkins started her role as the secretary of labor in 1933, there were cities that had stopped paying teachers and police, and people were going hungry because there was no way to cash their paychecks. Unemployment had spread to about one third of the population (Martin, 1976). Between 1930 and 1932, 773 national banks and 3,604 state banks had failed, closing their doors without people being able to withdraw their life savings (Cohen, 2009). Federal legislation to help people when they were out of work did not exist. The Supreme Court had previously ruled that federal assistance would be unconstitutional (Jansson, 2012). The new president, Franklin Delano Roosevelt (FDR), inherited quite a challenging situation. He began his popular "fireside chats" over the radio, at least partially, to try to reassure the nation. He tried to bring back the people's confidence in the banking system and slow the foreclosure of their homes, while beginning emergency programs and work programs through the newly formed Federal Emergency Relief Administration (FERA) in 1933, soon after he took office as president (Jansson, 2012).

The impact of the Great Depression was long lasting. It was not until the outbreak of World War II that industry began to regain stability and was able to employ many of those who had previously lost positions. This included women who had joined the workforce in large numbers due to many of the men being deployed overseas for the war and the need to produce ammunitions and other war-related materials. While the economic recovery during World War II brought jobs back to the country, working conditions and support for those who did not have employment had been changed by the legislation that FDR and Frances Perkins put in place during the depression.

CHILDHOOD AND EARLY LIFE

Perkins's family lived on the East Coast for hundreds of years. Her ancestors were "heroes of the American Revolution" (Gore Schiff, 2011, p. 26). Both Perkins's parents came from Maine, where they had a family history of farming and brick making (Cohen, 2009). However, Perkins was born in Boston on April 10, 1880. This was almost exactly 15 years after the Civil War ended (Colman, 1993). She was named Fannie Coralie Perkins. It was not until about age 25 that she began to introduce herself under the name most people know, Frances Perkins (Martin, 1976). Soon after her birth, the family moved to Worcester, Massachusetts, to open a stationery business that became well known in the area. Young Fannie Perkins and her sister Ethel spent every summer with their grandmother back in Maine. Their great-grandmother, Cynthia Otis, who had been alive before the Revolutionary War, would tell them vivid stories of pre-revolution times. Perkins was particularly proud of the connection to the Otis side of the family, who had been active in the Revolutionary War. Her relative James Otis is credited with having said "no taxation without representation" (T. Coggeshall, personal communication, May 23, 2017). The family kept a canoe and small boats on an inlet of the Atlantic ocean.

The family had a comfortable life. A maid and cook were usually on hand to help with the household. Mrs. Susan Perkins tended to be emotional, enjoyed sewing, and was skilled at working in clay. Once, when their family house in Maine was robbed, most of what was stolen was her handmade china (Martin, 1976). Perkins got along better with her quiet, white-haired father, Frederick. He began to teach her Greek when she was around the age of 7 or 8. He enrolled her in the Classical High School, which had few female students at the time. It was always assumed that she would attend college. Perkins was generally shy. She was too shy to go into a library to ask for a book (Colman, 1993). However, she enjoyed taking positions opposite of what she believed just to shock the other person. In a family of Republicans, she would sometimes insist that she was a Democrat, likely long before she knew what the two parties stood for (Martin, 1976). Her father encouraged her to speak directly and definitively, and not to be "talky." Perkins learned to develop a crisp and direct manner of speaking, which was highly useful for her later in life (Colman, 1993). Another somewhat distant relative from the Otis side of the family, General Howard, hired her to work as his scribe for a summer while he was writing a book, as he had lost his arm during the war and was unable to write (T. Coggeshall, personal communication, May 23, 2017).

Perkins was generally thought of as plain but intelligent. There is one fairly common story of Perkins shopping with her mother at the age of 12. While they were looking for a new hat for Perkins, her mother grabbed a tricorn hat (a small hat with the brims turned up to make something of a triangle) of Milan straw. She said, "My dear, this is your hat. You should always wear a hat something like it. You have a very broad face" (Martin, 1976, p. 5). After this, Perkins always had at least one tricorn hat in her closet. This event, and her mother's description of her and why she needed to wear something of this nature, reinforced to Perkins that she was not necessarily pretty in the traditional manner. The hat became almost a signature for her, with reporters later commenting on the fact that she always wore similar hats.

Perkins graduated from Worcester Classical High School in 1898 (Colman, 1993). She then attended college at Mount Holyoke College from 1898 to 1902, and enjoyed her time there. Her teachers challenged her to take more difficult courses, and she ended up majoring in chemistry (Martin, 1976). She took a course in American history that included the teacher leading the students on controversial field trips to the factories in town to survey the working conditions. This course first showed

Perkins how one major accident in the workplace could end a person's working career, and that poverty was not always due to a person's moral failures (Cohen, 2009). One of the more exciting activities for female students was to play basketball in bloomers! The school was started as a nondenominational female seminary, which matched Perkins' upbringing in the Congregationalist church. Perkins graduated from Mount Holyoke College as a class president. Even though she was not a stellar student, she was popular among the other students (Trattner, 1986).

WORKING LIFE BEFORE THE WHITE HOUSE

Perkins's parents had hoped that after graduating she would return home until she was married. Perkins, however, had other ideas. After hearing Florence Kelley of the National Consumers' League speak at her school, Perkins decided she wanted to go into social work. She went to New York to try to work with the New York Charity Organization Society (COS), and asked directly for the head of the program, Edward T. Devine. He gave her a case study: What would she do if she visited a family who had a dirty house, a mother with a black eye, and a father who was drunk? She said she would have the man arrested. This was not what the COS would recommend, as this would remove the only wage-earning parent from the home. Devine said she needed more life experience before doing this kind of work and sent her away with a list of books to read (Martin, 1976).

Although she was offered a job as a factory chemist, her family did not approve of the work (Cohen, 2009). Instead, Perkins spent 5 years teaching, first at a private girls' school, then at a school near Chicago (Gore Schiff, 2011). There she was able to spend time working at Hull House and the other nearby settlement house, Chicago Commons. She spent any weekends she could get away from school and her vacations at one of the two projects. She would make rounds visiting families with the nurses and eventually began to work at collecting wages from employers who would not pay their workers. These experiences led her to the conclusion that this should be her life's work. She later stated, "I had to do something about unnecessary hazards to life, unnecessary poverty. It was sort of up to me. . . . The circumstances of the life of the people of my generation was my business, and I ought to do something about it" (Martin, 1976, p. 64, as quoted from the Frances Perkins Oral History at Columbia's Oral History Research Office, Book 1). In 1907, Perkins took a job as executive secretary at the Philadelphia Research and Protective Association (Gore Schiff, 2011). She worked to protect young immigrant and African American girls from being preyed upon by men at the docks and railways, who would take the girls to a place to live—often a brothel (what we would now call human trafficking situations). She investigated the rumors and was then charged to either prevent the trafficking from taking place or to find legislation at the local or state level to stop it (Colman, 1993).

Perkins eventually went back to school. Although there were not yet degrees in social work and her job had no educational requirements, she wanted to know more. She started taking night classes in 1908, and eventually obtained a master's degree in political science from Columbia University in 1910 (Trattner, 1986). She received a fellowship from the Russell Sage Foundation to do survey research in Hell's Kitchen, which became her thesis. While there, she lived in a settlement house right in Hell's Kitchen (Gore Schiff, 2011). Her thesis paper focused on malnutrition in school-aged children in that area of New York (Trattner, 1986). Her first published article was a short summary of this thesis. Perkins first met Franklin Delano Roosevelt (the future president with whom she would work for much of her life) in 1910, at a tea dance at the home of a friend of hers while she was studying for her master's degree (Perkins, 1946).

In 1910, Perkins accepted a job offer as the secretary of the New York City Consumers' League, allowing her to work with Florence Kelley, whose speech from her college years inspired her to go into social work (Martin, 1976). Her salary was $1,000 a year. One of her major projects was to work on a bill to limit the number of hours that women and children were allowed to work to 54 hours a week—the "54-hour bill." The bill had failed when it attempted to limit men's working hours, but it was considered possible for women due to the "special health needs" of women and was several years in the making (Cohen, 2009). The bill was eventually passed in 1912, at least partially due to her hard work and advocacy. She also surveyed hundreds of factories and bakeries to learn about conditions and fire hazards. Perkins became one of the leading experts in fire safety after her work during this period. Perkins was active in the suffrage movement, working to give women the right to vote. She was even known to take a soap box (literally) to the street corners and share her views. Perkins's parents were sympathetic. Her father, after hearing a speech by Dr. Anna Shaw, announced to his family that she was a great orator and decided women should vote (Martin, 1976). In 1917, the state of New York gave women the right to vote in state elections, and finally in 1920 women were given the vote in federal elections.

Perkins continued to work to improve safety conditions in the workplace. In 1911, she witnessed the Triangle Shirtwaist factory fire in which 146 women died, with many jumping from windows when they became trapped (Berg, 1989). Perkins and other guests had just been sitting down to dinner when they heard the sound of fire alarms and went outside to find out what was happening. Across the street they could see the Triangle Shirtwaist factory on fire. She ran toward the fire, seeing people in the windows, trapped by the fire. Perkins watched people fall or jump out the windows. There was only one fire escape, and it quickly collapsed (Gore Schiff, 2005). Perkins was deeply troubled by this experience, especially knowing the workers had previously asked for help with safety conditions and had been roughly denied. She took this event as a call to act. A journalist and friend later said that "what Frances Perkins saw that day started her on her career" (Downey, 2009, p. 36). In 1912, she took a position at the Committee on Safety of the City of New York and continued to work on factory safety. The years 1911 to 1915 were later considered a time of revolution in the labor field, as many bills were passed adding protections and moving toward social responsibility. These changes gave Perkins the long-term conviction that the best way to improve conditions in factories and for the working people in general was through legislation (Martin, 1976). Perkins was later quoted as having said that "the New Deal was born on March 25, 1911," the night of the Triangle Shirtwaist factory fire (Mitchell, 2011, p. 55).

FAMILY LIFE AND BALANCING WORK

Perkins married Paul Wilson, an economist for the reform mayor in New York, in 1913, at the age of 33 (Cohen, 2009). No one knew she was about to get married. Perkins and her fiance did not even invite any of their friends or family members to the ceremony. Two female strangers were brought in to be witnesses. Although the marriage seemed unusual to some people, the couple appeared to be very much in love with each other. When Perkins vacationed away from Wilson, she wrote letters to him once or twice a day (Martin, 1976). Perkins did make a point to keep her own name, at least for work purposes. Since people knew her as Frances Perkins, changing her name would mean losing some of her recognition. Wilson did not seem to object. In some ways, this was help-ful to him, as he could remain separate from her when her political moves did not fit in with his. However, many other individuals, both in business and politics, did not approve of this decision. At one point Perkins was forced to hire a lawyer to prove that changing one's last name to the hus-band's was not a law, but a custom.

Wilson continued working with the mayor of New York (Cohen, 2009), where they lived at the time. Perkins planned to finish her con-tract with the Committee on Safety and then begin volunteering a few days a week in order to have time to begin a family. In 1915, she had a child who died shortly after birth. Her father died the next year, in 1916 (Gore Schiff, 2005). At the end of 1916 her only living child, a daughter named Susanna, was born. With the help of a nurse, Perkins continued with her work. After she completed her assignment with the Committee on Safety in 1917, she became a volunteer director for a women's organi-zation, which led to the directorship of The Maternity Center Association. Here she was involved in what she called the "most successful piece of social work I have ever seen organized" (Martin, 1976, p. 133). The pro-gram worked to lower the high death rates of mothers and infants. They began by opening a maternity center where low income pregnant women could see a doctor and learn how to take care of children. The association also provided support for legislation to provide maternal and child health services.

In 1918, Perkins's life took a dramatic and unexpected turn. Her husband Wilson had a mental health disorder, which showed itself clearly at this time. Perkins said that he "suffered from an up and down illness. . . . He was sometimes depressed, sometimes excited. The cycle was terribly irregular. . . . Sometimes he was hospitalized, sometimes not" (Martin, 1976, pp. 135–136). In the beginning, they thought it was a short-term illness. For about 10 years, Wilson was able to work at least part of the time. However, it became clear that he would not be able to continue working, and he lost all his money gambling, which the family referred to as the "accident" (T. Coggeshall, personal communication, May 23, 2017). Perkins now held the position of primary wage earner of the household, while balancing the needs of a young child and her hus-band. Perkins was eventually offered a position as a member of the Industrial Commission of the State of New York (Berg, 1989). This posi-tion was higher in the government than any woman had ever been appointed!

Perkins entered into a male-dominated world of politics with a position and salary that many resented her holding. Perkins spent the next 15 years (1918–1933) working on labor issues in New York, first under Governor Al Smith and then under Governor Franklin Delano Roosevelt (FDR)—both of whom she admired tremendously (Martin, 1976). Perkins was extremely intelligent in her strategies to work with the men in politics. She spoke briefly and to the point, as her father had taught her. She had an excellent sense of humor that helped diffuse what could be uncomfortable situations. Perkins intentionally began to dress in a motherly fashion (perhaps at the suggestion of FDR's mother) so that the men would see her as someone to trust and confide in, instead of a sexual figure (T. Coggeshall, personal communication, May 23, 2017; Gore Schiff, 2011). In her work, Perkins witnessed and helped resolve strikes, advocated limited working hours for women and workmen's compensation, and worked on election campaigns for both Smith and Roosevelt. She helped the 54-hour bill become legislation, although she compromised by allowing an exception for women to work more than 54 hours in canneries, hoping to change that at a later date. The lesson of taking what you can at the time stayed with her, and she became a "half-loaf girl," willing to come back for the changes she still hoped to see (Gore Schiff, 2005). Over time she moved into different positions, but continued to stay in the area of labor issues, becoming a national expert in several areas. In 1929, FDR appointed Perkins as the Commissioner of the New York State Department of Labor to give her more power in the labor movement. In this position she was granted a salary of $12,000, the highest government wage in the state. This was necessary for the family as her husband was no longer able to work at all, and their daughter Susanna needed funds for school and eventually college. The position required that she move to Albany, as she would need to be in the office every day. This meant that she was not able to spend as much time with her husband or child, both of whom stayed in New York. For the next 4 years she worked on labor issues for the state of New York before moving on to her most well-known position as the national Secretary of Labor.

SECRETARY OF LABOR, 1933 TO 1945

On February 28, 1933, President Franklin D. Roosevelt publicly appointed Perkins as the new secretary of labor. Perkins agonized over accepting the appointment, especially as her husband and daughter were settled in New York (DeWitt, 2011). Coggeshall recounts that on the night before the acceptance, Perkins recalled her grandmother's words to her: "If a door is open for you, my dear, you must walk through it and do your best on the other side" (T. Coggeshall, personal communication, May 23, 2017). During her acceptance speech, Perkins thanked Florence Kelley, who had become a mentor to her (Colman, 1993). Women from many different movements celebrated the appointment, but many others were deeply unhappy with her selection for this post. Her gender seemed to confuse many. Many simply did not know what to call her. Most people of the cabinet were referred to as Mister, and the Speaker of the House of Representatives had to instruct reporters to call her Madam Secretary. When using her name, she suggested Miss Perkins, which confused them more because she was married but had kept her maiden name for common use. Reporters and others continuously used her name incorrectly, sometimes intentionally.

Even though Perkins attempted and requested to keep her family out of the media, there were reports about her family, in particular her daughter Susanna. One human interest story about a runaway dog even listed Susanna's address as she did not live with her parents, which raised safety concerns. In 1928, the baby of Charles Lindbergh had been kidnapped, and Perkins feared a similar situation could happen to Susanna, although it never did (Martin, 1976). Wilson, her husband, was concerned about publicity and that someone might find out about his condition (Cohen, 2009). Coggeshall, her grandson, remembers a story that he was told of how she had been known to take the film out of the cameras of photographers if they took a picture of her at an event without permission (T. Coggeshall, personal communication, May 23, 2017). Although it is likely that many political figures of the time received a great deal of unwanted attention from the press, Perkins probably had more scrutiny due to her gender and her position as the first female cabinet member.

The move to take on this role included some personal challenges for Perkins. As her husband Wilson went to reside in a mental health facility in 1933, she was the only source of income for the family. She decided to keep their apartment in New York so that her daughter Susanna could return home from school and they would all have a location to live there. Perkins was in a position where her $13,000 a year salary had to pay for housing in both New York and Washington, DC, and also any bills from the mental health facility or Susanna's school that were necessary

(Martin, 1976). Fortunately, an old friend whose husband had died, Mary Rumsey, had a home in Washington and invited Perkins to live with her. This provided her with a place to entertain as well as reside. Perkins also found a new church home, St. James, which, although a Protestant church, followed a fair amount of the rituals of Catholicism. The rector referred Perkins to a nearby community of Episcopal nuns as a place for solitude and prayer, and Perkins began to stay there for a few days at a time to rest, usually for 1 day per month. The nuns had a rule of silence for all except 2 hours a day that Perkins found refreshing (Mitchell, 2011).

One of the first issues Perkins had to face in her new role as secretary of labor—besides the giant cockroaches in the offices—was the corruption within the Bureau of Immigration, which at the time fell under the Department of Labor. A segment of the workers had taken to illegal activities regarding the deportation of non-legalized residents. Raids were commonly being performed and money was changing hands in highly inappropriate ways (Cohen, 2009). Perkins was able to solve this first problem when she discovered that the funds dedicated to paying the men in this department were gone and simply did not ask for more money. The resulting layoffs cleared out the corrupt workers. Perkins also ended other unfair practices at the bureau. When she heard complaints from White workers that there were African Americans eating in the "Whites only" lunchroom, she declared that the policy was in fact to separate blue- and white-collar workers, and soon abolished separate eating areas altogetherr. She also hired African American workers, many in clerical positions (Guzda, 1980). Perkins chose to strengthen the status of the other bureaus within the department, including Labor Statistics, Women, Children, and Employment Bureaus. She gave President Roosevelt (FDR) a list of policies dealing with unemployment that she wished to focus on. Minimum wages, federal aid to states for relief, old age insurance, and the abolition of child labor were all on that list (Berg, 1989). The only thing on her list that was not accomplished was universal health care.

Perkins felt that FDR's main talent was that he was able to make people feel at ease and get them to talk about the things they knew in order to gain a better understanding of various situations as well as the people involved (Perkins, 1946). He looked to his staff to present concrete actions to solve the needs of the people. The "New Deal" was not so much a specific plan that FDR developed as it was a phrase to help people feel assured that there was hope, at least in 1933 (Perkins, 1946). Perkins was instrumental in developing some of the emergency aid legislation to alleviate the desperation of the people during the Great Depression. Perkins was aware of how overarching the situation was. She stated, "The depression has brought home to us not only an unemployment of unforeseen dimensions but a realization of the large amount of unemployment and underemployment which is chronic even in normal times" (Perkins, 1934, p. 769). Two social workers, Hopkins and Hodson, brought her a plan to create a joint federal–state program to begin providing relief, which Perkins then took to the president, and it became the Federal Emergency Relief Act (Cohen, 2009). Perkins also assisted in relief legislation with the Emergency Conservation Work Act of 1933. This act created the Civilian Conservation Corps and relocated three million 18- to 35-year-old urban men to rural camps where they were paid one dollar a day to work on conservation efforts on public lands (DiNitto & Johnson, 2016). The young men were provided with room and board and often sent much of their salary back to their families. Another one of Perkins' main concerns near the beginning of the depression was unemployment insurance. While objecting to some of the unemployment policies that did not support what she thought needed to happen, Perkins asked FDR if it was okay for her to be outspoken on the topic. FDR said to her, "Frances, this is the best politics you can do. Don't say anything about politics. Just be an outraged scientist and social worker" (Martin, 1976, p. 218). Perkins continued to do this and work on her list of policies to implement.

In 1934, Perkins created the Division of Labor Standards to work together with the states on labor-related issues such as health and safety. Although this department no longer exists, many of the policies do, through the more familiar name of Occupational Safety and Health Administration (OSHA). One state commissioner told her she was the first secretary of labor to show an interest in state departments (Colman, 1993). Perkins traveled between states, spending time advocating for and educating people on social reform around labor issues. She was becoming better known around the country, which also meant that she was featured more in the media, which was not something she enjoyed. There were even cartoons depicting her at work, often showing her as the fearless individual standing up for others' rights. In 1934, FDR also appointed a committee of cabinet members to develop the Social Security program, including unemployment and old-age insurance. Perkins was the head of the committee.

Perkins threw her energy into developing the Social Security Act. She gathered statistics, looked at what other countries were doing, and explored ways to fund the massive program. One of the challenges was how to consider tracking personal information of the millions of people who would be involved in receiving Social Security. At some point she was told of a new machine that would be able to coordinate the massive amounts of information—the IBM computer (T. Coggeshall, personal communication, May 23, 2017; Lasewicz, 2011). Throughout her efforts, she knew that it was possible that the Supreme Court would still find the Social Security Act unconstitutional, as it was really the first federal level legislation providing assistance for those in poverty, and several smaller previous bills had not been allowed. However, the mood of the country had shifted during the Great Depression, and middle- and upper-class people were beginning to realize that poverty was not always due to a fault or moral flaw of the individual. The act eventually grew to include aid to the blind, children, elderly, and people with disabilities along with the unemployment insurance. The committee was slow to debate and decide on the details of the bill. The president gave the committee a dead-line of December 25, 1933, to present him with a bill. Several days before the deadline, when the bill had not yet neared completion, Perkins called the committee of men to her house, put a bottle of Scotch on the table, and told them they could not leave until the work was done. They pre-sented the bill to the president on December 24, one day before the deadline (Downey, 2011). On August 14, 1935, the Social Security Act was signed into law with a small ceremony for those who had advocated for the bill. Perkins herself brought pens to be given along with copies of the bill for each person to receive and keep. However, she didn't bring one for herself. The president had to ask for an extra pen to sign a copy for her, and then presented both to Perkins (Colman, 1993). Photographers took official pictures of the ceremony. Perkins was the only woman present. Unfortunately, Perkins was not able to enjoy the ceremony as much as she might have. She had received a phone call just before leaving for the event that her husband Wilson had disappeared. She went to New York right after the ceremony was completed. Wilson was found unharmed (Cohen, 2009).

To Perkins's disappointment, the Social Security Board was not placed under her jurisdiction. It was also without funding for some basic necessities, such as some of the leadership positions, offices, and furniture. When Perkins was made aware of the situation, she rose out of her own chair and pushed it over to the staff member to use. She also turned over some of her best staff members to the new Social Security Board to ensure it would progress well (DeWitt, 2011). Perkins continued to run the Department of Labor, even while dealing with personal challenges. Her friend Mary, with whom she lived, had an accident while hunting. She fell off her horse, which then rolled on her. She was taken to the hospital where she caught pneumonia, and died a month later. Perkins lost both a friend and a home (Cohen, 2009). She didn't have the funds to live independently, and ended up moving into the house of a couple who were traveling in Europe. Her daughter Susanna (who had gone on to college at Bryn Mawr) often exasperated her. She pestered Perkins so much about the poor situations of out-of-work artists that Perkins eventually proposed a plan to FDR to put these artists to work painting murals and works for public display (Martin, 1976). By 1937, her husband Wilson was able to live outside of institutions with the help of a male nurse (whom they called a *secretary*). It is possible that someone else was helping with the medical bills, as these bills were high at that time without medical insurance (Martin, 1976). Perkins continued to visit Wilson on as many weekends as possible. In 1938, Susanna had left college and was planning her wedding to an artist named David Hare. Perkins was very involved with the wedding. She kept track of those who responded to invitations and sent gifts. She mentioned that the "emotional upheaval that mothers go through on such an occasion is undoubtedly a helpful purge, but extremely difficult" (Martin, 1976, p. 397). The couple left for Santa Fe for Hare's work, and Perkins occasionally was able to visit them overnight while traveling for her own work.

Progress continued with the application of labor standards in the workplace with the Fair Labor Standards Act. In 1937, legislation was finally passed that set a basic minimum wage (of $0.25 an hour) and a 44-hour work week (dropping to 40 hours after 3 years). When the bill went into effect in 1938, over 11 million people were impacted (Martin, 1976). The last of FDR's New Deal measures was an act to abolish child labor, which was eventually put into effect with a Supreme Court ruling in 1941 (with the exception of agricultural work). Most of what Perkins had set out to do as secretary of labor had been accomplished. Perkins tried to retire from the position once again as FDR went into his third term as president, but her resignation was refused.

Instead of the honor that Perkins should have received for all her work and accomplishments, Congress and those in Washington began to accuse Perkins of disloyalty to the country and even tried (and failed) to impeach her. At one point Perkins had listed her birthdate in the wrong year, making her 2 years younger than she actually was. Perkins's grandson (T. Coggeshall, personal communication, May 23, 2017) suggests that she may have changed her birthdate so that she would not be older than her boss! The birthdate change combined with her not using her husband's last name was enough for some to say she was not who she claimed to be, and that she might even be a communist or a "Jew." Perkins stated, "There were no Jews in my ancestry. If I were a Jew, I would make no secret of it. On the contrary I would be proud to acknowledge it" (Martin, 1976, p. 399). Anti-Semitism was rising throughout the country as well as in Europe as World War II began.

WARTIME CHANGES

With the rise of the war, the lingering impact of the Great Depression and the smaller recession at the end of the decade ended as Americans went to work in the wartime economy. So many more workers were needed in the factories that women were hired into these positions, especially as more and more men went overseas with the military. Keeping the standards of labor that had been won from all the years of hard work was a challenge during war time (Perkins, 1946). Many industries and government contractors wanted to suspend the labor laws for the duration of the war, if not repeal them outright (Perkins, 1946). However, Perkins insisted that "maximum production for war cannot be achieved unless full consideration is given to the conditions under which the human factor in industry functions best" (Perkins, 1942, p. 54). Perkins issued a statement that the War and Navy departments agreed with. The 40-hour work week, 8 hours a day for up to 6 days, was still a principle that must be followed. The labor standards remained in place (Cohen, 2009).

At the start of the war overseas, immigration fell under the Department of Labor. As a part of her department, Perkins worked hard to allow as many endangered people from European countries (especially those targeted due to their identity as Jewish) into the country through the immigration process. Perkins was a firm supporter of bringing

German refugees to the United States legally and tried to find sections of the law that would allow her department to issue visas. She also stood up to FDR, advocating for the loosening of immigration laws to bring in refugees. For example, there was a law that stated that those given visas had to be able to support themselves. Perkins found a loophole in an older law that allowed others to put up bonds to support immigrants, and she advocated for its use (Zucker, 2001). Unfortunately, in 1940 the decision was made to move immigration to the Department of Justice. This kept Perkins from having as much of a role or voice in immigration matters during the war, when it may have been a safe haven for thousands of those persecuted in Europe. Many social workers advocated bringing more people to the United States. Perkins once described a conversation that Hull House cofounder Jane Addams had with FDR. Addams had mentioned that the price of wheat had fallen in part due to the surplus of the grain, but that it was "about what a million immigrants a year would have eaten up" (Perkins, 1946, p. 348). Several years later FDR mused that a large population didn't make a country unprosperous, and that someday the country may need to think of immigration policy through that lens. However, many other factors and fears, including a fear that some immigrants could be spies or Nazis, imposed a limit on immigration. Perkins believed that the United States was becoming more and more isolationist (Perkins, 1946). She noted how during this time of war, many people in the United States preferred to pull back from the global situation and only protect themselves. She strongly opposed legislation that advocated for the fingerprinting of citizens (which she thought impinged on their right to privacy) and the internment of Japanese American citizens during the war (Berg, 1989). Although Perkins wanted to increase immigration during these years and opposed some of the less positive moves from Congress, once the department was removed from her jurisdiction she was not able to have much of an influence in these areas.

After working through the Great Depression and through World War II, Perkins planned to retire from her position as the secretary of labor at the beginning of FDR's fourth term of office. The president asked her to remain briefly, which she did. Then, on April 12, 1945, FDR died unexpectedly from a cerebral hemorrhage. Although his health had apparently been declining, no one seemed to have expected his death to happen at that time. Perkins had been one of only two cabinet members who worked with FDR for his entire time as president (Cohen, 2009).

Perkins stayed in her position until a transfer to the newly chosen secretary could be arranged, several weeks later. Perkins spent a summer back in Maine, with only a trip to Paris for the International Labor Organization meeting in October remaining to wrap up her time with the White House (Martin, 1976).

"RETIREMENT" FROM PUBLIC OFFICE

At the age of 65 Perkins left her position as the secretary of labor. However, she was still healthy and believed in work. She also needed an income, as she was still supporting herself, her husband, and often Susanna, who had separated from her husband. Her relationship with her daughter was difficult, and Perkins often disapproved of her decisions. Susanna eventually found work at the Metropolitan Museum of Art, married another artist named Calvert Coggeshall, and had a son, Tomlin, in 1954 (Downey, 2009). Perkins loved being a grandmother! Tomlin Perkins Coggeshall, her grandson, shared memories of going to church with her as a young child. It was just the two of them, without Tomlin's mother (T. Coggeshall, personal communication, May 23, 2017). Perkins's faith continued to be very important to her. Coggeshall also remembered a time when he was about 7 and in New York with his grandmother, and they went to F.A.O. Schwartz, the toy store. After that they continued to Grand Central Station and walked down the platform to the engine. The engineer recognized her and invited the two of them to come up into the engine—a great treat for a 7-year-old! Coggeshall later remembered Perkins's swollen legs and how much effort it must have taken her to have done this day trip with him (T. Coggeshall, personal communication, May 23, 2017). During these years her husband, Paul Wilson, was able to leave the mental health institutions in 1951 to live with her in Washington until his death in 1952. At the age of 70, this was his first time in Washington, and Perkins found him to be very dependent and "without passion" (Martin, 1976, p. 479).

Perkins' first work in "retirement" was to write a book about President Roosevelt. The writing appeared to be difficult for Perkins. She dictated much of it, and had a secretary and an editor helping her. The book became a popular biography and soon had editions published in England, France, Germany, and Austria (Martin, 1976). After finishing the book, the new President Truman asked her what position she would like to have, and she eventually worked with the Civil Service Commission. She stayed there for the next 7 years as a much quieter figure who provided support to those she worked with and entertained only her closest friends in her home (Downey, 2009). Perkins stayed in this position from 1946 until 1952, when President Eisenhower was elected. She sold her house in Washington when she left the position.

After retirement from her 7 years at the Civil Service Commission, Perkins gave up government work completely. Perkins moved into a new area for her—teaching. Perkins's many years in a pivotal position in the cabinet during the 1930s and 1940s gave her a unique standing as a living historian of the times. Her first teaching job was a 6-week temporary lecturing position at the University of Illinois (Downey, 2009). Other temporary posts were offered to her, but nothing permanent. Even though she had previously turned down even deanship positions at major universities, now there did not seem to be anyone who wanted to hire her. Perhaps she had developed too much of a reputation as a radical (Downey, 2009). Eventually, in 1955, Cornell University's new Industrial and Labor Relations School offered her a full-time visiting lecturer position teaching U.S. labor history and the New Deal policies (Gore Schiff, 2005). Her classes became quite popular, with students hearing firsthand how these policies had actually been developed. For a time, she lived in residential hotels, not having a permanent home. An old friend, Margaret Poole, offered to let her stay in their home when she was in New York (she had previously given her old apartment to Susanna's family), and Perkins spent a good deal of time there—including most Christmases, as her relationship with her daughter Susanna never became very close (Downey, 2009).

Perkins, having become accustomed to working in all-male environments, was soon invited to live at Telluride House. The house was an old mansion that was formed into a student residential center. It was an honor to be invited to live in the home, and visiting scholars often came to dinner. Perkins's grandson related a story in which Perkins shared her excitement on being invited to live there and said she felt like a "bride on her wedding night" (T. Coggeshall, personal communication, May 23, 2017; Cohen, 2009). The president of Telluride House had decided that the first woman to live in the house should be "the most important career woman the United States had produced" (Downey, 2009, p. 384). Perkins moved into a small yellow room upstairs and enjoyed living with and getting to know the students. Her thrifty nature also appreciated that the home was endowed and that there was no cost to living there. Perhaps, fortunately for all involved, her hearing had become somewhat poor, so living with 30 noisy college students didn't bother her. She tended the house garden and had the students bring cuttings of heirloom flowers from other properties to make the garden a place of beauty again (Downey, 2009). Coggeshall says that Perkins had a wonderful last 5 years of her life working and living with the students there. He remembers visiting her there on one occasion, when the college students in the home taught him to play ping pong (T. Coggeshall, personal communication, May 23, 2017). The students were more than welcoming to her.

While teaching at Cornell and living at the Telluride House, Perkins became frail. She was, after all, now 83 years old. Her traveling was now most often to funerals for friends and past coworkers. Her hearing was poor and her eyesight was quickly lost when a blood vessel burst in her eye while she was giving a lecture. She had a heart condition and dizzy spells. But she was financially unable to retire. All of her previous income had gone to support her husband and daughter, Susanna. Susanna had a mental health episode in 1964 that required her to have additional care, which her artistic husband could not provide. Perkins paid for it, even though by 1965 the family didn't visit and had in fact told her she was not allowed to visit her beloved grandson Tomlin. Frances still felt she had to assist them. Her income from her book, *The Roosevelt I Knew*, was put into a trust fund for Susanna's family (Downey, 2009).

In April 1965, Perkins took a trip to see an eye specialist, visited the convent where she had previously been for a retreat while she was secretary of labor, and stayed with her friend Margaret Poole. She also went to address a lung issue, possibly from the pneumonia she had contracted the previous fall. The doctors admitted her to the hospital, and she quickly deteriorated, having several strokes (Gore Schiff, 2005). Susanna was notified and visited, but Perkins was unable to speak to her (Downey, 2009). On May 14, 1965, Perkins died at the age of 85. Perkins had planned out exactly what was to be included in her funeral service, which was held in New York City. Some of the male students from the Telluride House served as pallbearers (Martin, 1976). Although she was much missed at Cornell University, by this time, sadly, much of Perkins's life and work had been forgotten by the general public. She was buried in the family plot in Newcastle, next to her husband and parents.

LESSONS LEARNED

Although Frances Perkins is often not given the credit she deserves for her role in developing Social Security, it was through her work that more Americans have received assistance than from any other federal program. FDR's grandson, James Roosevelt, Jr. (2011), called Social Security the most successful government program of the past 75 years, with about 52 million Americans receiving funds each month. Without Perkins, it is possible that this assistance would not be available to the millions of Americans who depend on it to live. The core of many of our current systems of legislation for worker protection, minimum wage standards, unemployment insurance, and Social Security all came from the work of Frances Perkins. Her ability to network with legislators and provide clear interpretations and examples of the meaning of legislative bills to those in Congress, her sacrifice of her personal life to her work, and her passion improved the lives of millions of Americans, and continues to do so today. Frances Perkins gives us an example of a "wholesale" or macro social worker at his or her best, with the ability to make major policy changes to improve entire systems for populations that are most vulnerable, especially those in poverty. She worked on the political level with various other groups of people to intervene in the lives of individuals and families. To finish this chapter, read through the following text of CSWE's Competency 8. Then you will be ready to go through the classroom exercises and discuss what you saw through Perkins's life and work throughout this chapter. The section reads:

Competency 8: Intervene With Individuals, Families, Groups, Organizations, and Communities

Social workers understand that intervention is an ongoing component of the dynamic and interactive process of social work practice with, and on behalf of, diverse individuals, families, groups, organizations, and communities. Social workers are knowledgeable about evidence-informed interventions to achieve the goals of clients and constituencies, including individuals, families, groups, organizations, and communities. Social workers understand theories of human behavior and the social environment, and critically evaluate and apply this knowledge to effectively intervene with clients and constituencies. Social workers understand methods of identifying, analyzing, and implementing evidence-informed interventions to achieve client and constituency goals. Social workers value the importance of interprofessional teamwork and communication in interventions, recognizing that beneficial outcomes may require interdisciplinary, interprofessional, and interorganizational collaboration. Social workers:

- Critically choose and implement interventions to achieve practice goals and enhance capabilities of clients and constituencies

- Apply knowledge of human behavior and the social environment, Person-in-Environment, and other multidisciplinary theoretical frameworks in interventions with clients and constituencies

- Use interprofessional collaboration as appropriate to achieve beneficial practice outcomes

- Negotiate, mediate, and advocate with and on behalf of diverse clients and constituencies

- Facilitate effective transitions and endings that advance mutually agreed-on goals (CSWE, 2015, p. 9)

Perkins had the opportunity to work within the scope of many of these areas during her career as a social worker. Although the work she is most remembered for is primarily legislation around Social Security, she also had periods where she worked to intervene with individuals in the prevention of human trafficking situations or those in need of worker's assistance. What areas can you remember and discuss? Are there any points you don't see her using during her career?

CLASSROOM ACTIVITIES

1. Go to the library and read newspapers from the 1930s and 1940s to get a feel for what real life was like in that era, especially during

(continued)

the Great Depression and World War II. If you have relatives who lived through this time, consider interviewing them to see what they remember!

2. Perkins broke many barriers as the first woman to be involved in the political arena as an appointed member of the cabinet. What challenges did she face as a female in this position? In what ways did the other women you have read about pave the way for her to do this work? Do you think women have made much progress since this time? Why or why not? Find specific cases of women in the workplace or in politics to provide evidence for your thoughts. In some authors' opinions, Perkins was able to become such a successful leader because she was, in a way, forced to be the primary income earner for the family. Thinking back on some of the other women in this book, do you see similar patterns?

REFERENCES

Agnew, E. N. (2004). *From charity to social work: Mary E. Richmond and the creation of an American profession.* Chicago: University of Illinois Press.

Berg, G. (1989). Frances Perkins and the flowering of economic and social policies. *Monthly Labor Review, 112*(6), 28–32.

Cohen, A. (2009). *Nothing to fear: FDR's inner circle and the hundred days that created modern America.* New York, NY: Penguin Books.

Colman, P. (1993). *A woman unafraid: The achievements of Frances Perkins.* New York, NY: Atheneum.

Council on Social Work Education. (2015). *2015 educational policy and accreditation standards for baccalaureate and master's social work programs.* Alexandria, VA: Author.

DeWitt, L. (2011). Frances Perkins and the administration of Social Security. In C. Breiseth & K. Downey (Eds.), *A promise to all generations: Stories and essays about Social Security and Frances Perkins* (pp. 91–102). Newcastle, ME: The Frances Perkins Center.

DiNitto, D., & Johnson, D. (2016). *Social welfare: Politics and public policy* (8th ed.). Boston, MA: Pearson.

Downey, K. (2009). *The woman behind the New Deal: The life and legacy of Frances Perkins—Social Security, unemployment insurance, and the minimum wage.* New York, NY: Anchor Books.

Downey, K. (2011). Frances Perkins conceives a plan. In C. Breiseth & K. Downey (Eds.), *A promise to all generations: Stories and essays about Social Security and Frances Perkins* (pp. 69–79). Newcastle, ME: The Frances Perkins Center.

Gore Schiff, K. (2005). *Lighting the way: Nine women who changed modern America.* New York, NY: Hyperion.

Gore Schiff, K. (2011). An advocate comes of age. In C. Breiseth & K. Downey (Eds.), *A promise to all generations: Stories and essays about Social Security and Frances Perkins* (pp. 25–39). Newcastle, ME: The Frances Perkins Center.

Guzda, H. P. (1980). Frances Perkins' interest in a new deal for blacks. *Monthly Labor Review, 103*(4), 31–35.

Jansson, B. (2012). *The reluctant welfare state: Engaging history to advance social work practice in contemporary society* (7th ed.). Belmont, CA: Cengage.

Lasewicz, P. (2011). A fierce determination to improve: Social Security and the IBM. In C. Breiseth & K. Downey (Eds.), *A promise to all generations: Stories and essays about Social Security and Frances Perkins* (pp. 105–124). Newcastle, ME: The Frances Perkins Center.

Martin, G. (1976). *Madam Secretary: Frances Perkins.* Boston, MA: Houghton Mifflin.

Mitchell, D. (2011). Frances Perkins and the spiritual foundation of the New Deal. In C. Breiseth & K. Downey (Eds.), *A promise to all generations: Stories and essays about Social Security and Frances Perkins* (pp. 43–58). Newcastle, ME: The Frances Perkins Center.

Perkins, F. (1934). Unemployment and relief. *American Journal of Sociology, 39*(6), 768–775. doi:10.1086/216618

Perkins, F. (1942). Labor standards and war production. *The Annals of the American Academy of Political and Social Science, 224,* 54–57. doi:10.1177/000271624222400109

Perkins, F. (1946). *The Roosevelt I knew.* New York, NY: Viking Press.

Roosevelt, J., Jr. (2011). The mythology of fear. In C. Breiseth & K. Downey (Eds.), *A promise to all generations: Stories and essays about Social Security and Frances Perkins* (pp. 199–215). Newcastle, ME: Frances Perkins Center.

Trattner, W. I. (Ed.). (1986). *Biographical dictionary of social welfare in America.* New York, NY: Greenwood Press.

Zucker, B. A. (2001). Frances Perkins and the German-Jewish refugees, 1933–1940. *American Jewish History, 89*(1), 35–61. doi:10.1353/ajh.2001.0018

Whitney Young at the White House, 1964.
Source: Photo by Yoichi Okamoto.

CHAPTER 6

Whitney Moore Young Jr.: A Civil Rights Mediator

July 31, 1921–March 11, 1971

"If America is really serious about freedom and equality, it will have to prove that by allowing black people to be free and to be equal. That means that America must share with black people the power and the privileges now held only by white Americans. It cannot ask the black man to be responsible without giving him the responsibility for his own destiny; it cannot as him to exercise discipline unless it allows him the power to control his own life."

—Young (1969, pp. 254–255)

Whitney Moore Young Jr. was a social worker and a race relations expert best known for his role in bringing the National Urban League into the civil rights movement of the 1960s (Jansson, 2012). Although other civil rights leaders such as Martin Luther King Jr. and Malcolm X are better known for their leadership in the marches, protests, and movements of the 1960s, Whitney Young worked quietly in the background. One of his primary methods of working within the civil rights movement was to work with White businessmen and community leaders to help African Americans gain access to employment and other rights in the community. He spent much of his time (and social work skills) to bring more equal treatment through working with those who could be seen as being the oppressors. While some thought he was betraying his community through his association with Whites, he was able to be a bridge between the two segments of the population. As Jesse Jackson described it, Young's difficult job was to sell "civil rights to the nation's most powerful whites" (Weiss, 1989, p. xi). He worked hard to bring equality in housing, employment, rights to eat or go to the movies in the same places as Whites, and social services to the African American community by working within the current power structure and helping them see how these equal rights would benefit all of those in the community, not just African Americans. As you read through his life and work, consider Council on Social Work Education (CSWE) Competency 9: Evaluate Practice With Individuals, Families, Groups, Organizations, and Communities. Young worked primarily within the organizational and community settings; however, this required a great deal of skill at an individual level. Think about how he must have evaluated this work in each setting to be able to make progress and change.

CONTEXT OF THE TIMES: THE CIVIL RIGHTS ERA

The 1940s to 1970s was a tumultuous era in the United States. The Second World War brought on both a new set of challenges and a new awareness of the inequality that some portions of American society were experiencing. When America entered the war, African American soldiers were still segregated from White solders, and often given menial jobs (Harris, 1967). Segregation broke down in the armed forces, eventually through a 1948 order from the president. However, when African American soldiers returned home and found they were still not considered equal, several decades of intense work and fighting for civil rights ensued. A large number of African Americans moved from the South to the North (Jansson, 2012). Protests took the form of marches, bus and other boycotts, and even simple individual protests such as Rosa Parks refusing to give up her seat on the bus (Harris, 1967). Dr. King preached that the people are "tired of being segregated and humiliated" (Harris, 1967, p. 45). In 1957, nine African American children were sent to the previously segregated school for White students, Central High School in Little Rock, Arkansas (Harris, 1967). Four hundred local people turned up to guard the entrance of the school from these students, showing the resistance of the overall population to allow desegregation to take place.

In 1963, around 250,000 African Americans and White allies attended the March on Washington when Dr. King gave his "I Have a Dream" speech. The Civil Rights Act of 1964 gave the federal government power to enforce desegregation laws (Jansson, 2012). African Americans were split on how to best address their rights. Should they follow the nonviolent path that Dr. King and Whitney Young suggested, or was a more militant approach more likely to succeed?

EARLY LIFE, EDUCATION, AND LESSONS IN SEGREGATION

Whitney Moore Young Jr. was born on July 31, 1921, in Shelby County, Kentucky, to two very highly educated African American professionals (Dickerson, 1998). His father was a faculty member and the eventual president of the Lincoln Institute, a boarding vocational high school for African American students in Kentucky. In his youth, Whitney Young Sr. had attended this school before studying engineering. Young's mother, Laura Ray, was the first female postmistress in Kentucky and had also attended Lincoln Institute, where she met her future husband (Weiss, 1989). The couple taught briefly at the institute before moving to Detroit. Whitney Young Sr. enlisted in the army in 1918 and was sent overseas for the end of the First World War. Upon his return to the United States, the family moved back to Kentucky and he resumed teaching at the Lincoln Institute. Whitney Young Jr. and his younger sister Eleanor were born while the family was there. His older sister Arnita had been born in Detroit. Due to the family's position in the school and community, Young was sheltered from much of the racism that other African Americans grew up being very familiar with. At Lincoln, both Black and White faculty and students interacted freely with each other (Weiss, 1989).

One of Young's earliest memories was of his first major encounter with racism at the age of 5 (Weiss, 1989). His parents took the family to a nearby town to see a movie. While his parents were purchasing the tickets, he wandered into the main lobby, where an usher yelled at him, questioning why he was in there. His parents scolded him, grabbed him, and took him up to the balcony where African Americans were permitted to sit. Young was confused. He did not understand why the man had yelled at him and why his family had to sit upstairs. This was his first experience with segregation. Young later stated that he was slow to realize what limitations were placed on African Americans (Weiss, 1989).

Perhaps because of this upbringing, Young said he never felt inferior to Whites. This undoubtedly helped him later in life when he negotiated with Whites in powerful positions to gain rights for other African Americans.

While growing up, Young had an excellent example of how to negotiate though the segregated world in a manner that would bene-fit those he worked for. Young Sr. had the challenge of trying to edu-cate young African Americans in what they would need for the future while keeping White members of the board happy with the "voca-tional" tracks. When these board members would come to visit the campus, the students left their regular classes. The boys went into the fields for farming and the girls went into home economic classes. As soon as the board members left, the students would return to classes on history, science, and math. This was one way that Young Sr. "honored the rules of the white man's game" while still accomplishing his own purpose of educating students (Weiss, 1989, p. 13). Young Sr. trained his children to be knowledgeable, eloquent, and not hate oth-ers, no matter what took place. Young's mother, Laura, taught her children to love and respect people. Young was once spanked for not speaking to someone on the street (Weiss, 1989). The family was involved in campus activities such as movies and basketball games. The family tended a garden together, played cards, did homework together, and went for walks.

At the age of 12, Young began attending the Institute as a student himself (Weiss, 1989). Even from this age, he was remembered by his classmates as a negotiator and leader. One student said, "He was always sure of himself" and his sister Eleanor said "if he couldn't talk his way out of [a situation] he'd just walk away from it" (Weiss, 1989, p. 17). His mother said that he had a way of sweet-talking himself out of trouble, and that when he spoke she would "forget what she was fussing about" (Weiss, 1989, p. 17). She said he "was a manipulator from way back" (Weiss, 1989, p. 17). Young was lucky enough to be a student during a time when many people were losing their homes, in the middle of the Great Depression. He was able to study, play sports such as tennis and basketball (he was smaller than many other students at this age, although he grew to over 6 feet tall later in life), and be involved in campus life. He graduated from high school at the age of 15 as the valedictorian of the class. His sister Arnita was the salutatorian. His father was said to be embarrassed and was afraid others would think he had shown favoritism, but the other faculty members would not allow this to be changed (Dickerson, 1998).

In 1937, Young began attending one of the few 4-year schools that allowed African American students, Kentucky State Industrial College, along with his sister Arnita (Dickerson, 1998). Many Lincoln graduates attended the school, and it was a fairly friendly location for Young. He had previously met an African American physician and was impressed by both his bearing and the respect that others gave him, so Young's first thought was this would be his path. He studied for a bachelor of science, with a minor in education (Weiss, 1989). Although he was not a particularly great student, with a B average and occasionally lower grades, he was again remembered for his personality and leadership. A fellow student said that "anywhere Whitney was, was fun. He was radiant and just carried happiness with him" (Weiss, 1989, p. 26). Another student stated that "everyone spoiled him to death. He was the kind of person you just had to love. He was like a big brother to everyone" (Weiss, 1989, p. 26). He continued playing sports, was involved in the Alpha Phi Alpha fraternity, and was elected as class president (Dickerson, 1998). When Young was a junior, he met one very special woman, Margaret Buckner. Although she had hoped to study journalism at a larger university, due to family financial constraints during the lingering effects of the Great Depression Kentucky State was a better option (Weiss, 1989). One Sunday, Whitney left her a note that said "Please forgive me for staring at you in church this morning. But I couldn't take my eyes off you. I would very much like to meet you" (Weiss, 1989, p. 28). At that time she was dating someone else, so she did not respond. They got to know each other over time, and by Young's senior year they were inseparable. Young graduated in 1941 (Jansson, 2012). He applied to the only two medical schools that accepted African American students, but was denied by both schools (Dickerson, 1998). Young and Margaret continued dating from a distance while he worked to raise money for tuition. Then, Pearl Harbor changed his plans.

MILITARY LIFE

Once Pearl Harbor was bombed in 1941, Young decided he needed to enlist in the army—the still-segregated army. While he hoped they would send him for medical training, he was sent to Massachusetts Institute of Technology (MIT) for engineering training instead. He was assigned to be roommates with two White men, one of whom complained to the officers that he could not share a room with an African American man. The officer ordered him to do so, and at first the roommate would not speak to Young. However, over time they became good friends. Young was even the best man at his wedding (Weiss, 1989). In 1944, Young finally married Margaret. On New Year's Day they had a wedding at her parents' house. Young's mother, Laura, told him, "I always thought that no girl would be good enough for my son. But there is one, and I'm glad you found her" (Weiss, 1989, p. 32).

Young was assigned to a segregated African American company and sent overseas to England in October 1944. The unit worked with White officers, with a great deal of strain and animosity. The company was armed and angry about the unequal treatment they received. The situation was so bad that the officers were "terrified of the men, afraid to speak to them, even afraid to come out of their tents at night" (Weiss, 1989, p. 34). Some of Young's most important life experiences came out of this situation. Young became the negotiator between the two sides. Over time he was able to get the officers to treat the company with more respect and give them more rights (such as rights to the liquor allowance), and the men were more willing to take orders. Young was given several awards for being able to form the peace between the two sides. More importantly, he found his life's work. Instead of being a doctor, he would dedicate his life to improving race relations using his skills in interracial mediation (Dickerson, 1998). Young's time serving overseas in the Second World War was a pivotal moment in his life, as it brought him into his life's work.

The end of the war did not bring an end to the strain between Whites and African American men who had served. If anything, it was intensified. African American men returned home from Europe where they were treated on equal footing with the White soldiers. They had won a huge victory and thought they were returning home as heroes. They quickly discovered that their treatment in the United States had not changed, and became angry. Why fight for the rights of others overseas that they were not granted at home? The experience of these African American soldiers contributed to the rising of the civil rights movement of the 1950s and 1960s.

GRADUATE STUDIES AND DISCOVERING THE URBAN LEAGUE

With his new focus on race relations, Young decided it was time for graduate school. He was encouraged to get a master's in social work. He went to join his wife Margaret who was finishing her master's degree in counseling at the University of Minnesota and was accepted to the MSW program there in 1946. He attended school on the GI bill, and concentrated his classes on the group work curriculum (Dickerson, 1998). His first internship was at a public welfare agency, but it was his second internship that set his career on the path he would follow for most of his life. This internship was at the Minneapolis Urban League, a branch of the national program working to provide social services and advocate for the rights of African Americans. For his master's thesis, Young chose to focus on the history of the St. Paul Urban League and prepared a 90-page report of the history and current activities of the branch (Weiss, 1989). After completing his MSW in 1947, he was offered a position at this branch (Jansson, 2012). Young knew that the Urban League's mission was focused on improving the conditions of African Americans, and that his interpersonal and mediation skills that he had learned in the army and in his MSW program would be a great asset to the organization (Dickerson, 1998). Job discrimination was one of the main issues the St. Paul office focused on. Many employers would only hire Whites, or limited the jobs for African Americans to menial or behind the scenes jobs. Young worked to build connections with the White businessmen and to encourage them that it would be beneficial to hire employees from the African American community.

Young's early married life was busy outside of his studies and work at the Urban League. He was involved in many boards and local associations, such as the National Association for the Advancement of Colored People (NAACP) and the Young Men's Christian Association (YMCA). He was an active member of Alpha Phi Alpha (Dickerson, 1998). His wife, having completed her graduate studies while pregnant with their first child, chose not to work full-time, but worked part-time with teenagers and youth. Their social life was full, as they were friends with many of the local African American professionals. They went to picnics, parks, watched sports games, played cards, or had potluck dinners (Weiss, 1989). Young was well liked by friends and peers at work. He continued to learn how important the support of influential Whites in the community was for the advancement of the African American population. Attending the Unitarian church in town helped him have connections for broader fellowship in an interracial setting. Young became increasingly committed to racial integration (Dickerson, 1998).

By 1950, Young had accepted a position as the executive secretary at the Omaha branch of the Urban League and moved the family out of Minnesota (Dickerson, 1998). Margaret spent her time volunteering and taking care of the family, enjoying reading, and sewing. Their daughter Marcia started nursery school in Omaha. The family had difficulty finding housing there. Much of the housing available for African Americans in this community barely met minimum standards. A survey determined that about 15% of the homes needed to be condemned. About one third of the homes had no indoor bathrooms (Dickerson, 1998). Desegregated housing quickly became a focus in Young's work. Young's challenges in his new position were somewhat similar to the issues in St. Paul—employment, housing, and social services. However, the conservative nature of this new location brought new challenges. In some situations, staff members were reluctant to bring an African American director to meet with the businessmen in the city (Weiss, 1989). Young went anyway and won them over. Many positions in these settings, such as telephone operators and architects, were filled for the first time by African Americans (Jansson, 2012). More teachers were placed at mixed race schools instead of segregated schools only, and by the end of the first 2 years all hotels and diners in the area would serve both races equally (Weiss, 1989). Young made connections with both African American and White leaders to promote the idea that equal access and equal hiring practices were good for all, not just one particular group. The skills in running this branch gave Young a foundation for the work he was to accomplish in the future.

DEAN OF SOCIAL WORK

Young had kept his connection to social work education throughout his earlier positions at the Urban League, often supervising field education internships (Weiss, 1989). He taught classes at several schools while in Omaha. In 1954, Young was offered the position of dean at the Atlanta University School of Social Work. The school had trained some of the first African American social workers and placed them all over the country. Margaret was not happy with the idea of the move into a new part of the country (Weiss, 1989). However, she knew that Young would accept the position if it was offered to him. Young saw this as a chance to practice his ideas about training social workers as well as to be involved in the new civil rights movement that was picking up in that area of the country. Young joined the School of Social Work as their dean at the age of 32, possibly the youngest member of the faculty.

Young made many advancements in the program. He worked to expand financial aid to students to stabilize enrollment. He admitted White students into the program for the first time in 1956. He expanded the budget and hired more full-time faculty members. He encouraged faculty to attend conferences and participate on boards. The curriculum of the program was updated to fit the guidelines of the CSWE, which brought in new specializations such as psychiatric and medical social work (Dickerson, 1998). Katherine Kendall (see Chapter 7), while working with CSWE, visited the program and stated that the work on developing the curriculum was remarkable and praised the faculty's up-to-date information (Dickerson, 1998). During an invited visit from Kendall in 1958, an incident involving a nearby school's intent to stay segregated even after the Supreme Court case of *Brown v. Board of Education* outlawed this practice took place. Because of Young's invitation and their discussion, Kendall worked with CSWE to add the standard that discrimination in education was inconsistent with social work education (Kendall, 2004). In addition to work at the university, Young continued to spend time on civil rights issues, and succeeded in desegregating the Atlanta public library (Weiss, 1989). When the Montgomery Bus Boycott took place in 1955 and 1966, Young traveled there and met with Martin Luther King Jr. (Dickerson, 1998). Young was a board member for the NAACP in Atlanta. Young thrived in this challenging Southern community.

Young's family was not as pleased with the setting. Although Margaret found work teaching at a local college, she did not enjoy living in Atlanta. She later stated, "I hated it down there. I was angry all of the time" (Weiss, 1989, p. 68). The heightened segregation felt humiliating, and was not the experience she wanted for her two daughters. The practice of only allowing African Americans to ride on the back of the bus was one example she could not deal with. She said, "I tried it once, taking

Marcia to town on the bus, and when I got on the bus and saw this sign, 'Blacks seat from the back,' I got off . . . I think it hit me too suddenly" (Weiss, 1989, p. 69). The oppressive nature of the Southern culture was more than she could deal with. After only 4 years as the dean, Young decided to explore ways to move out of Atlanta. He accepted a research fellowship that allowed him to study at Harvard, Boston University, and MIT, putting together his own unique program focusing on race relations (Dickerson, 1998). The family moved to Cambridge, where both of Young's daughters were able to attend a private school and Margaret volunteered at the International Student Center, enjoying the cultural activities that were not available in Atlanta. The fellowship was offered to Young as part of a greater plan. One of the leaders of the National Urban League board, Lindsley Kimball, saw a great deal of potential in Young. He was instrumental in helping Young obtain the fellowship in order to better prepare him for the eventual role as director of the National Urban League (Weiss, 1989). Young was able to spend a year studying race relations and social planning from four different universities in the Boston area to better prepare him for his next position as a national director (Dickerson, 1998).

DIRECTOR OF THE NATIONAL URBAN LEAGUE

In 1961, Young took over as the executive director of the National Urban League. He started by asking the directors of the local offices (and other African American leaders and academics) what direction the national branch should move into (Weiss, 1989). Young knew that as a professional social work agency, the Urban League could focus on areas that the other civil rights groups could not, particularly in the areas of research and communication between the various groups (Dickerson, 1998). The family moved to New York, although not without some issues. The home they decided they wanted to buy was in a White community, and some of the people there had previously objected to an African American family moving in. However, the real estate agent shared with the neighbors that many other prestigious communities wanted the Young family to move to their neighborhoods, and tensions were avoided. The Young family thought it was important to show from the beginning that interracial living was a part of their practice and could be done (Weiss, 1989). Even Young's daughter Marcia worked on these principles. On her first day of school, she was invited to sit with a group of African American students at lunch, and accepted. But on the days after that she refused, and sat alone for a week until a White student joined her at the table. Weiss (1989) states that by the end of the month the pattern of sitting at segregated tables at lunch had ended. Changing the long-standing patterns was something that needed to be accomplished through daily life in society, not just at work.

One of Young's first tasks as the new director of the Urban League was one of the more unpleasant aspects of running an agency, fund-raising. The program had been left in poor shape, without the funds needed to work toward its mission. Young used his connections, particularly with foundations, to raise the income substantially. The national office was restructured, and connections with the local affiliates were strengthened (Weiss, 1989). Only then could Young refocus the agency on expanding its activities in new directions. This included a great deal of growth. In his time as director, Young added 35 new locations, grew the staff from around 300 to over 1,200, and increased the budget significantly (Weiss, 1989). Throughout this growth, the Urban League found a new focus as a civil rights organization. Young believed that it was vital that the organization be a part of the growing civil rights movement, in part to influence the direction of the movement away from the more militant segments and toward greater cooperation (Dickerson, 1998). Young also supported a domestic Marshall Plan, with a focus on providing funds to low-income African American communities (Jansson, 2012). Some of the long-standing ideas of this plan can still be seen today, in what is more commonly called affirmative action (Early, 2011). Young called for "special emergency aid" to be given to African Americans to compensate for 300 years of discrimination (Kinlock Sewell, 2004). However, Early (2011) notes that in some ways the turn to affirmative action has hurt the African American community, as it has been extended to all nonmajority groups and has not been focused as much on bringing the African American community out of poverty as the domestic Marshall Plan had hoped to do.

EARLY CIVIL RIGHTS

The Urban League was founded in 1910 by both African American and White men and women to strive for equal opportunities for the

African American population (Young, 1965). The improvement of civil rights was left to the NAACP and the Congress of Racial Equity (CORE). The Urban League focused more on research, negotiation, and community organization (Young, 1965). In the late 1950s, a shift in the civil rights movement included a leadership that was more militant than those previously in charge. These leaders were not content to move through court systems for changes to take place. These new leaders and organizations tended to believe that the older system was too slow and cautious. The National Urban League, in particular, was thought to be out of touch with the current situation (Weiss, 1989). Young slowly began to change that opinion. He believed that the Urban League could not afford to stay out of events such as the planned March on Washington.

The 1963 March on Washington (where Dr. Martin Luther King Jr. gave his famous "I Have a Dream" speech) became a focal point for many of the civil rights agencies, militant or not. The demand was for economic justice, which had always been a key area of concern for the Urban League. However, there were differing ideas on how the march should be shaped. Some wanted it to be a show of civil disobedience. Some thought it should be only African Americans. Young insisted that it should be interracial and free from violence, making sure it was an event the Urban League could support (Dickerson, 1998). He worked with leaders from each of the related agencies, persuading them that the march would be more effective as a general show of concern and support for change. To ensure that the other agencies would move from this perspective, he invited them to be involved in the planning of the event (Weiss, 1989). He also reassured President Kennedy that the march would not interfere with the progression of the civil rights bill that Kennedy had sent to Congress. Young helped form a plan that placed African American police officers in around the march itself but White officers in areas where White supremacist groups such as the Ku Klux Klan were likely to be present (Weiss, 1989). Instead of organizing the speakers, Young suggested that the speakers form their own timeline of who would speak when to ensure their buy-in. When one speaker submitted a speech filled with material that went against the overall message, Young suggested that the speaker might consider that "we've come this far together, let's stay together" (Weiss, 1989, p. 108). Young had a central position in shaping the march to form a peaceful protest that would promote the rights of African Americans without causing undue fear or resistance from the rest of the population. The march was considered a great success. Although Young's speech was not as memorable to many, his solid plan of what to do next made an impact. Partially due to Young's efforts in organizing the march as a peaceful show of concern, Dr. King was able to give his inspiring speech to millions.

Young took a different approach to promoting civil rights than many other leaders in the era. For example, Young was one of the few who was never arrested. He said, "I do not see why I should have to go to jail to prove my leadership" (Weiss, 1989, p. 110). He managed to be present and often highly involved (along with the Urban League) in critical settings throughout the movement. Young was among the speakers from the march from Selma to Montgomery in 1965 (Weiss, 1989). However, when violent forms of protest or "Black power" separatism were present, Young and the National Urban League stayed away. He said, "I have no intention of retreating into a reverse kind of segregation and abandoning my efforts to get true equality" (Weiss, 1989, p. 112). Young often acted as a mediator between the leaders of the different civil rights organizations, and helped bring the more militant sections to at least talk to other organizations. He was able to identify and speak to the student movements, and had connections that even helped with funding for events such as the March on Washington. In some ways, Young helped the National Urban League become the preferred agency to work with for many Whites and leaders in power. They were thought to be easier to deal with, and perhaps less dangerous. He would encourage the leaders to make progress in the civil rights movement in the ways the Urban League would suggest, with the alternative being the chaos that the militant movements could bring. For example, Young had a relationship with Malcolm X, who had no interest in a nonviolent strategy. Malcolm X once said that "I have to play the role I play in order for them to listen to people like Martin and Whitney" (as quoted in Weiss, 1989, p. 123). If a corporate executive called Young saying that Malcolm X wanted to speak to him, Young would suggest that that person had better do something for the African Americans in the community so he would be able to answer to Malcolm X (Weiss, 1989). In this way, the different approaches to obtaining civil rights sometimes played off of each other. However, if the sets of leaders did not speak to each other, it is unlikely this could have been the case.

THE LANDSCAPE BEGINS TO CHANGE: THE CIVIL RIGHTS ACT OF 1964

The Civil Rights Act of 1964 changed the landscape. It was now illegal to discriminate in employment due to race. Public facilities were required to be desegregated. Voting rights were protected, especially for African Americans in the South (Jansson, 2012). The act even provided a course of action for victims if the laws were broken, providing a way to enforce the law (Bent-Goodley, 2014). Unfortunately, a great deal of racial violence followed. African Americans were angry that while the laws had changed, their social and economic situations had not (Weiss, 1989). Young was again able to be a bridge between the sides. Both African Americans and Whites trusted him. President Kennedy, President Johnson, and President Nixon all looked to him for guidance. Young was particularly close to President Johnson. He even advised Johnson on his 1965 State of the Union address (Dickerson, 1998). Young turned down direct appointments with two administrations to be able to continue his work at the National Urban League (Sims, 1971). Young did visit Vietnam in 1966. The trip was funded by the National Urban League to assess the welfare of the African American soldiers and learn how to better assist the soldiers when they returned home (Dickerson, 1998). Young's refusal to take a position in the antiwar climate of the 1960s separated him from many of the other civil rights leaders, who were primarily antiwar. It may have also contributed to his ability to continue to advise three presidents on how to continue their work to improve civil rights within the country. Other moderate civil rights leaders refused to take a position, saying that the war and civil rights were separate issues (Hall, 2003).

The National Urban League continued to grow. Young published his book *To Be Equal* in 1964. In this book, Young continued his themes of asking for better employment, education, housing, and healthcare for the African American community (Young, 1964). He also called attention to the discrimination gap that existed, even when laws made official discrimination illegal. He said, "Equal opportunity, if it is to be more than a hollow mockery, must also mean the opportunity to be equal, to be given a fair chance to achieve equality" (Young, 1964, p. 23). Funding from large foundations, such as a $1,500,000 grant from the Ford Foundation in 1966, allowed Young to pursue many of his projects (Dickerson, 1998). They were able to work on improving housing in the cities that hosted Urban League offices. Funding also allowed the organization to be involved in expanding the agency to 32 additional cities (with more joining every year) and to be more involved in social activism around the country.

Young's busy schedule kept him traveling often. He attended many of the main civil rights movement activities, including boycotts and marches, sometimes as an individual instead of as the head of the agency. Sometimes he would visit two or three cities in the same day. Although he was close to his family, his schedule took a toll. His daughter Marcia noted that Young did not know how to stop and relax. Young was still close to his wife Margaret, who helped him as an editor, sounding board, and advisor. He was said to have had a flirtatious nature and a weakness for the temptations of other women. Nevertheless, for their 25th wedding anniversary Young gave Margaret a brooch modeled after the Urban League's equal sign and recited poetry to her in front of the 400 guests at their anniversary dinner (Weiss, 1989).

Young sought to change the system from within, which was not always the most popular method. Other African Americans criticized him for taking this role. He continued to advocate for the involvement of White supporters and advocates, especially businessmen who might employ the community (Dickerson, 1998). The more militant segment of the movement considered Young a sellout, some calling him "Whitey" Young. Others preferred Young's tactics of racial cooperation and dialog (Dickerson, 1998). The drastic events of the late 1960s gave Young and the organization enough support to change the direction toward being more directly involved in supporting the civil rights movement from the forefront. The assassination of Martin Luther King Jr. in 1968 shocked the nation and caused massive riots. This event in particular allowed Young to direct the National Urban League to change its policies so that direct action, community organizing, and lobbying became a part of its practice (Weiss, 1989). This reorientation became known as the New Thrust. One of the primary areas of concern for the New Thrust was the ghettos, and how to bring inner city grassroots leadership from this segment of the population into power and partnering with the National Urban League (Dickerson, 1998). While still working within the system, this allowed for more involvement in areas that most African Americans saw as necessary for change and brought greater commitment from some segments of the population. By 1970, the National Urban League received over $5 million from foundations, showing the investment from the philanthropic arena (Dickerson, 1998). Another $21 million in contracts with the federal government increased its ability to provide housing and other infrastructure changes (Dickerson, 1998). However, by 1971, Young was preparing to turn 50 and ready to retire from the National Urban League, having seen most of his goals attained.

A SUDDEN DEATH

Young's trip to Nigeria to participate in the African and American dialog took place before he was able to decide what was next for him. Many said he should not have taken the trip. His health was poor and Margaret had just returned from her father's funeral (Dickerson, 1998). However, he decided it was important to attend. Africans respected Young for his work in the civil rights movement. On the fourth day of the conference Young and several others decided to go swimming in the ocean. The water was dangerous, but Young loved to swim. When the rest of the group returned to shore, they noticed that Young was not with them. Several men tried to pull him in and revive him, but were not successful. Young had died in the water. The date was March 11, 1971 (Jansson, 2012). The president had to call Margaret to tell her the news (Weiss, 1989). Young was buried in Lexington, Kentucky, next to his mother. Thousands of people lined the street to watch the funeral go by. President Nixon offered the eulogy for the ceremony, where about 4,000 people filled the cemetery. Nixon said that Young's genius lay in that "He knew how to accomplish what other people were merely for" (Nixon, 1972, p. 42). He also remembered Young always having an "equal" button on his jacket, and said that "he didn't just wear that in his lapel; he wore it in his heart" (Nixon, 1972, p. 44). Young had spent his adult life working for equality in America. Sims (1971), who took over as the interim director of the National Urban League, said that Young "was a man who formed a human bridge between the rich and the poor, the white and the black, the conservative and the liberal" (p. 71). Young was able to work with people from all backgrounds to improve society for all, but especially for African Americans.

LESSONS LEARNED

Whitney Young's name is not one of the first that comes up when people talk about leaders in the civil rights movement. However, Young was perhaps the strongest individual working within the system to involve both African Americans and supportive White allies. He was a leader in many areas. He developed his leadership in running local offices of the Urban League. He was the dean of the Atlanta University School of Social Work and even the National Association of Social Workers (NASW) president in 1969 (Dickerson, 1998). He led the National Urban League through the tumultuous times of the 1960s. Young was an advisor to Presidents Kennedy, Johnson, and Nixon, helping them to improve civil rights at a national level. Young was able to bring new opportunities to many African Americans in the areas of employment and housing, partially due to his ability to speak with the White business leaders and obtain buy-in from them. However, he could equally well interact with the militant and separatist members of the movement. The leaders of other civil rights programs often relied on Young for advice, contacts, and resources (Dickerson, 1998). From behind the scenes, Young was involved in supporting boycotts and setting up marches—even the 1963 March on Washington where Dr. King presented his "I Have A Dream" speech. Young had a talent in getting both sides to come together for the greater good of both. Young may be the greatest influence that few people have heard of from the civil rights era. Now that you have read more about Young's life, consider CSWE Competency 9.

The section reads:

Competency 9: Evaluate Practice With Individuals, Families, Groups, Organizations, and Communities

Social workers understand that evaluation is an ongoing component of the dynamic and interactive process of social work practice with, and on behalf of, diverse individuals, families, groups, organizations, and communities. Social workers recognize the importance of evaluating processes and outcomes to advance practice, policy, and service delivery effectiveness. Social workers understand theories of human behavior and the social environment, and critically evaluate and apply this knowledge in evaluating outcomes. Social workers understand qualitative and quantitative methods for evaluating outcomes and practice effectiveness. Social workers:

- Select and use appropriate methods for evaluation of outcomes

- Apply knowledge of human behavior and the social environment, Person in Environment, and other multidisciplinary theoretical frameworks in the evaluation of outcomes

- Critically analyze, monitor, and evaluate intervention and program processes and outcomes

- Apply evaluation findings to improve practice effectiveness at the micro, mezzo, and macro levels (CSWE, 2015, p. 9)

Whitney Young did not speak directly to evaluation of services in his work, but he undoubtedly used extensive evaluation methods to make the changes he did within multiple systems. From directing a social work program at a university to running a nationwide agency, evaluation of the issues within the many platforms would have been necessary to see the strengths and areas that were in need of growth. In what ways do you think Young used evaluation methods and knowledge of theoretical frameworks in his work?

CLASSROOM ACTIVITIES

1. Watch the documentary *The Powerbroker: Whitney Young's Fight for Civil Rights*. What do you think of his approach to changing society? Do you think the approaches of other civil rights leaders were more or less effective than his? What do you think is the lasting impact of Young's work?

2. If your class is in an area where there is a chapter of the Urban League, consider either having a guest speaker attend the class or having a student interview someone from the organization and report back to the class. What is the mission of this agency now? Has it changed since Whitney Young was the director? How do you see the Urban League impacting the surrounding community? For an extended project, consider having the class volunteer to work with the Urban League.

REFERENCES

Bent-Goodley, T. (2014). Social work and the Civil Rights Act of 1964. *Social Work, 59*(4), 293–295. doi:10.1093/sw/swu040

Council on Social Work Education. (2015). *2015 educational policy and accreditation standards for baccalaureate and master's social work programs.* Alexandria, VA: Author.

Dickerson, D. (1998). *Militant mediator: Whitney M. Young Jr.* Lexington: The University Press of Kentucky.

Early, G. (2011). The two worlds of race revisited: A meditation on race in the age of Obama. *Daedalus, 140*(1), 11–27. doi:10.1162/DAED_a_00055

Hall, S. (2003). The response of the moderate wing of the civil rights movement to the war in Vietnam. *The Historical Journal, 46*(3), 669–701. doi:10.1017/S0018246 X03003200

Harris, J. (1967). *The long freedom road: The civil rights story.* New York, NY: McGraw-Hill.

Jansson, B. (2012). *The reluctant welfare state: Engaging history to advance social work practice in contemporary society.* Belmont, CA: Brooks/Cole.

Kendall, K. (2004). Unforgettable episodes in fighting discrimination. *Reflections: Narratives of Professional Helping, 10*(1), 56–62. Retrieved from https://reflections narrativesofprofessionalhelping.org/index.php/Reflections/article/view/1182

Kinlock Sewell, S. (2004). The "not-buying power" of the Black community: Urban boycotts and equal employment opportunity, 1960–1964. *The Journal of African American History, 89*(2), 135–151. doi:10.2307/4134097

Nixon, R. (1972). *Four great Americans: Tributes delivered by President Richard Nixon.* New York, NY: Doubleday.

Sims, H. (1971). Whitney Young's open society. *The Annals of the American Academy of Political and Social Science, 396,* 70–78. doi:10.1177/000271627139600107

Weiss, N. (1989). *Whitney M. Young, Jr. and the struggle for civil rights.* Princeton, NJ: Princeton University Press.

Young, W. (1964). *To be equal.* New York, NY: McGraw-Hill.

Young, W. (1965). The Urban League and its strategy. *The Annals of the American Academy of Political and Social Science, 357,* 102–107. doi:10.1177/000271626535 700112

Young, W. (1969). *Beyond racism: Building an open society.* New York, NY: McGraw-Hill.

Katherine Anne Tuach Kendall.

Source: Photo courtesy of the Katherine A. Kendall Institute, Council on Social Work Education.

CHAPTER 7

Katherine Anne Tuach Kendall: Reforming a Profession

September 8, 1910–December 1, 2010

"Perhaps only the rare person can function equally well both as a reformer and as a helper, but the profession can and should make room for both."

—Billups (2002, p. 147)

It is not often we come across a person who is able to work across decades, within major trends and flows of social work and social work education, and across international lines. Katherine A. Kendall—who lived to be 100 years old—managed to do so, and to do so with much greater impact than one would expect. Although Katherine Kendall is a name that may not be familiar to the everyday social worker, her life's work has had a huge influence on every student who takes social work classes at an accredited institution. From her work with the United Nations (UN) in the late 1940s to leading the Council on Social Work Education (CSWE) as its first executive director, Kendall's contributions to the field of social work cannot be overlooked. As you read through this chapter, consider how Kendall's work applies to human rights. Consider how her work fits in with CSWE Competency 3: Advance Human Rights and Social, Economic, and Environmental Justice. What do you notice in her work that advances human rights?

CONTEXT OF THE TIMES

As with many of the other social workers in this book, it is difficult to limit Kendall's work to just one period of time. She began her social work education around 1940, but did not retire until 1978. The vast changes in the culture and in social work over time must have been astonishing! The focus of her later years was on international social work education during the 1960s and 1970s, so we explore this period. As noted in Chapter 6, the 1960s saw great changes in the United States through the civil rights movement. Jansson (2012) calls the time frame of 1968 to 1980 the "Paradoxical Era" due to the dynamics of the time. He notes particularly how Presidents Nixon, Ford, and Carter were relatively conservative presidents, yet major social reforms and expansions of social programs such as the Food Stamps program took place during this time. In 1973, *Roe v. Wade* legalized abortion (Jansson, 2012). The Vietnam War also had a major impact on American society during this time frame.

CHILDHOOD AND EARLY YEARS

Kendall was the only girl in a family of four children. She was born in Scotland during the Progressive Era, on September 8, 1910. She describes her happy childhood saying, "the cottage in which I was born is one of those that you see in fairy tales—a stone cottage, covered with roses, no indoor plumbing, no interior heating except for one huge fireplace in the kitchen, where we spent most of our time" (Watkins, 2010, p. 169). In the winter, a large tub was brought into the kitchen on Saturday nights for baths, and as the only girl in the family, Kendall bathed first (Healy, 2008). She was described as always having her head in a book, even as a child, and usually received books as presents. Thinking back, Kendall once stated "I must have been something of a nerd" (Healy, 2008, p. 222). Kendall's mother was a very strong figure, one who took care of the family while the father was away with his work for the military. She had a passion for music, and would sing and play on the small organ that was kept in the parlor. Kendall's father was a soldier, and often away for duty. Kendall shared about years when her father was away, and the strong role that her mother played in the family. She managed to keep the family well fed and healthy on a meager allowance from a soldier's pay. Her brothers planted potatoes and they lived off the garden, their chickens, and any rabbits they were able to catch (Kendall, 2000).

Kendall's father immigrated to Canada in 1913 to take advantage of a land grant. The family was to follow, but he later decided that Chicago offered better opportunities for the family (Healy, 2008). The family immigrated to Chicago after World War I, in August 1920, when Kendall was 10 years old. Kendall remembered not wanting to leave home, and the pile of the family's furniture outside the cottage being sent to auction before they left. She remembered the entire village coming out to say goodbye to them when they departed (Healy, 2008). When the family was boarding the ship to sail to the United States, Kendall tasted her first tomato! For a long time after this, she refused to eat tomatoes because they reminded her of the pain of leaving their home in Scotland (Healy, 2008). Kendall's parents eventually returned to Scotland during the Great Depression when work in the United States was difficult to find, and after the children were grown up and established in the United States. The family continued to visit Scotland often, and Kendall wrote that all members of the family returned to the Muir of Ord, the village the family left in the early decades of the 1900s, at least once. Kendall even specified that after her death, her ashes were to be buried in her parents' grave site in the beautiful churchyard in the Muir of Ord (Kendall, 2000).

Kendall grew up as an excellent student. After working in a factory to save money for school, she enrolled in the University of Illinois, where she received her degree in liberal arts in 1933. Attending college during the Great Depression was no easy task, but Kendall spoke highly of her mother's ability to "provide me with a wardrobe that was the envy of all my friends" even when there was "scarcely a nickel to spare" (Kendall, 2000). At the time, her interests lay in becoming a foreign correspondent. She enrolled in Spanish classes, where a "tall rather good-looking and obviously young man strode into the room, looked us over and immediately took charge" (Kendall, 2000, Sec. 2). After explaining how Spanish fit into her goals of becoming a correspondent, the professor handed her a note saying "Please come to my office. I think I can be of help to you as I have been a reporter for both the *Chicago Tribune* and the *Herald-Examiner*" (Kendall, 2000, Sec. 2). They began meeting weekly, discussing literature. She learned he was only 1 year older than her and was working on his doctorate degree. When their meetings were discovered she was switched to a different teacher in the second semester. After graduating, she became engaged to this former Spanish teacher, Willmore "Ken" Kendall (Watkins, 2010). They were married in London in 1935. Kendall later connected a book she read while on her honeymoon with influencing her to have a career as a social worker. She stated that it was the "silent voice of a person in a book": the book was *The Jungle* by Upton Sinclair, on the appalling conditions in the Chicago stockyards and the life of a Polish immigrant who lived there. The injustice of it was "so strong I couldn't leave it alone" and she "knew then that my work had to have something to do not only with fighting injustice, but also to working with the victims and helping them retain their dignity as human beings" (Kendall, 2000, Sec. 2).

BECOMING "PINK"

After graduation Kendall spent several years in Europe, first in London, and then in Madrid. The social movements taking place at the time had a major influence in Kendall's life. To her, this time period brought an awakening to the need of addressing the ills of society, or the variety of social injustices that her new group of friends (and her continued reading) made her aware of. The couple lived in Madrid before the Spanish Civil War, and became involved in the Popular Front Movement. Kendall, who was not able to attend university, felt she was in need of something to do. She persuaded the head of a millinery (hatmaking) shop to take her on as an apprentice (she was very fond of hats!). Although her sewing skills were negligible, her Spanish was quite good, and she learned a great deal about the lives of the women who were working alongside her, living in poverty. All these lessons made her "quite ideological . . . I was in the middle, left of center," which made some suspect her of being *pinko*, another (derogative) term for communist. She was once investigated for this suspicion, although she stated she was "never over the edge of communism" (Watkins, 2010, p. 171), no matter how much farther to the left she was than others. All these experiences gave her a new awareness of the need to become active in fighting social injustices. As she stated in an interview, "I needed to do something about all that was wrong in the world around us . . . but I had no idea what until I found social work" (Billups, 2002).

INTRODUCTION TO THE WORLD OF SOCIAL WORK

In 1938, Kendall and her husband left Spain to return to the United States for her husband Ken's new position at the University of Illinois, and then to the Louisiana State University (LSU). After his first day at work at LSU, he came home and told her, "You know they have something here called social work. It sounds like what you're interested in. Why don't you look into it?" (Watkins, 2010, p. 172). She did, and it was exactly what she wanted. She was quickly admitted and became the first graduate of the program. The new Department of Social Welfare was staffed mainly by more experienced social workers from the North. Her insistence on a focus on social reform was a challenge to the faculty, who focused more on individual casework. Fortunately, completing an internship had a major impact on Kendall, who recognized that "help with personal problems was just as important as changing social conditions and [I] ended up convinced that social work must be involved with both" (Watkins, 2010, p. 172). Kendall's mother, with whom she was very close, came to live with them for much of the time she was in school. Kendall said, "She made all my clothes. I was one of the best-dressed people at the university, although we had no money. . . . She, that's what she did. She dressed me; sent me off into the world as best she could, and that was it. But what I did in the world, I don't think she ever understood" (Watkins, 2010, p. 175). After receiving her masters' degree Kendall became the first trained social worker in the Baton Rouge welfare office, and received a special caseload of families she helped lead to independence.

When her husband returned to the University of Illinois to complete his doctorate, Kendall went with him to enter the University of Chicago to study for her doctorate under leaders such as Edith Abbott and Sophonisba Breckinridge (Billups, 2002). Her studies lasted some time, as she kept being offered unique employment positions such as the assistant director of the international unit of the U.S. Children's Bureau, as an officer with the UN, and as the executive secretary of the American Association of Schools of Social Work (AASSW; Watkins, 2010). Although it took her until 1950 (the same year as her divorce from Ken, which was at least partially due to her constant moving for employment), she eventually completed her PhD. She was also awarded four honorary doctorates due to her work in the social work field. She was appointed the executive secretary of the AASSW after completing her PhD, as well as being appointed to the board of the International Association of Schools of Social Work (IASSW). She eventually became the first Moses Distinguished Professor at Hunter College and taught at several other universities, including Howard University and the University of Hawaii (Billups, 2002). The separation from Ken took place after 15 years of marriage, and Kendall later wrote that "although we went our separate ways, we never ceased to cherish those early years of happy fulfillment as partners in search of an early life together" (Kendall, 2000, Sec. 2). Her time with Ken had brought her into an entirely new world.

WORKING WITH THE UNITED NATIONS

In 1945, Kendall was offered a position with the U.S. Children's Bureau, where she worked as a trainer in International Service until 1947. This job helped lead her to a position as a social affairs officer at the UN. This new position gave her the opportunity to become immersed in international social work education. The UN was still a relatively young organization, having been formed after World War II (Kendall called it "shining new and idealistic" in Billups, 2002, p. 148). The organization was beginning to focus its efforts on professional development and training for staff. A large portion of Kendall's work was the 3-year study of social welfare personnel published by the UN in 1950 as *Training for Social Work: An International Survey.* This also became the foundation of her doctoral dissertation. This study was considered groundbreaking, as it put together a "comprehensive picture of social work education" and continues to be a "significant historical document" (Healy, 2008, p. 224). The study led the Social Commission of the UN to pass a resolution calling for social welfare personnel to be trained as social workers through formal courses in social work. This further led to a high priority on training and the establishment of programs of professional education for social work (Kendall, 2000, Sec. 4). The report came out around the same time period when social work was growing immensely in the United States. World War II and its aftermath caused the necessity for many social workers to be hired by the Red Cross and other agencies to work with soldiers as they returned home (Jansson, 2012).

Kendall's work also led her to address both similarities and differences in social work around the world at the first professional meeting outside of the United States, which was held in Canada in 1951 (Goldstein

& Beebe, 1995). An international focus on social work also grew out of the study, with work groups, seminars, and faculty exchange programs formed to facilitate international professionalism. Kendall stated that "it was a tremendous relief and honor to have the commission pass the resolution declaring that social work was a professional function requiring professional preparation" (Watkins, 2010, p. 175). The international recognition of the profession and the education required continued to develop the field of social work.

Social work then, as now, struggled to maintain its identity as a profession. It is this work by Kendall that is acknowledged as the "definitive recognition of the profession" (United Nations, as cited by Watkins, 2010, p. 176). Kendall later said that it was her work at the UN that allowed her to have so many wonderful experiences later, as it "immersed me in social work education around the world and put me on track for the rest of my professional life" (Billups, 2002, p. 153). Her work also allowed the UN to see training programs as a necessity and social work as an actual profession that required specialized education. This in turn led to a higher priority and focus on social work as a profession, and assisted in its growth.

PARAGUAY MISSION AND INTERNATIONAL SOCIAL WORK

Kendall considered her short-term consultation on social work education in Paraguay to be one of her four greatest accomplishments, as well as one of the most challenging (Watkins, 2010). In the mid-1950s, Kendall was hired to review and provide recommendations on social welfare to the Ministry of Public Health in Paraguay. She worked with local schools and programs to explore their programs and problems and how they could draw from American experiences in social work to improve the program. A major problem revealed was the lack of guidance and financing from the Ministry of Health, under which these programs were defined. Fortunately, the minister was enthusiastic about making the recommended changes, and an expansion of the work went as far as renaming the department to the Ministry of Public Health and Social Welfare. Kendall's work was "social action at its very best—effecting drastic change in government structures" (Watkins, 2010, p. 177). This experience was so dramatic that it greatly increased her interest in international social work.

Kendall was also highly involved in a 6-year international family planning program from 1971 to 1977 (Watkins, 2010) as a part of her work at IASSW. This project worked to provide personnel and acceptance of family planning around the world. The project took place in such far flung corners of the world as Asia, eastern and western Africa, the Middle East, and Latin America. Local social work educators from more than 30 different schools were consulted, partially to try to learn how to promote the program with respect to the specific cultural contexts. Kendall's understanding of the need to include social workers to best work with varying cultural components became one of the core components of the Katherine A. Kendall Institute for International Social Work Education, created by CSWE in 2005 (Watkins, 2010).

COUNCIL ON SOCIAL WORK EDUCATION

Being a part of the "birth of CSWE" and being one of the key staff members in beginning the educational services was described as one of Kendall's most exciting experiences (Billups, 2002, p. 153). Kendall was the CSWE's first executive director, having been involved before the official start of the program in 1952. Before CSWE was formed, there were a variety of professional social work organizations with different areas of focus. Social work programs were developed in several different forms, also with separate areas of focus. As Kendall (2002) wrote:

> The first schools in the United States were established not by educational institutions but by practitioners in private social agencies. Their primary interest was to produce practitioners who were better prepared to work with individuals and families, using casework as a special kind of helping relationship. With practice as a central concern, casework in the classroom and supervised practice in the field became, and for many years remained, the hallmark of American social work education. (p. 6)

Most of the social workers teaching these students were part-time teachers who were working in the field full-time at the local social agencies (Kendall, 2002). Casework, or work at an individual and family level, was almost always the focus, with macro level classes such as policy having a lesser influence. Over time the focus on casework incorporated psychoanalytic theory and became more professional and more associated with graduate level work. There was also a split in thinking between those who believed social work was best taught at the graduate level and those who thought it could best be taught starting at the undergraduate level, with an additional year at the graduate level, so that students could have more of a broad base of related courses (such as biology, psychology, and other social science courses). This could give students a firm foundation in many areas that are related to social work practice. Kendall herself encouraged a much greater emphasis on this foundation at the undergraduate level, and was disappointed in the lack of emphasis in this area over time. There continued to be divergence in thinking regarding the primary role of casework versus the role of policy or macro level work, as was seen earlier with Mary Richmond (casework) and Jane Addams and Ellen Gates Starr (policy and macro/community work).

From 1918 through the 1940s, multiple organizations and associations were formed to attempt to regulate and strengthen social work education. This included the AASSW and the National Association of Schools of Social Administration (NASSA). While the AASSW was focused on preparing students for a lifetime career in the profession and the NASSA with a preparation for public service work (Kendall, 2002), these organizations were—with some difficulty-—able to merge with other existing ones to better serve the overall interests of the field. Kendall, as the executive secretary of AASSW starting in 1950, was highly involved in the negotiations in merging these and the other bodies into CSWE. In 1952 these organizations were combined into one primary program that became responsible for, as one author eloquently put it, "providing the forum, setting the agenda, and defining the nature, expectations, standards, qualifications, competencies and levels of social work education" (Mwansa, 2011, p. 7). CSWE is the organization that now allows for accredited social work programs in the United States, and sets the competencies that all social work programs must teach their students (the ones you most often see in your learning contracts for your field education internships).

Throughout her career, Kendall held the positions of Educational Secretary, Associate Director, and finally the executive director of CSWE from 1963 to 1966. During her time as executive director, several important changes were made to the organization's policies. This included a focus on quality (not just quantity) of social workers, more and better social workers to meet the needs of society, and renewed attention to international work (Kendall, 2002). In 2004, CSWE established the Katherine A. Kendall Institute for Social Work Education to encourage the mainstreaming of international social work education curriculum in the United States in honor of her work (White, 2008).

INTERNATIONAL ASSOCIATION OF SCHOOLS OF SOCIAL WORK

One of Kendall's major life passions was her work with the IASSW. When it was left in disarray after World War II, she vowed that she was going to "make American schools aware of the IASSW if it was the last thing I ever did. This was a little like my social action days back in my youth. The IASSW became a cause" (Billups, 2002, p. 150). Although she was officially employed with CSWE, she was in charge of multiple areas of IASSW, including accreditation, curriculum development, and educational consulting. She was told, "You can do it, if you do it on your own time and it doesn't cost anything" (Billups, 2002, p. 150). Kendall made it her mission to make sure that every social work program in the United States became a member (Healy, 2008).

Kendall and others within the program quickly began to involve developing countries in Asia, Latin America, and Africa. The family planning project was the creation of the Asian and Pacific Association for Social Work Education that they assisted in forming. Kendall had already traveled extensively, starting even before her work with the UN. When she spoke of what she had seen during her trips, she shared,

> I remember the misery I have witnessed first-hand in my work in Asia, Africa, and Latin America. There were so many women still in their 30s looking like women of 50, worn out from child-bearing. There was mighty little nourishment for babies suckling at their sagging breasts and very little to eat for the children who preceeded them. I remember, too the surge of relief and hope when they were introduced to family planning and helped to use the methods made known to them through programs. (Kendall, 2000, Sec. 6)

Seeing these individuals and their life circumstances helped encourage her to continue with her international social work. It was obvious that social workers were needed in all parts of the world.

In 1966 Kendall left her position at CSWE (but took the role of the director of international education) in order to be more involved in the IASSW (Watkins, 2010). She was the full-time secretary-general from 1971 until she retired in 1978, as well as the honorary president for many years. She recognized that social work in the United States had a "long history of off-and-on engagement with international movements and professional activities" (Abram & Cruce, 2007, p. 3) and was committed to bringing the international focus back to social work. Kendall was credited with "reestablishing the strength, vitality, and global prominence" (Watkins, 2010, p. 178) of the IASSW, partially due to her strong base in CSWE. She helped move the organization from a largely European group (which was already badly disrupted by World War II) into a worldwide organization strengthening social work education (Healy, 2008). Before World War II, the association had 75 member schools in 18 countries. By 1978, when Kendall retired from her position as the head of the organization, there were approximately 500 member schools in 70 different countries (Healy, 2008). The time under Kendall's leadership is often considered the "golden era" of IASSW.

"RETIREMENT"

Kendall officially retired from working in the field in 1978 (Watkins, 2010). However, her "retirement" seemed to have been from official positions only, as she continued to be highly active in writing, publishing, and consulting for more than 20 years. Kendall also continued her focus on international work with the CSWE and the IASSW. She was an honorary lifetime member of both of their boards. In 2002, Kendall published a book on the starting years of the CSWE (Kendall, 2002). One author (Watkins, 2010) noted that it was only after her 95th birthday that she stopped riding the Metrorail to come into the CSWE office! Reflecting on her many positions, Kendall stated, "I have never had a job I didn't love. Luck has smiled upon me again and again. Always, I seemed to be in the right place at the right time for good things to happen" (Kendall, 2000, Sec. 6). Kendall moved to a small cottage in Collington in 1988 and spent many productive years there, with a special den sufficiently hidden from the rest of the house for work, and never returned to her apartment in New York. For the completion of large writing projects, a study room in the Library of Congress was set aside for her use (Kendall, 2000, Sec. 6). Kendall appeared to have great fondness for this arrangement. She once stated,

> What a joy to be surrounded at the Library of Congress by hundreds and thousands, perhaps millions of books . . . whether you see them or not, you know the books are there, waiting to be handled and used not only by scholars but by all kinds and sorts of people. (Kendall, 2000, Sec. 6)

Kendall's love of scholarship and writing is evidenced by her multitude of publications, including several books.

PROFESSIONAL AND PERSONAL CHALLENGES

When asked about her life's challenges, Kendall stated some issues that many social workers will find all too familiar—juggling jobs, long hours, not enough time, and the necessity of doing things using your own money in order to get it done. She stated that "the ongoing challenge that all social welfare and social work organizations face is the challenge of finding money to do the job. It's not at all ennobling to be poor. It's a pain. And it keeps us from doing what really needs to be done" (Billups, 2002, p. 157). These issues are not uncommon for social workers. Many will also find that no matter how many wonderful opportunities are offered to them in the profession, there may well be one or several things that do not come to pass. For Kendall, one of these was a plan in the 1960s to expand international programs through the U.S. Congress's International Education Act. Kendall was to work in a position toward this goal half time through the IASSW and half time with CSWE. However, even though the act was passed, Congress never funded the act and the arrangement never took place (Healy, 2008).

Her personal life was also filled with trials. Many of them seemed to be physical, even though she lived to be 100 years old! Kendall had issues with both her hearing and sight, although hearing aids and corneal transplants took care of those problems. She also lost her stomach to cancer. Kendall seemed to have approached each of these medical challenges just as she did the challenges in her professional life. They were "inconvenient," but "not in any way a hindrance" (Billups, 2002, p.

157). Many people today could learn a lesson from this attitude toward what could be some pretty major problems! However, there were times when these medical conditions became an issue, not just in her personal life, but also professionally. It was only after she had been named the executive director of CSWE that Kendall was diagnosed with Fuchs dystrophy and recommended to have corneal transplants, or she would eventually become blind. Because this meant several years of impaired vision, Kendall tried to ignore the advice of her doctors, until several of them in different countries all told her the same thing. Kendall did eventually have the eye surgery, with successful results (Kendall, 2000).

Unfortunately, cancer was also a condition that Kendall was forced to face on several occasions. In 1979, Kendall found out that what she thought was an ulcer was actually cancer, and her entire stomach needed to be removed! On hearing this, Kendall asked if this was a death sentence (not knowing how one could live without a stomach) and was told by the doctor that "you can manage very well without a stomach. We simply rearrange your insides" (Kendall, 2000, Sec. 5). Fortunately, he was correct, as Kendall lived for another 30 years. Kendall stated that she had "managed very well without a stomach and without a spleen . . . it has made me wonder why we were so constructed in the first place" (Kendall, 2000, Sec. 5). Her aliments did not end there, as she also had lung surgery for suspected cancer, and earlier in life, ear operations for hearing loss. However, as her long life shows, these trials did not stop her.

Challenges are balanced by the things in life that are of particular enjoyment, and Kendall had many loves in life. In addition to her obvious love for scholarship and writing, she was happily involved in the life of her family and extended family, particularly her godchildren. Three of her godchildren had lost their parents in childhood. Kendall had informally agreed to be their guardian, but due to a lack of this in writing the children ended up living with relatives. Kendall enjoyed gardening, particularly with one of her godchildren, Andy, who was a master gardener (Kendall, 2000). Kendall was an excellent swimmer, and once won a diving competition while living in Spain (Kendall, 2000). One of Kendall's favorite activities, however, was cooking. She spoke of the years when her mother moved back to the United States to live with her after her father had passed, and how Kendall would enjoy making dinner for them every night. Kendall spoke of cooking as a work of art:

Sometimes cooking can be as creative as painting a picture or composing a poem or a symphony. Well, perhaps not a symphony, but a concerto. That is what I am thinking as I contemplate the production of a Spanish paella. Fortunately, I was introduced to the real thing in Madrid and know how it should taste and what it should look like. Properly put together it is a masterpiece of harmonious color and contrasting ingredients. (Kendall, 2000, Sec. 6)

Like every good social worker, Kendall found balance in people and hobbies outside of her work. She had numerous self-care activities.

CONTRIBUTIONS TO THE FIELD

It is difficult to truly highlight the major contributions of such a leading figure in social work. From her early work establishing the need for social work professionals and training with the UN to many years of leading not only the IASSW but also CSWE, to her multitude of publications—educational, historical, and reflective-—her list of accomplishments is one any social worker could aspire to. The core of her work centers on promoting social work education, especially on an international platform, in order to assist social workers on the front lines to have the tools needed to promote social justice at an individual level, as well as at macro levels. Kendall feared one of her failings was that she was not able to add a broad social science curriculum into social work's undergraduate degrees. Although they did some of this, she did not feel that it was enough. With the multitude of issues that social workers assist their clients with, she felt they needed to know more about society, economics, politics, and more (Billups, 2002). She suggested that in looking toward the future, social work education should become more interdisciplinary, as well as more international.

ADVICE TO SOCIAL WORKERS

When Kendall was asked, in 2003, what her advice was to social workers who are now working in the field, she said:

To be a social worker, you have to care deeply about people and what happens to them. There are values we must uphold, and those values should influence our views on current events, such as the social and economic policies of the present administration. You have to *care* what happens to the world and be concerned when the United States uses its great wealth and influence for destructive ends instead of helping to reduce worldwide poverty. You have to care about the world hating us and this unilateral approach to foreign relations. You have to think clearly about the racial question—to be sure you're not tainted by underground racial prejudice. (Brandwein, 2005, p. 109)

This advice applies just as much to social workers now as it did then. Although it may not be easy to continue to care for others in the face of all the issues we now encounter, to be a good social worker one must care deeply about the people we work with and the rest of the world outside of our immediate community.

LESSONS LEARNED

To finish this chapter, read through the following text of CSWE Competency 3. Then you will be ready to go through the classroom exercises and discuss what you saw in Kendall's practice throughout this chapter. The section reads:

Competency 3: Advance Human Rights and Social, Economic, and Environmental Justice

Social workers understand that every person regardless of position in society has fundamental human rights such as freedom, safety, privacy, an adequate standard of living, healthcare, and education. Social workers understand the global interconnections of oppression and human rights violations, and are knowledgeable about theories of human need and social justice and strategies to promote social and economic justice and human rights. Social workers understand strategies designed to eliminate oppressive structural barriers to ensure that social goods, rights, and responsibilities are distributed equitably and that civil, political, environmental, economic, social, and cultural human rights are protected. Social workers:

- Apply their understanding of social, economic, and environmental justice to advocate for human rights at the individual and system levels

- Engage in practices that advance social, economic, and environmental justice (CSWE, 2015, pp. 7–8)

Discuss how you noticed Kendall working to advance human rights in her many different roles. How did she do this at the UN? How did she advance human rights in her leadership roles in social work education? How else do you see this competency applying to her work?

CLASSROOM ACTIVITIES

1. In 1947, Kendall worked with the UN to determine what social work training programs were available and used in different countries. This study led the UN to set standards for professionals to have social work education for their work. As a class or in small groups, learn more about the UN. Learn about its history. How and why was the UN formed? What were some of its main goals? How is the UN working at a global level now? Has this changed over time? Does it seem to support the necessity of social work in the same way now as it did around 1950? What are some of the primary declarations from the UN that may assist in advancing human rights and social, economic, or environmental justice?

2. This chapter discussed how Kendall, while massively productive in her professional life, also had a balance of family and hobbies to provide for her self-care. We know self-care is essential in finding the balance needed to become a stable social worker. What are your self-care practices? Have these changed since you became a student or started your field placement? Spend some time writing out a self-care plan for yourself, and how you will implement this over

(continued)

the next few weeks or months. Reflect on this plan with your classmates. How can you hold yourself accountable to doing this?

REFERENCES

Abram, F., & Cruce, A. (2007). A re-conceptualization of "reverse mission" for international social work education and practice. *Social Work Education, 26*(1), 3–19.
doi:10.1080/02615470601036393

Billups, J. (Ed.). (2002). *Faithful angels: Portraits of international social work notables.*
Washington, DC: NASW Press.

Brandwein, R. (2005). Katherine Kendall: A social work institution. *Affilia, 20*(1),
103–110. doi:10.1177/0886109904272115

Council on Social Work Education. (2015). *2015 educational policy and accreditation
standards for baccalaureate and master's social work programs.* Alexandria, VA: Author.

Goldstein, S., & Beebe, L. (1995). National Association of Social Workers. In R. L.
Edwards (Ed.), *Encyclopedia of social work* (19th ed., Vol. 2, pp. 1747–1764). Washington, DC: NASW Press.

Healy, L. (2008). Historical SW&S portraits: Katherine A. Kendall (USA), honorary
president since 1978. *Social Work & Society, 6*(1), 220–233. Retrieved from http://
www.socwork.net/sws/article/view/109/398

Jansson, B. (2012). *The reluctant welfare state: Engaging history to advance social work
practice in contemporary society.* Belmont, CA: Brooks/Cole.

Kendall, K. A. (2000). *Jottings & random thoughts on a long life.* Unpublished. Located
in the Social Welfare History archives at University of Minnesota. Folder 1:2 Clip-
pings, 1961–2006. SW 97.

Kendall, K. A. (2002). *Council on Social Work Education: Its antecedents and first twenty
years.* Alexandria, VA: Council on Social Work Education.

Mwansa, L.-K. (2011). Social work education in Africa: Whence and whither? *Social
Work Education, 30*(1), 4–16. doi:10.1080/02615471003753148

Watkins, J. (2010). Katherine A. Kendall: The founder of international social work.
In A. Lieberman (Ed.), *Women in social work who have changed the world* (pp. 167–
181). Chicago, IL: Lyceum Books.

White, B. (Ed.). (2008). *Comprehensive handbook of social work and social welfare. The
profession of social work.* Hoboken, NJ: John Wiley & Sons.

Dr. Nazneen Sada Mayadas.
Source: Printed with permission from Dr. Doreen Elliott.

CHAPTER 8

Dr. Nazneen Sada Mayadas: A Truly International Social Worker

July 24, 1932–June 1, 2015

"Celebrating diversity is a recognition and positive acceptance of the natural differences among humankind. . . . Celebrating these differences is an open affirmation of respect for all creatures."

—Mayadas (1997, p. 230)

D r. Nazneen Sada Mayadas was a social work educational innovator, an advocate for refugees and those of diverse backgrounds, and an international practitioner. She worked and traveled in over 150 countries over the span of her 50 years as a social worker (Dignity Memorial, 2015b). Although she was born and began her social work career in India, Mayadas practiced in Canada and the United States before (and after) her time with the United Nations High Commissioner for Refugees (UNHCR), where she served as the chief of social services and worked to improve conditions for refugees. She taught extensively on cultural issues and was one of the first professors to use video feedback in interviewing classes. Lieberman, who has an edited chapter in her book about women in social work, said of Mayadas, "I will always remember her not so much walking into a room, as levitating in, sari flowing, and totally mysterious to us unpolished Texas rubes (sic). She was the kind of person you wished you were, but knew that the raw material was JUST NOT THERE. There will just never be anyone like her" (Dignity Memorial, 2015b). Mayadas made her impact on the world as a well-published scholar, professor, and a community and international social worker. Her work in bringing international social work to social work students, as well as her time in the United Nations (UN), contributes greatly to our understanding of Council on Social Work Education (CSWE) Competency 2: Engage Diversity and Difference in Practice. As an individual from another country, she brought new perspectives into her practice. She managed to work across cultures as a bicultural social worker.

CONTEXT OF THE TIMES

Even though it is difficult to describe the era of practice for a social worker whose work spans over 50 years, for this chapter we focus on the 1980s, around the time Mayadas was working with the UNHCR and shifted her teaching focus to international issues. According to Jansson, the unemployment and inflation of the 1970s together with the rise of conservativism led to the election of President Reagan in 1980 (2012). President Reagan was particularly harsh toward people who lived in poverty, and decreased the budget of many welfare programs. The early 1980s saw a deep recession (Jansson, 2012). This conservative era lasted throughout the 1980s, through the presidencies of Ronald Reagan and George H. W. Bush. President Bush followed the overall path that Reagan had set out, including large military spending. The decade also saw the explosion of the space shuttle *Challenger,* the melt-down of the Chernobyl nuclear power plant in the Soviet Union, and the fall of the Berlin Wall in Germany as the Soviet Union fell apart (National Geographic, 2013). Social workers continued to reach out to minority and impoverished populations, primarily those working in nonprofit or government programs. The licensing of social workers contributed toward the trend of social workers moving toward private practice during this decade, and continued to be an area of debate for the profession (Wenocur & Reisch, 2001).

CHILDHOOD IN INDIA

Nazneen Sada Mayadas was born on July 24, 1932, to Dr. James and Mrs. Shanti Williams (V. Anand, personal communication, August 6, 2017). She was born in Lucknow, India, a large multicultural city in Northern India. People in this region speak both English and Urdu. Hindi was not introduced until later. Mayadas grew up in the time of British rule in India, but also during the time when Mahatma Gandhi was inspiring the Indian Independence Movement, ending when India became independently governed in 1947. Mayadas's grandfather, Isa Charan Sada, was a known Lucknow Urdu poet who, among other things, authored the only existing Urdu translation of Milton's work: *Paradise Lost, Paradise Regained,* and *Samson Agonistes.* Dr. Williams had a thriving family practice treating the elite members of the city, while also providing medicine and treatment to indigent clients free of charge (Segal, 2010). Mrs. Williams was not only a homemaker, but was also very involved in the community and in the Christian church. The couple financed a wing of their local Anglican church and were considered pillars of the community (V. Anand, personal communication, August 6, 2017). Young Mayadas was the baby of the family. She was 15 years younger than her only sister, Shahla (Segal, 2010).

Mayadas had a comfortable childhood as the youngest child of a physician in a large Indian city. Unfortunately, at the age of 10, tragedy struck the family. Mrs. Williams died of tuberculosis after a 3-year quarantine, leaving young Mayadas alone with her grieving father, as her sister by then had married and moved to Bombay (Segal, 2010). The family lived in a compound typical of what an Indian family of their socioeconomic status would have. There were two separate households, one for her father and one for her maternal aunt, who was also a physician in the family practice and had a large family (N. Mayadas, personal communication with U. Segal, July 17, 2009). The family medical practice, including operating rooms, was in a separate building in the compound. Mayadas's nephew recalls seeing patients in the waiting room for treatments or consultations and bringing their medications to be dispensed in containers they brought from home to avoid the added costs for bottles (V. Anand, personal communication, August 6, 2017). Mayadas likely witnessed similar activities as she was growing up. The family had a variety of servants, including a cook, butler, maid, driver, watchman, and others. As the oldest female in the house, Mayadas assumed the management of the house at the age of 12 after her mother died (Segal, 2010). Mayadas enjoyed summer vacations in the mountains, specifically in Naini Tal, where the family spent the months of May and June. They usually stayed at the Grand Hotel with a small group of servants who were housed in the hotel's quarters specifically built for that purpose (V. Anand, personal communication, August 6, 2017).

Mayadas attended the local schools that had been founded by British and American missionaries. Although her family was Christian, she made many friends from other religions, particularly Hindi students (Segal, 2010). There was evidence of Mayadas's commitment to social justice back in her school days. Her father was once asked to remove her from school when she was found standing on a table "instigating a rebellion" among the students (Segal, 2010). After graduating from high school, Mayadas continued to live at home and attended a nearby women's college, the Isabella Thoburn College. She studied English literature, history, and economics for her bachelor's degree (Segal, 2010). She was also active in the National Christian Student Movement (V. Anand, personal communication, August 6, 2017).

While she was in college, her father died. Young women in India do not generally live on their own, so the family house was sold and Mayadas moved to live on campus. She completed her bachelor's degree and went to the University of Allahabad to complete a master's degree in medieval Indian history (Mayadas, 2003). Indian history may have been a particularly interesting topic at this time, right after India's independence from British colonial rule. Much of the history had to be reinterpreted at this time (V. Anand, personal communication, August 6, 2017).

INTRODUCTION TO SOCIAL WORK

After completing her master's degree, Mayadas was offered a position on the executive staff of the Young Women's Christian Association (YWCA) of India in Calcutta, working as both the international guesthouse superintendent and the director of education from 1956 to 1959 (Segal, 2010). She initially lived with the family at the vicarage of St. Paul's Cathedral, which was the seat of the Metropolitan of the

Anglican Church of India, Pakistan, Burma, and Ceylon. In 1957, when her sister attended Columbia University in New York City to do her master's in English literature, Mayadas moved to the YWCA hostel (V. Anand, personal communication, August 6, 2017). She had the opportunity to learn a great deal in this position. She learned about management and leadership, international service organizations, and interacted with people from many countries. She was also very interested in Mother Teresa's Nirmal Hriday (Pure Heart), the home for those who were homeless and dying, and visited the home with her family. Working with Calcutta's most disenfranchised individuals may have helped guide Mayadas toward social work (V. Anand, personal communication, August 6, 2017). Mayadas always had an interest in helping others, but this position introduced her to a more formal system of helping others. In 1959, Mayadas was offered a scholarship through the YWCA to study social work at Case Western Reserve University in Cleveland, Ohio (Segal, 2010).

Living in the United States was a new experience for Mayadas. Her living and financial situation was quite different than what her upbringing prepared her for. Mayadas grew up in a relatively affluent family. However, when she came to the United States, the Indian government's laws only allowed her to bring $8 with her! She now had to think very carefully about how she spent her money. She had to tell her friends she could not eat out with them and return to the dorms instead of spending money on going out (Segal, 2010). Her Indian culture would not allow her to tell her friends that she did not have the money. Like most immigrants, Mayadas experienced the many cultural adjustments that have to be made upon entering a new country (V. Anand, personal communication, August 6, 2017). In India, she had always been driven wherever she needed to go. Learning to drive was a new experience! Another big decision for an Indian woman was cutting her hair. Mayadas made these adjustments to life in the United States and became truly bicultural (D. Elliott, personal communication, September 25, 2017).

After graduating, Mayadas was offered a position as a neighborhood worker in Cleveland at the Friendly Inn Settlement (Segal, 2010). She worked with individuals and families struggling with poverty. Unfortunately, her visa only allowed her to work in the United States for 2 years. She moved to Canada in 1963 to work with the Family Service Agency in Vancouver (V. Anand, personal communication, August 6,

2017). This position involved more group work and family therapy. Mayadas was briefly married to an Indian man while in Canada. When the marriage deteriorated, Mayadas decided to return to the United States to work on her PhD at Washington University in St. Louis (Segal, 2010). Mayadas decided she wanted to go into teaching and that she could better fend for herself as a single woman with a doctorate degree. She worked part-time at Catholic Family Services in St. Louis supervising students and in family practice while in school (N. Mayadas, personal communication with U. Segal, July 17, 2009).

TEACHING SOCIAL WORK

Mayadas was hired to teach at St. Louis University once her PhD was complete. Her classes became very popular! Students began camping outside of the registrar's office to be first in line when they opened to ensure a spot in one of her classes (Segal, 2010). Some students even caught a cold after spending the night outside in their sleeping bags (N. Mayadas, personal communication with U. Segal, July 17, 2009). After 2 years of teaching, Mayadas was offered a position at the University of Texas in Arlington. Even as she began her teaching career in the 1970s, she was an innovator in the classroom (Segal, 2010). At a time when most teachers used lectures almost exclusively, she enjoyed leading in-depth classroom discussions. She would model her skills in the clinical classes to give the students a better idea of what clinical practice was like in real therapy sessions. Mayadas introduced video feedback into her clinical classes (Segal, 2010). By taping the sessions and providing detailed feedback, students were able to better understand the areas where they needed improvement. In addition, she required students to teach the skills they learned to clinicians in the community, providing agency presentations. This gave students practice in public speaking and increased their identification as social workers in addition to thoroughly learning the skills themselves. She developed a set of videotapes for the classroom that demonstrated interviewing skills for students that were popular in the classroom for decades (Segal, 2010). These tapes are still sold and used in the classroom now (V. Anand, personal communication, August 6, 2017). Mayadas was also one of the first professors teaching distance education through video, with the professor in one location and the students in another. Although this is common today, at that time it was quite innovative! Mayadas was one of a few professors using technology in such a variety of ways to provide instruction for students. She stated that one of her contributions to academia was the integration of using videos for teaching and practice (N. Mayadas, personal communication with U. Segal, July 17, 2009). She was also highly active in research and publication in a wide variety of areas, including the use of videotapes in education, group work, and leadership skills.

THE UNITED NATIONS

Mayadas was offered a position as the chief of social services to the UNHCR in 1981. A friend of hers knew the person vacating the position and recommended her for it. She went to New York and spoke with the person who was retiring. Mayadas applied for the position, and after a very lengthy interviewing and vetting process was hired (N. Mayadas, personal communication with U. Segal, July 17, 2009). She took a 1-year leave of absence from teaching that turned into 4 years. She was the primary advocate for social services in a field that did not always fully appreciate the need for these services (Segal, 2010). Mayadas traveled extensively to refugee camps around the world, visiting 15 countries in Africa, seven in Asia, 10 in Europe, and seven in Latin America (Segal, 2010). As a part of this position, she oversaw the approximately 200 social work units in every country that had an office. She noted the difficulty in working in this role. When there was an emergency in some part of the world, an emergency unit was sent out before the social work units, but then the social work units were supposed to know what could be done about the troubles there (N. Mayadas, personal communication with U. Segal, July 17, 2009). She noticed that few of the people providing social services had a background in social work. The workers were primarily indigenous people hired by the country itself. Anyone with an MSW degree was quickly placed in an administrative position, often at the international level. Providing quality social services to those in the camps was a huge challenge.

Social services was charged with both survival tools and adaptation tools, such as counseling and recreational programs such as language or handicrafts. One of the biggest challenges in adapting to life in the refugee camp was dealing with the problem of boredom. As Mayadas said in an interview with Segal, "the day is very long in the camp, and there is nothing to do" (Segal, 2010, p. 46). In one example, Mayadas shared about a visit to a camp in Africa where the women waited despondently with their children for their food to be cooked. Mayadas asked them if they would rather cook their own food, and they said yes. The program was then able to be rearranged to allow the women to make food to provide for their families—an excellent empowerment tool. This also allowed the camp staff to spend their time working on other issues (Segal, 2010). Education also fell under social services, and so was a part of Mayadas's work. Education was often the biggest request from refugees. Education provides refugees with an activity to do and gives the families and children the possibilities for future employment (Gladden, 2013).

Mayadas discovered that there was no handbook to guide the social services segment of the UNHCR. One of her major projects was the development of a manual to provide to the field offices (Segal, 2010). It was tricky to account for the differences between sites and cultures, but having a guide helped calm the ambiguity and anxiety of staff at the offices, giving them a way to approach situations without needing to reinvent the wheel. Mayadas especially advocated for the needs of special groups, such as those with disabilities, who would have been overlooked without her attention. Mayadas also noted the challenge of dealing with compassion fatigue. By the 1980s, countries were getting tired of dealing with refugees, especially since many of the refugees were no longer European or White. Resettlement had changed and the refugee camps became more like little prisons. People were no longer welcomed into new countries as they had been after World War II. Part of Mayadas's job was meeting with the government offices or ministers in each country to advocate for what that camp needed, whether it was expanding programs or funding for the refugees (N. Mayadas, personal communication with U. Segal, July 17, 2009). In 1981, the Nobel Peace Prize was awarded to the UNHCR overall, with each employee receiving a copy (Segal, 2010). Mayadas said this was the "most exciting thing in the work." The money from the prize was used as seed money for a program for handicapped refugees, and some was spent on prostheses for people who had lost limbs due to land mines. Other agencies donated to the fund once they saw the need (N. Mayadas, personal communication with U. Segal, July 17, 2009).

A SHIFT IN TEACHING

After a 4-year leave of absence from the University of Texas at Arlington, Mayadas was given the choice to resign or return to teaching. Leaving a tenured position would have been a difficult decision, especially for a single immigrant woman. Mayadas said that returning to teaching was at first a depressing experience. No one was very interested in her great international experience of 4 years at the UNHCR. She had to start over with her salary and seniority (N. Mayadas, personal communication with U. Segal, July 17, 2009). Mayadas found upon returning to Texas that some of her priorities in teaching had shifted. Instead of teaching clinical classes, Mayadas shifted to more macro work to bring awareness of global issues, oppression, and diversity. She said, "As you will see in my publications after my return from Geneva, there is now a much broader world orientation. Much of my later work is focused on social work and social development" (Segal, 2010, p. 49). Mayadas wrote more on working with refugees and international social welfare after her experience with the UNHCR. For example, she wrote an article "Psycho-Social Welfare of Refugees: An Expanding Service Area for Social Work" in 1983, when the current system of refugee resettlement in the United States was fairly new. In the 1990s, Mayadas was one of three editors, along with Doreen Elliott and Thomas Watts, who published a series of three international handbooks. They wrote one on social policy, one on social work theory, and a third on social work education. These included *The World of Social Welfare: Social Welfare and Services in an International Context* and *International Handbook on Social Work Education*, which filled a gap in research regarding what was taking place in social work education in more than 23 countries on five continents (Watts, 2008). Katherine Kendall (see Chapter 7) wrote about the importance of this last book in the forward, stating that it reflected the global nature of both social problems and how social work as a profession works with these problems in different areas of the world (Kendall, 1995). Watts, one of the editors of the handbook, states that Mayadas is known internationally for her expertise in both international and comparative social welfare

(Watts, 2008). Through much of Mayadas's career, from the early 1980s when she worked with the UN and after, she wrote on issues facing refugees in addition to this broader international perspective. For example, in 2000 Mayadas and Segal published a chapter about the treatment of refugees in the United States during the 1990s, and how the treatment of different refugee people groups was (and is) often unequal. The chapter also focused on refugee strengths and needs and how social services can assist the population (Mayadas & Segal, 2000). Her later research included more strategies of how to assist the population. Segal and Mayadas (2005) focused on the problems of refugees and immigrants arriving in the United States and how to assess and work with these families.

Mayadas was known as a hard taskmaster and had high expectations of her colleagues. One of her peers, Dr. Duehn, spoke about what it was like to work with her. He said that if they were not teaching, they were always either gathering data or writing about the data. They met together every day! While Mayadas was applying for U.S. citizenship, the immigration officer asked Duehn and his wife how often they saw her. The officer was suspicious about the response and questioned it, saying it was impossible. Duehn's wife retorted, "Believe me, it's daily!" Their hard work resulted in numerous publications. Duehn says that in 3 years, they had published 16 articles or chapters in books (W. Duehn, personal communication, September 27, 2017). Even though they worked incredibly hard, her friends spoke about Mayadas as also being very fun-loving. She loved to party and socialize (D. Elliott, personal communication, September 25, 2017). Duehn shared that Mayadas had methods of interjecting fun to help keep everyone motivated through their hard work. Her love for margaritas was well known! Every day at 5:00 p.m., to keep them working, Mayadas would start the blender and mix up a pitcher (or several!) of frozen margaritas (W. Duehn, personal communication, September 27, 2017). Tea was not the only drink she served!

Mayadas also assumed leadership roles in the National Association of Social Workers (NASW) and CSWE, including serving on both the Publications Committee and as chair of the NASW Book Committee. She coedited a journal,*Social Development Issues* for 6 years (D. Elliott, personal communication, September 25, 2017). She received many awards, including the Lifetime Achievement Award by the NASW of the State of Texas, the CSWE Partners in International

Social Work Education Award, and the Distinguished Alumni Award from Washington University George Warren Brown School of Social Work (NASW Foundation, 2017). Her teaching and guidance was described as never judgmental, but always accepting and then challenging others to be their finest selves (V. Anand, personal communication, August 6, 2017). She continued to teach social work and guide students through their dissertation work. Students and colleagues alike appreciated her support. Although she was involved in several activities, she always made time for other people. Catheleen Jordan, a colleague, shared in the guest book at her funeral that one could stop by her office at any time for a cup of tea and some advice (Dignity Memorial, 2015a). Mayadas was remembered for her elegance and dress. Duehn remembered how at their university, her chic and sophisticated saris were legendary, and that some people even said she "floated." She always wore her hair in a perfectly coiffed beehive. Duehn remembered one event while presenting at a conference in San Francisco when they were caught in a rainstorm. While they were halfway across the Bay Bridge, their car stalled and they had to abandon the car. He said that because of the rain and driving wind, "her beehive hairdo collapsed almost immediately. Ever conscious of her appearance, she screamed, 'I must look like a drowned rat!' This was one of the very few times that I saw Nazneen lose her composure" (W. Duehn, personal communication, September 27, 2017). Mayadas was not one to sacrifice her fashion due to the amount of hard work she was involved in!

Mayadas had a great deal of advice for students who wanted to enter the field of social work. Most importantly, she said that there needs to be more awareness of diversity (N. Mayadas, personal communication with U. Segal, July 17, 2009). She suggested learning at least one other language and to learn more about other countries, including their geography. She suggested that social work schools need to better prepare students for international social work and the needs of people around the world. Mayadas commented that "a whole lot of thinking that the third world is not much different from what happens in our own backyard . . . there's a third world in our backyard, too" (N. Mayadas, personal communication with U. Segal, July 17, 2009). When looking at many of the events of recent years, it is difficult to argue with this opinion! Mayadas and her colleagues also argued for social work educators to integrate a global perspective in the classroom and remove the split in thinking between domestic and international social work. Many Americans have a lack of global perspective that does not prepare students for the world arena or the interdependence of nations at a professional level (Asamoah, Healy, & Mayadas, 1997).

RETIREMENT AND END OF LIFE

Mayadas was unfortunately diagnosed with Parkinson's disease in 1992. She persevered through this challenge as she had many others in her life, with fortitude and determination. For many years her medical issues were kept under control through medications, but in later years the Parkinson's caused severe pain and spinal deterioration (D. Elliott, personal communication, September 25, 2017). She did not allow this condition to slow her down, and taught classes and attended conferences while in a scooter. She even traveled to India and Russia while using the scooter, where she attracted a great deal of interest and amusement—electric disability scooters were not a common sight there! By 2006 the Parkinson's had affected her voice to the point where she could not project her voice in the classroom. However, when her close friend Dr. Duehn was retiring in 2007, Mayadas participated in speech therapy for weeks so that she would be able to give the tribute at his farewell dinner. As Elliott shared, "she did not allow disability to curtail her style and she bore it with great courage and fortitude for many years" (D. Elliott, personal communication, September 25, 2017). Mayadas continued to show strength through her medical challenges.

Mayadas retired from teaching in 2006. After retiring, Mayadas continued to be an avid reader. Elliott said that Mayadas was "a truly bicultural individual who could appreciate equally Urdu ghazels, and American and British poetry and music, always able to quote prolifically from all" (D. Elliott, personal communication, September 25, 2017). She loved the theater and movies. She also enjoyed watching her favorite Hindi soap operas on television. She loved her naughty little dog Clarence as well as her family and friends. Mayadas kept up with her family in India until she passed away. When she visited India, which was quite often, she usually invited her many friends to dinner at hotels in Delhi and Lucknow. These were happy occasions that the relatives and friends still recall (V. Anand, personal communication, August 6, 2017). Elliott stressed how important family and friends were to Mayadas. She said, "She loved both unconditionally. She always made a point of keeping in touch with her wide group of friends, and in particular she had a small group of longtime friends in New Delhi, all accomplished women in their different walks of life who were college friends and one who was a friend from kindergarten." Elliott shared how "whenever Nazneen visited New Delhi they would all get together at one house or another and there would be great celebrations" (D. Elliott, personal communication, September 25, 2017). Mayadas had a full and long life. She was once asked what the key to her longevity was. Mayadas responded "clean living and high thinking" (N. Mayadas, personal communication with U. Segal, July 17, 2009). She said that it was ironic that her body was giving way but not her mind. She said, "The mind wants to do it but the body has cut me off" (N. Mayadas, personal communication with U. Segal, July 17, 2009).

Mayadas became ill and died of a hospital infection on June 1, 2015. She had many friends in Arlington who were with her, as well as her niece and nephew (V. Anand, personal communication, August 6, 2017). Her nephew stated that her funeral service was very well attended and that many friends, colleagues, and students from around the world spoke at the reception or wrote personal thanks and messages.

Mayadas was truly an international social worker. She obtained four academic degrees, two in India and two in the United States (Watts, 2008). She practiced social work in India, Canada, and the United States before working with the UNHCR and traveling to refugee camps in many countries, including but not limited to: Kenya, Ethiopia, Ghana, Sudan, Thailand, Malaysia, Croatia, Hungary, Argentina, Peru, and Venezuela. She presented papers in countries around the world. Her work at the UN included writing a manual to standardize the social work being done in camps around the world (N. Mayadas, personal communication with U. Segal, July 17, 2009). She excelled in all areas of social work, including practice, teaching, research, and service (Segal, 2010). Even the clothing she wore spoke to her international identity. In Segal (2010), she spoke of students' reactions to her saris (the traditional clothing of India). She said that at first, students may have been surprised, but that it was not a barrier. Mayadas said, "Perhaps clothes and race make a cursory difference at the beginning, but if one related genuinely to people, then one is generally accepted" (Segal, 2010, p. 50). She continued by speaking to the importance of being genuine with the people one is working with. She stated, "If I had adopted Western clothing, I would have been uncomfortable, and that would have evidenced itself in my behavior and make others uncomfortable too" (Segal, 2010, p. 50). By being yourself, you are better able to relate to and serve your clients. Elliott summarized her sunny personality as someone who had a "fine brain, was an accomplished and productive scholar and could assess a situation and summarize it very aptly and quickly. She had a great sense of humor and a quick wit." She said that Mayadas "was highly committed to her chosen profession and was regarded as an excellent teacher. In her address in receiving the NASW State of Texas Lifetime Achievement Award, she called the profession of social work 'a noble profession'" (D. Elliott, personal communication, September 25, 2017). Nazneen Sada Mayadas was a noble contributor to social work as a profession, and her ideas and work are as applicable today as they were during her life.

LESSONS LEARNED

After exploring the life and work of Dr. Nazneen Mayadas, you are ready to read through the text of CSWE Competency 2. You can then compare what you have seen through her life with this competency. Mayadas contributed to many areas of social work, with one major area being international social work and cultural sensitivity. This section reads:

Competency 2: Engage Diversity and Difference in Practice

Social workers understand how diversity and difference characterize and shape the human experience and are critical to the formation of identity. The dimensions of diversity are understood as the intersectionality of multiple factors including but not limited to age, class, color, culture, disability and ability, ethnicity, gender, gender identity and expression, immigration status, marital status, political ideology, race, religion/ spirituality, sex, sexual orientation, and tribal sovereign status. Social workers understand that, as a consequence of difference, a person's life experiences may include oppression, poverty, marginalization, and alienation as well as privilege, power, and acclaim. Social workers also understand the forms and mechanisms of oppression and discrimination and recognize the extent to which a culture's structure and values, including social, economic, political, and cultural exclusions, may oppress, marginalize, alienate, or create privilege and power. Social workers:

- Apply and communicate understanding of the importance of diversity and difference in shaping life experiences in practice at the micro, mezzo, and macro levels

- Present themselves as learners and engage clients and constituencies as experts of their own experiences

- Apply self-awareness and self-regulation to manage the influence of personal biases and values in working with diverse clients and constituencies (CSWE, 2015, p. 7)

Discuss how you see Mayadas and her work fitting into this competency. How does she show the value of diversity in her life? How did her work impact diversity, especially the understanding of diversity for her students?

CLASSROOM ACTIVITIES

1. Read the 1951 Refugee Convention from UNHCR and the Universal Declaration of Human Rights from 1948. What do you think about these documents? Do you think all countries are following these guidelines? Is the United States following all of these guidelines?

(continued)

2. Does your university have a partnership program where you can work with students from another country? Consider pairing up with an international student (or a nonstudent immigrant or refugee in your community) and learn about what it is like to be an immigrant or refugee while assisting him or her to adjust to this country. How does this experience help you understand Competency 2? Talk about this experience in class.

REFERENCES

Asamoah, Y., Healy, L., & Mayadas, N. S. (1997). Ending the international-domestic dichotomy: New approaches to a global curriculum for the millennium. *Journal of Social Work Education, 33*(2), 389–401. doi:10.1080/10437797.1997.10778879

Council on Social Work Education. (2015). *2015 educational policy and accreditation standards for baccalaureate and master's social work programs.* Alexandria, VA: Author.

Dignity Memorial. (2015a). Guest book. Retrieved from http://www.legacy.com/guestbook/dignitymemorial/guestbook.aspx?n=nazneen-mayadas&pid=174994861

Dignity Memorial. (2015b). In memory of Dr. Nazneen Sada Mayadas. Retrieved from http://obits.dignitymemorial.com/dignity-memorial/obituary.aspx?n=Nazneen-Mayadas&lc=2348&pid=174994861&mid=6468285

Gladden, J. (2013). Coping strategies of Sudanese refugee women in Kakuma Refugee Camp, Kenya. *Refugee Survey Quarterly, 32*(4), 66–89. doi:10.1093/rsq/hdt017

Jansson, B. (2012). *The reluctant welfare state: Engaging history to advance social work practice in contemporary society.* Belmont, CA: Brooks/Cole.

Kendall, K. (1995). Foreword. In T. Watts, D. Elliott, & N. Mayadas (Eds.), *International handbook on social work education* (pp. xiii–xvii). Westport, CT: Greenwood Press.

Mayadas, N. (1997). Should social work celebrate unity or diversity? Diversity! *Journal of Social Work Education, 33*(2), 230–234. doi:10.1080/10437797.1997.10779172

Mayadas, N., & Segal, U. (2000). Refugees in the 1990s: A U.S. perspective. In P. Balgopal (Ed.), *Social work practice with immigrants and refugees* (pp. 198–227). New York, NY: Columbia University Press.

National Association of Social Workers Foundation. (2017). NASW social work pioneers: Nazneen Sada Mayadas. Retrieved from http://www.naswfoundation.org/pioneers/m/nazneensadamayadas.htm

National Geographic. (2013). The 80s timeline. Retrieved from http://www.national geographic.com.au/history/the-80s-timeline.aspx

Segal, U. (2010). Nazneen S. Mayadas: An advocate for refugees worldwide. In A. Lieberman (Ed.), *Women in social work who have changed the world* (pp. 38–52). Chicago, IL: Lyceum Books.

Segal, U., & Mayadas, N. S. (2005). Assessment of issues facing immigrant and refugee families. *Child Welfare, 84*(5), 563–583. Retrieved from http://citeseerx.ist.psu .edu/viewdoc/download?doi=10.1.1.467.4575&rep=rep1&type=pdf

Watts, T. (2008). Tribute: International social work pioneer: Nazneen S. Mayadas. *Hispanic Health Care International, 6*(1), 51–54.

Wenocur, S., & Reisch, M. (2001). *From charity to enterprise: The development of American social work in a market economy.* Chicago: University of Illinois Press.

The Honorable Barbara Mikulski, MSW.
Source: United States Senate.

CHAPTER 9

The Honorable Barbara Mikulski: A Leader of Women

July 20, 1936–Present

"I decided I would rather be opening doors from the inside than knocking on doors from the outside.
I realized that politics was social work with power."

—Mikulski, as quoted in Collins and Lazzari (2010, p. 18)

The Honorable Barbara Mikulski was the first social worker and the longest serving woman elected to Congress. Mikulski was the first Democratic woman to hold a Senate seat that had not previously been held by a husband and the first Democratic female to serve in both the House of Representatives and the Senate. In 1994, she was the first woman to be elected to a Democratic leadership position in Congress (Mikulski et al., 2000). She served five terms as a U.S. Representative from Maryland from 1977 to 1987. Mikulski was then elected to the U.S. Senate in 1986, serving as a senator from 1987 to 2016. She worked under seven different presidents: President Gerald Ford when she started in 1977, President Jimmy Carter from 1977 to 1981, President Ronald Reagan from 1981 to 1989, President George H. W. Bush from 1989 to 1993, President Bill Clinton from 1993 to 2001, President George W. Bush from 2001 to 2009, and President Barack Obama from 2009 until she retired from office in 2016. Mikulski broke many gender stereotypes and glass ceilings to become a Congresswoman. She was a longtime champion for civil rights, women's rights, and science. As one of the earliest women to serve in Congress, Mikulski was a mentor to many other women as they were elected, helping them to know how to work within the "good old boys club" of Washington, DC. As a social worker, she utilized skills and an understanding of the real life situations that many Americans live with so that, while in office, she could pass legislation that would make a difference in people's lives. As you read through this chapter, see how much you can apply Council on Social Work Education (CSWE) Competency 5: Engage in Policy Practice to Mikulski's life and work.

CONTEXT OF THE TIMES

Mikulski served in Congress through several highly varied political climates and some major transitions for women. The Reagan, Bush, and Clinton eras had very different areas of focus when addressing the welfare of the people in the United States. The Reagan and Bush presidencies were characterized by a highly conservative era (Jansson, 2012). Baby boomers, born in the postwar boom and not experiencing the Great Depression, tended to be more preoccupied with gathering personal wealth, and populations were shifting into the suburbs (Jansson, 2012). Unfortunately, the rise of Reaganomics eventually brought America into a recession with the highest percentage of the population (15.3%, or 35 million people) in poverty since the 1960s (Trattner, 1999). The 1980s also saw the decline of the Cold War and the fall of the Berlin Wall. The 1990s began to move toward a more supportive environment for some of the nonmajority populations. Bush passed the Americans with Disabilities Act to help individuals with disabilities find work (Trattner, 1999). Clinton enacted the "Don't Ask, Don't Tell" legislation, which prevented military leaders from questioning members of the armed forces about their sexual orientation, although it did not prevent them from dismissing members who claimed they identified as anything other than heterosexual (Jansson, 2012). Major events were happening overseas during this time period. In 1991, the first Gulf war, Operation Desert Storm, began the occupation of some Middle Eastern countries by the U.S. military.

Jansson (2012) called President Clinton's time in office a period of uncertainty. Liberal, moderate, and conservative ideologies were all struggling to gain power over the others. This certainly was a time of change for the overall welfare state. The Personal Responsibility and Work Opportunities Act of 1996 and the enactment of the Temporary Assistance to Needy Families caused a major shift in the enrollment of people in welfare programs, but not due to a decreased need (Cummins, Byers, & Pedrick, 2011). These acts unfortunately replaced 60 years of entitlements to needy children and their caretakers, with limits on time and conditions on receiving assistance (Reisch, 2014). Just the enactment of the Personal Responsibility and Work Opportunities Act of 1996 reduced the welfare rolls by 50%, leaving many without support (Jansson, 2012).

Shifts were happening in the political climate as far as who was coming into office. In 1992 and again in 1996, Congress gained more African Americans, Latinos, and women than ever before (Trattner, 1999). Women did not traditionally have a role in office, even entering the later part of the 20th century. The first woman to run for office was Elizabeth Cady Stanton, who attempted to win a seat in Congress in 1866, but lost (Thomas, 2005). In 1917, Jeanette Rankin won a congressional seat, but it was not until 1978 that a woman was elected to the Senate without filling an unexpired term (usually that of her husband). Barbara Mikulski was the first Democrat elected to the Senate in 1987 (Thomas, 2005). Although the numbers of women in politics at all levels were on the increase, the overall percentage of women to men was still quite negligible. In 2004, women had 13% of the seats in the House of Representatives and only 14 women were in the Senate (Thomas, 2005). Although 1996 was a challenging year, more women were voted into Congress than ever before. Twelve new women were brought into office in that election!

CHILDHOOD AND GROWING UP POLISH

Barbara Ann Mikulski was born on July 20, 1936, in Baltimore, Maryland, to a Polish immigrant family (Collins & Lazzari, 2010). Her great-grandparents had moved to Baltimore from Poland. She was the oldest of three girls. Her parents, Christine and William Mikulski, ran a family grocery store, Willy's Market. Her relatives opened the first Polish bakery in Baltimore, Mikulski's Bakery, where her grandmother made her famous jelly doughnuts and raisin bread (Mikulski et al., 2000). One of Mikulski's chores was to deliver groceries to people who were homebound and could not get to the store. Mikulski attended the Sacred Heart of Jesus Elementary School and the Institute of Notre Dame High School

(Jansson, 2012). She considered becoming a nun when she grew up, but said she could not deal with the rule of obedience. She was too much of a protester (Malcolm & Unger, 2016). At the age of 16, she attended the Catholic High School and joined the Christophers' movement to provide service to the poor and advocate for social justice (Mikulski et al., 2000). Her family worked hard to provide their daughters with education, and taught them they could do anything. However, Mikulski later laughed at the thought of her considering public office as a child, saying that she "didn't sit around in my little sandbox in a Baltimore ethnic neighborhood saying, 'oh, one day I'm going to be a U.S. Senator'" (Mikulski et al., 2000, p. 26). Mikulski did not have female role models for that kind of work in her youth.

Mikulski said the nuns who taught her were some of her role models, especially in loving your neighbor and caring for others. They taught her that women could be smart and effective (Collins & Lazzari, 2010). She cites Jane Addams of Hull House and Florence Kelley, who founded the National Consumers League to fight for better wages for women, as her role models. Her Polish American identity was important to her. Most of the people in her community were first- or second-generation Polish Americans. Mikulski discussed how the community created ethnic organizations such as "Polish Hill" and that people attended local ethnically based parish churches to both preserve their culture and to organize community services such as nursing homes. She also mentioned the reasons why her family emigrated to the United States. She said her great-grandmother came here "not in search of guarantees, but in search of opportunities" (Duszak, 1998, p. 51), and encouraged forming more opportunities for the youth of the community.

BECOMING A SOCIAL WORKER

Mikulski received her first degree, a Bachelor of Arts, from Mount St. Agnes College in 1958. Since she had an interest in social justice and advocacy was rooted in her back in her childhood, she decided she wanted a social work degree to help with President Kennedy's war on poverty. Mikulski graduated from the University of Maryland School of Social Work in 1965, with a focus on community organizing and social planning (Haynes & Mickelson, 2006). Her first job in social work was as a foster care worker at Catholic Charities (Collins & Lazzari, 2010). She then moved on to a position at the Department of Social Services as a child abuse worker. Mikulski stated that some of her commitments to work on protection for women and children against violence came out of this time period and what she saw on the job (Collins & Lazzari, 2010). She also worked for a VISTA training center (Jansson, 2012). During the 1960s, Mikulski was involved in registering African Americans to vote, organizing strikes, and desegregating the residents in Baltimore (Jansson, 2012). Mikulski wrote an article for the *New York Times* that spoke of America's ethnic groups as being forgotten and being unfairly branded as racist, and gained national recognition for the article (Malcolm & Unger, 2016). At the age of 27, Mikulski shocked her parents by moving into her own apartment in a mixed area of Baltimore. Her parents believed children should live at home until they were married (Jansson, 2012). Mikulski was considering going back to school for a postgraduate program when she ended up in the middle of her first political battle. Although she did eventually earn her doctorate degree, at this point in time her life was about to take a different shift.

FINDING POLITICS

While working as a social worker, Mikulski learned that a 16-lane highway project was scheduled to destroy the neighborhood where her family had first lived when they arrived in the United States. The area of Baltimore was home to a variety of ethnicities, including African American, Polish, Italian, and Greek. Mikulski was quoted as saying, "We didn't let the British take Fells Point, we didn't let the termites take Fells Point, and we're not going to let the state roads commission take Fells Point" (Haynes & Mickelson, 2006, p. 28). Mikulski and others in the community began some truly grassroots organizing. They talked to planners and politicians, organized the neighborhood, and ran bake sales to raise money to rent buses to take people to the State House and Washington, DC. They intentionally gave the community and residents a militant name so that they would be taken seriously. They were called the Southeast Council Against the Road (SCAR; Collins & Lazzari, 2010). With time and a great deal of effort, they won the fight and the highway was routed away from the neighborhood (Haynes & Mickelson, 2006). They thought the fight to keep the highway out of the neighborhood would take about 3 months. Instead, it took 2 years (Collins & Lazzari, 2010).

After this experience, Mikulski decided she wanted to be able to create change from the inside of City Hall. In 1971, she campaigned for a seat on the city council. Her parents helped by handing out flyers at the family grocery store encouraging people to vote for her (Jansson, 2012). Mikulski said, "I knocked on 15,000 doors that summer, wore out five pairs of shoes, I got mugged by fourteen Chihuahuas, and I won my seat on the city council" (Haynes & Mickelson, 2006, p. 29). She was then able to do the work from the inside as she wanted, using her social work skills. While serving on the city council, Mikulski also taught sociology classes at Loyola College to encourage students to become engaged in social justice and activism issues (Collins & Lazzari, 2010). She served on the city council from 1971 to 1976. She introduced and passed legislation to help lower the cost of bus fares for older adults and established a commission to study the impact of sexual assault on the survivors (Jansson, 2012).

CONGRESS: POLITICS AT THE NATIONAL LEVEL

Very few women were involved in politics in the early 1970s, and fewer still at the national level. The glass ceiling was alive and strong, limiting the possibilities for women. Mikulski was the first woman elected to the Senate who was not taking over the seat of her husband. In 1996, an unprecedented 12 women were elected to national office (Collins & Lazzari, 2010). Social workers are also underrepresented in office, even though social workers often have a better understanding of social needs and have excellent training and skills to work in political positions. Karger and Stoesz (2014) noted that in 2010, only five social workers were in national positions: Barbara Mikulski from Maryland, Debbie Stabenow from Michigan, Barbara Lee from California, Susan Davis from California, and Allyson Schwartz from Pennsylvania. Their analysis of 250 social workers serving as elected officials showed that 69% were involved in local offices, 29% in state positions, and only 2% in federal offices. Most of them found their social work education instrumental in public service (Karger & Stoesz, 2014).

As noted when discussing Frances Perkins's role in politics (see Chapter 5), the media is often unkind toward women in political positions. Mikulski was asked why she was not married. She responded with great humor and said, "Cause nobody ever asked me!" (Collins & Lazzari, 2010, p. 19). In her first national election, she was accused of being a fascist feminist, anti-male, and a radical lesbian (Kamber, 2003). In addition to the media issues, she was often disrespected by the men who worked with her. Once, while she was in the Senate, a coworker joked about women throwing their underwear at him, and insinuated that Mikulski was one of them. She was furious and called him out on it, and helped him draft the apology statement that the media would run (Malcolm & Unger, 2016). One male senator commented that "She understands it's still an all-boys club, and she's going to be a player. She already is" (Malcolm & Unger, 2016, p. 86).

Mikulski's personal life and appearance were often under discussion. Mikulski described herself as klutzy and frumpy, not necessarily what is pictured from a woman in power. She stood at a "stocky" 4 feet 11 inches (Malcolm & Unger, 2016). Mikulski said that one of the biggest fights was that she did not fit the stereotypes for a female candidate, someone who was "short, clunky, and mouthy" (Malcolm & Unger, 2016, p. 73). But the voters in her constituency wanted someone that they knew, someone who looked like they did and would fight for them. She would say, "I'm counting my calories, I'm counting my votes, and I'm counting on you on Election Day" (Malcolm & Unger, 2016, p. 74). She was even able to win the backing of the African American community, although there were some ethnic tensions in the area. Mikulski's strengths lie in her sense of humor, her authenticity, and her down-to-earth approach. She was able to move between the working class people in her district and the elite wing of the Democratic Party (Malcolm & Unger, 2016). This ability made her an effective leader and representative. She became known as one of the toughest but most effective Democrats in Congress.

Mikulski's first attempt at winning a seat in the U.S. House of Representatives failed. Her 1974 election was the only one she lost in her entire career (Collins & Lazzari, 2010). However, she ended the election in good spirits, saying her political career was not dead, as she had become a household name (Malcolm & Unger, 2016). In 1976, she ran again and won a landslide victory for a seat in the U.S. House of Representatives (Malcolm & Unger, 2016). Funding a campaign is a challenge for anyone, particularly women, and in order to raise funds for the election Mikulski called for the support of women, getting smaller checks than men usually did. She did everything from having bake sales to letter writing campaigns with help from supportive groups such as EMILY's list (Malcolm & Unger, 2016). She obtained a reputation for being not only a natural born Polish descendent but as a feisty urban populist who understood what the local people were going through. Mikulski worked to be available to her constituents. She did not have a desk in her office at Congress so that there would not be a barrier between her and the people, and joked that she would get calls from people at three in the morning—people who were standing by their refrigerator in the middle of the night and wanted to talk to people with their same problems (Robson, 2000). Being overly available was sometimes an expectation of a female representative, but Mikulski turned it into a strength rather than a weakness. People knew her as "Barb" and felt they had a personal relationship with her. An attack on her was seen as an attack on the people themselves (Robson, 2000).

Ten years after she won her seat in the House of Representatives, she ran for and won a seat in the Senate. She was the first Democratic woman in the Senate to hold a seat not previously held by a husband, among several other firsts for a woman. As she said,

> I am the first social worker in the United States Senate. Now I have a caseload of four million Marylanders! And though I am practicing in a different forum, those skills and values I learned as a community organizer in the streets of Baltimore are what make me an effective leader in the corridors of Congress. (Mikulski, as quoted in Haynes & Mickelson, 2006, p. 176)

Even before winning a seat in the Senate, Mikulski was smart enough to begin to position herself for committees with influence, such as the Senate Appropriations Committee, which oversees budgets (Malcolm & Unger, 2016). From 2012 to 2015 she was the chair of this powerful committee.

MAJOR ACCOMPLISHMENTS IN CONGRESS

Mikulski was dedicated toward improving the lives of her constituents as well as the American people in general throughout her career. She was involved in the passage of funding for shelters for survivors of domestic violence, supported the equal rights amendment, supported raising the minimum wage, and fought for the Homemaker IRA, which eliminated the penalization of women who had to stay home to raise children by restricting the allowable deduction (Mikulski et al., 2000). She advocated for the working people and for jobs to come to her constituents in Maryland. Mikulski was a strong proponent for healthcare, especially for women. Before her term, the National Institutes of Health (NIH) provided little funding for women's issues such as breast cancer. Mikulski brought attention to this and made sure it was changed. Funding for breast cancer has increased by 700% since 1990, in part due to Mikulski's efforts (Collins & Lazzari, 2010). Mikulski teamed up with other women in the Senate to work on this, making it a bipartisan effort by working with Republican Senator Olympia Snowe (Epstein, Niemi, & Powell, 2005). As a member of the NIH Appropriations Committee, Mikulski launched an effort to create the Women's Health Research Initiative, the first of its kind in the country (Malcolm & Unger, 2016). She also introduced the Paycheck Fairness Act and supported the Lilly Ledbetter Fair Pay Act to provide protection for women against pay inequities (Swers, 2013). Mikulski worked to try to pass universal healthcare (also like Frances Perkins), although this was not accomplished. Mikulski also fought to expand civil rights issues, continuing her work for racial equity from the 1960s. She was one of the leading sponsors for the Lilly Ledbetter Fair Pay Act to expand the Civil Rights Act of 1964. The bill allowed employees to sue for discrimination issues more easily (Malcolm & Unger, 2016).

Mikulski served on multiple committees, including the Senate Appropriations Committee (which controls the budget), the Labor and Human Resources Committee, and the Small Business Committee, among many others (Jansson, 2012). As the head of the Appropriations Committee, the budget was a major concern. This committee handles the budgets for the National Science Foundation, the National Aeronautics and Space Administration (NASA), the NIH, and the Food and Drug Administration, all very large budgets that are highly important to continue the work relating to science and safety ("The Hand on Your Purse Strings," 1994). This position allowed her to have input in the effort to support research for women's issues, particularly health issues, and in supporting the space station for NASA.

Mikulski was a long-time supporter of science and funding for science programs. She was very concerned about the digital divide in the United States, separating those who have access to technology and those who do not (Mikulski et al., 2000). In 2000, she introduced a bill to help close the digital divide. She also worked with a joint venture between

NASA and the Greater Baltimore Alliance to bring a project called Space Hope to Maryland. Space Hope is a training program to provide new technologically based skills to workers to keep them from being left behind (Mikulski et al., 2000). Due to her longtime support of science and technology, NASA named one of the world's largest astronomy databases after her. In 2012, NASA also named an exploding star "Supernova Mikulski" in her honor (Space News, 2012).

A FEMALE GUIDE TO OTHERS

Mikulski was the woman who had been in the Senate the longest. Due to this and her mentoring activities, she has been called the "Dean of Women" (Collins & Lazzari, 2010). When new female members were elected to the Senate, Mikulski mentored them in how to be effective. She did not limit this mentorship to only Democrats, but worked with women from both parties (Collins & Lazzari, 2010). The women senators recognized their status as a minority and tried to support each other (Swers, 2013). Mikulski hosted monthly bipartisan dinners for the women, and the women got to know each other as individuals as well as representatives. They discussed "home and family, but they also talk about issues and how to make things happen in this male-dominated institution," said one staffer (Swers, 2013, p. 242). Mikulski advocated for more women to be elected, and wanted to be one of many women in Congress. She considered women in Congress to be a force, not a caucus. This enabled them to get things done across party lines. Mikulski said that women were able to do what men could not. She said that the women "listened to each other and functioned with maximum respect" (Malcolm & Unger, 2016, p. 291). This allowed deeper and more trusting relationships than others and gave the women a solid basis for working together. Mikulski said the women worked toward creating sensible approaches, and that although they came from very different standpoints, they were more likely to work toward the "felt need" to find a resolution (Mikulski et al., 2000).

As a leading woman in the Senate, Mikulski was able to provide an example to the many women who would follow her. Sometimes this was done through supporting women's issues through specific bills, sometimes it was done through meeting and mentoring newly arrived representatives, and sometimes symbolic gestures took place. Early in her days at the Senate, Mikulski and several other women all wore pants instead of skirts and dresses to the Senate meetings, breaking a long-standing tradition. She was considered a transformational leader who helped teach others how to become leaders in their own way (Mikulski et al., 2000). Mikulski suggested being as practical as possible. She said, "When you go out and try to solve a problem, you have to have strategies to make it happen. If you only talk and don't produce, you are just one more disappointment. You contribute to the cynicism" (Mikulski et al., 2000, p. 32). Often, Mikulski's strategies came from listening to her constituents. She also listened to others in the Senate, asked for help to learn what she needed to know, read all the reports, and became known as a reliable representative. Mikulski used another creative idea to mentor other women in politics. She became an author of a fictional series that featured a new senator who had the misfortune to stumble into murders and chilling plot lines. The novels featured the challenges and guidance that Mikulski also gave to new senators in real life (Mikulski et al., 2000).

PERSONAL IS POLITICAL

Mikulski is one of the first to say that as a social worker, you make the personal political. Your own experiences will shape what is important to you and what you will fight for. She gave one example of this from her own life, and detailed what happened to her family when her father had Alzheimer's. When the family had to look for a nursing home because of his illness, they learned about the unfortunate guidelines from the government regarding how many resources the family could hold and still receive assistance for the nursing home costs. At the time, the guidelines stated that the family would have to sell or spend all of their assets except for $3,000. Families who had saved their whole lives were required to use their funds before receiving assistance, causing the spouse to live in poverty. Mikulski spoke with many other people about how this regulation had impacted them, and then worked to change the legislation. She said her "proudest accomplishment as a United States Senator" was that she was able to get legislation passed to lessen the burden of this on the spouse, letting couples keep their assets and obtain assistance in long-term care at the same time (Haynes & Mickelson, 2006, p. 190). Just that one change helped many people to live better lives.

ADVICE TO SOCIAL WORKERS

Mikulski stated that leadership is really a state of mind (Haynes & Mickelson, 2006). To become a leader, you will use that first social work skill that you learned—to listen to people and their stories. This will help people who may have been left behind, and you will be able to work to empower people. She said, "We must always lead the way toward equality and human dignity" (Haynes & Mickelson, 2006, p. 205). For social workers who may be considering going into public office, she (and the other women senators) has a list of suggestions. She said to consider:

1. When someone says, "Why you?," think "Why not me?"
2. Remember who you are, and where you came from.
3. Create a team effort.
4. Don't take it personally—and don't make it personal.
5. Identify the felt need (have a cause or a principle).
6. Respect your losses.
7. Control your agenda.
8. Ignore the babble.
9. Pass it on (Mikulski et al., 2000).

Mikulski said that many of the early women involved in politics did so because they were tired of hearing no on issues that were important to them. She said that over time a motto was developed: "Don't get mad. Get elected" (Malcolm & Unger, 2016, p. 63).

RETIREMENT FROM OFFICE

In 2016, Mikulski stepped down from office, having been the longest serving woman in the history of Congress. She was awarded the Presidential Medal of Freedom from President Barack Obama in 2016, and received two honorary doctorate degrees. She is now a professor of public policy at Johns Hopkins University and an advisor to the university president (Hub, 2017). At her current age of 81, she still has passion and energy for her work. She said, "I am excited to teach and encourage the next generation. . . . Being at Johns Hopkins enables me to continue to play a role locally in shaping Baltimore's future while promoting a national agenda of innovation, leadership, and service" (O'Shea, 2017).

After over 40 years in office, Mikulski continues to contribute to social work and policy today.

LESSONS LEARNED

Now that you have read through Congresswoman Mikulski's life and work, you can refer to CSWE Competency 5. This competency reads:

Competency 5: Engage in Policy Practice

Social workers understand that human rights and social justice, as well as social welfare and services, are mediated by policy and its implementation at the federal, state, and local levels. Social workers understand the history and current structures of social policies and services, the role of policy in service delivery, and the role of practice in policy development. Social workers understand their role in policy development and implementation within their practice settings at the micro, mezzo, and macro levels and they actively engage in policy practice to effect change within those settings. Social workers recognize and understand the historical, social, cultural, economic, organizational, environmental, and global influences that affect social policy. They are also knowledgeable about policy formation, analysis, implementation, and evaluation. Social workers:

- Identify social policy at the local, state, and federal level that impacts well-being, service delivery, and access to social services

- Assess how social welfare and economic policies impact the delivery of and access to social services

- Apply critical thinking to analyze, formulate, and advocate for policies that advance human rights and social, economic, and environmental justice (CSWE, 2015, p. 8)

In what ways can you identify Congresswoman Mikulski's work in these different areas of the competency? How did she work through local, state, or federal levels? What social work skills could you use in micro settings that might also apply very well to the macro work that Mikulski engaged in? As you have seen, Mikulski greatly advanced women in politics. However, there is still more work to be done. There are still far fewer women in politics, and stereotypes abound. How can you work within this competency to help women or other minority groups progress closer toward equality?

CLASSROOM ACTIVITIES

1. What kind of legislative work does your state chapter of the National Association of Social Workers (NASW) engage in? Do they have policy statements regarding specific issues? See if you can find a policy statement and suggested advocacy activities and lay out a plan to engage in one of these activities with your classmates. Consider having a representative from NASW speak in your classroom.

2. Watch the video *14 Women* (Boxer & Lambert, 2007) about the 109th Congress. Mikulski speaks of these political positions as being social work with power. Do you agree or disagree with this statement? What do you observe that the women in this video have in common? Do you think you could ever hold a position such as these?

REFERENCES

Boxer, N. (Producer), & Lambert, M. (Director). (2007). *14 Women* (Motion picture). United States: Vertical Films.

Collins, K., & Lazzari, M. (2010). The Honorable Barbara Mikulski: Fighting for social justice in the U.S. Senate. In A. Lieberman (Ed.), *Women in social work who have changed the world* (pp. 14–25). Chicago, IL: Lyceum Books.

Council on Social Work Education. (2015). *2015 educational policy and accreditation standards for baccalaureate and master's social work programs*. Alexandria, VA: Author.

Cummins, L., Byers, K., & Pedrick, L. (2011). *Policy practice or social workers: New strategies for a new era*. New York, NY: Allyn & Bacon.

Duszak, T. (1998). Polish American women: Tracing ethnic achievement in published U.S. government sources. *Journal of Government Information, 25*(1), 47–71. doi:10.1016/S1352-0237(97)00085-3

Epstein, M., Niemi, R., & Powell, L. (2005). Do women and men state legislators differ? In S. Thomas & C. Wilcox (Eds.), *Women and elective office: Past, present, and future* (2nd ed., pp. 94–109). New York, NY: Oxford University Press.

The hand on your purse strings. (1994). *Science, 264*(5156), 192–194. doi:10.1126/science.8146645

Haynes, K., & Mickelson, J. (2006). *Affecting change: Social workers in the political arena* (6th ed.) New York, NY: Pearson.

Hub. (2017). Former Senator Barbara Mikulski, now a Johns Hopkins professor, to receive two honorary degrees. Retrieved from https://hub.jhu.edu/2017/05/12/barbara-mikulski-receives-honorary-degrees-mica-nyu

Jansson, B. (2012). *The reluctant welfare state: Engaging history to advance social work practice in contemporary society* (7th ed.). Belmont, CA: Cengage.

Kamber, V. (2003). *Poison politics: Are negative campaigns destroying democracy?* New York, NY: Insight Books.

Karger, H. J., & Stoesz, D. (2014). *American social welfare policy: A pluralistic approach* (7th ed.). Boston, MA: Pearson.

Malcolm, E., & Unger, C. (2016). *When women win: Emily's List and the rise of women in American politics*. Boston, MA: Houghton Mifflin Harcourt.

Mikulski, B., Hutchison, K. B., Feinstein, D., Boxer, B., Murray, P., Snowe, O., . . . Whitney, C. (2000). *Nine and counting: The women of the Senate*. New York, NY: HarperCollins.

O'Shea, D. (2017). Longtime Congresswoman Barbara Mikulski joins Johns Hopkins faculty. Retrieved from https://hub.jhu.edu/2017/01/12/barbara-mikulski-hopkins-professorship

Reisch, M. (2014). U.S. social policy and social welfare: A historical overview. In M. Reisch (Ed.), *Social policy and social justice* (pp. 5–42). Los Angeles, CA: Sage.

Robson, D. C. (2000). Stereotypes and the female politician: A case study of Senator Barbara Mikulski. *Communications Quarterly, 48*(3), 205–222. doi:10.1080/01463370009385593

Space News. (2012). Hubble archive, supernova named in honor of Mikulski. Retrieved from http://spacenews.com/hubble-archive-supernova-named-honor-mikulski

Swers, M. (2013). *Women in the club: Gender and making policy in the Senate*. Chicago, IL: The University of Chicago Press.

Thomas, S. (2005). Introduction. In S. Thomas & C. Wilcox (Eds.), *Women and elective office: Past, present, and future* (2nd ed., pp. 3–25). New York, NY: Oxford University Press.

Trattner, W. (1999). *From poor law to welfare state: A history of social welfare in America* (6th ed.). New York, NY: The Free Press.

"Clearly, social work has a secure future. In some ways, it prospers under diverse conditions—when times are good, governments want to spend more for social services. When times are bad, we want to spend more to address human problems. Social workers are involved in both."

—Ginsberg (2005, p. 15)

CHAPTER 10

A New Century: Leaders in Recent Years

2000–2018

The previous chapters in this book have each focused on one individual, that individual's life, and his or her contributions to social work. However, as the field of social work has expanded greatly in recent decades, it can be difficult to determine "leaders" in social work overall. The individuals who have been discussed so far have had lasting impacts in a wide variety of areas, including the overall physical and mental health treatment of people diagnosed with mental health disorders, civil rights, social work education, and international social work. This final chapter is set up a bit differently.

We examine five areas of social work that have been primarily developed in more recent social work eras: lesbian, gay, bisexual, transgender, and queer (LGBTQ) rights; ethics; environmental social work; trauma; and neuroscience. Some basic information on these areas is provided, along with one individual who had contributed to this area of social work. These individuals have been selected as examples of leading areas of social work, but are by no means the only leaders in the field during this new century. It would be impossible to recognize here all of the people who are creating, developing, and inspiring the field of social work today. Social workers are moving into new areas of the field, and are collaborating with professionals from many other areas related to mental health and social justice. By working with other fields, social workers are evolving into multidisciplinary practitioners with an incredible variety of skills and strengths. One of the joys of working in social work is that there are so many options for practice! By reading these examples, it is hoped that you will begin to see some of the possibilities that lie ahead. As you learn about each of these areas and individuals, think about Council on Social Work Education (CSWE) Competency 6: Engage With Individuals, Families, Organizations, and Communities. Most if not all of these people started social work by engaging at a more micro level of work. With their experiences, they applied a macro framework to the situations they encountered to develop different specialties and segments of social work. However, even in the macro practice we encounter we see the impact on the individual. How can you see this competency being applied?

CONTEXT OF THE TIMES: A NEW CENTURY

The 21st century has seen a vast amount of progress as well as times of concern. We have seen the rise of the Internet, the war in Iraq, the September 11 terrorist attacks, the first African American President of the United States, the Great Recession, the Affordable Care Act, amazing developments in technology, and the Supreme Court ruling in favor of same-sex marriage (Cummins, Byers, & Pedrick, 2011; Jansson, 2012). The poverty rate continues to rise, while the current political climate is calling for less support for those in need, not more. Managed care, including limits set on how long and for what reasons social workers can provide treatment, is becoming more and more common. The elderly population is growing rapidly, and more and more are in need of support (Carlton-LaNey, 1997). College students are incurring more debt than ever simply to obtain a bachelor's degree.

Social work has a new set of challenges to work through. Dominelli (2017) discussed the rise of Islamophobia as well as continued and accepted racism and other social inequities as an area that causes struggles for social workers. In addition to social policies that provide more support for the wealthy than the vulnerable, we are seeing a rise in people not wanting to accept those who are different from them, especially in terms of country of origin. Despite these challenging areas, there are exciting new developments that have made their way into the social work world. We have seen a greater acceptance of the population that identifies as LGBTQ, and the ruling in favor of gay marriage (Jansson, 2012). We have seen a greater acknowledgment of the role of ethics in social work (Reamer, 1997). With a greater scientific understanding and advanced technology, we are able to apply new skills to social work. Services can now be provided from a distance using phone, video, or chat platforms. Social justice can be seen through the lens of environmental social work, allowing for the development of policies and practices that are sustainable for the earth in addition to the people who live on it. Advances in medical technology allow us to have a greater understanding of both trauma and neuroscience, and the connection between the two. All of these areas contribute to social workers being able to improve interventions to clients.

LGBTQ RIGHTS: DR. LORI MESSINGER

Social work has aimed to procure services and rights for underrepresented groups of people since the settlement house movement. Unfortunately, many social workers, especially those who completed their degrees before the mid-1990s, had little education relating to understanding and serving sexual minority populations (Morrow & Messinger, 2006). While some nonmajority groups have gained acceptance, according to Jansson, "gays and lesbians still encounter virulent prejudice" (Jansson, 2012, p. 482). Some social workers and other mental health practitioners still think it is okay to say that they will not work with individuals who identify as being a part of the LGBTQ population, not realizing that denying treatment in this manner is not consistent with social work's core ethics. Other workers may think that working with this population is just like working with any other group, and that no special training is necessary. However, education on the lived experience of individuals in this group is extremely important. Dr. Lori Messinger has been working on behalf of people who identify as a part of the LGBTQ population since her MSW internship with parenting teens. She has been involved in researching, publishing, and educating others about the experiences of people who identify as LGBTQ and how to improve services to them since she was in her doctoral program. Some of these publications are specific to social work students and interns, and would be extremely helpful for schools of social work.

Messinger's mother grew up in the American Baptist tradition, but because her father was Jewish, her mother converted to Judaism when they decided to get married. Her mother had to work to get her own family to accept her husband. Messinger was born in Philadelphia but only lived there until she was 6 years old. She had two younger siblings. When her family moved to Willingboro, New Jersey, she entered a neighborhood with a very diverse population. The city had lost a court case on racial segregation and had been intentionally integrated. Messinger said she learned many lessons about being White and having friends from different backgrounds while growing up in this neighborhood. When she was 6 years old a young African American girl who lived next door to her invited Messinger to meet her at the swimming pool. When she arrived she saw a "sea of black faces, with the girls wearing brightly colored swim caps, and I couldn't recognize her . . . after looking around, somewhat bewildered and embarrassed, I told my mother I wanted to go home." The next day her friend asked why she did not come, and she admitted she could not identify her. Messinger said she still cringes when she thinks about that, but at the time her friend laughed and said that "all the white girls looked alike" to her, too. After getting to know her, she said she could not imagine mistaking one Black person for another, but that this had been a good lesson in becoming a cross-cultural friend (L. Messinger, personal communication, September 12, 2017).

In high school, Messinger was involved in drama club and was a "choir geek." She was very involved in children's theater and eventually high school drama. Messinger said she had no balance, hand–eye coordination, or athletic ability, but she loved to sing and act! She also loved to argue, so much that she thought about being a lawyer; hence she was in mock trial and Olympics of the Mind (L. Messinger, personal communication, September 12, 2017). Messinger and her sister both dated interracially as teenagers, but bringing home African American boyfriends was not acceptable to her parents. Messinger's father even considered moving the family to the suburbs to keep them from dating men from a different race. She stood up to them by openly dating and inviting her boyfriends to the house.

Messinger says she did not really suspect that she was a lesbian until college, when she realized that she had always preferred spending time with her female friends. She read everything she could find on lesbian identity. Realizing she was attracted to a lesbian classmate, she acknowledged that she was more attracted to women than men, and more comfortable in relationships with them. Once Messinger realized this is what was right for her, she did what she now suggests others do not—she came out to everyone she knew all at once! Within a month, she had told everyone, and later said this was not the best idea. This quick and thorough disclosure had injured her support system, as she did not yet have answers to the questions they asked. After dating only two women, she met a third, Boo, the woman who became her wife. They met through friends in

1991, but really connected over New Year's Eve of 1991/92. Because of the ever-changing state and federal laws, Messinger shared that the couple has multiple important dates. They had a commitment ceremony in 1999, officially became domestic partners in 2007, were legally married in 2009, and finally had the marriage nationally recognized in 2013. They have been together for over 25 years, and Messinger says that Boo is "the most important person in my life, and I love her deeply" (L. Messinger, personal communication, September 12, 2017).

College life and finding social work was a journey for Messinger. Since she was a first-generation college student, she did not really know what to look for in a college. Messinger started attending the University of Pittsburgh since it was close enough to get home, but far enough so that her parents could not just drop in. She tried to get acclimated by joining the university choir and singing with a jazz band (University of North Carolina Wilmington, 2015). Nonetheless, the school was not a good fit, as many White students were from small towns and Western Pennsylvania and seemed uncomfortable with Black people. Moreover, they seemed to be more interested in a place to party than a place to learn. During her third year, her favorite aunt died. Messinger said she was heartbroken and lonely, and did not feel like she fit in. She withdrew from her classes when she returned home for the winter break. She eventually transferred to Douglass College at Rutgers to finish her undergraduate degree in philosophy, then immediately went into graduate school there for political science, with a specialization in women in politics. She met Boo while she was in this program. Boo was just finishing a social work degree, and once Messinger heard about what social work was, she realized it was a better fit. She finished her master's degree in political science, moved in with Boo in North Carolina, and applied to the social work program at the University of North Carolina at Chapel Hill, where she received her MSW and PhD. This program was a much better fit for her. She said switching to social work was the best decision of her academic career, as social work "focused on people in need, equity and equality, and the integration of knowledge, skills, and practice" (L. Messinger, personal communication, September 12, 2017).

Messinger had her first experiences within social work at a domestic violence and sexual assault crisis program. She later worked in a program for parenting teens that helped them finish school and plan for the future. She remembered working with a lesbian teenage mother who shattered her own stereotypes. She did not realize the client was a (closeted) lesbian for several months! She specialized in macro practice in her MSW program, doing a second placement conducting program evaluations of antipoverty agencies. After completing her MSW, she worked with the North Carolina Governor's Crime Commission doing program planning with agencies that served victims of crime. During Messinger's doctoral program, the staff at the school sent a lesbian MSW student who was having issues in her field placement to see her. She realized that many other LGBTQ students in the field were likely struggling with similar issues, and began a long career of research on the experiences of LGBTQ students, faculty, staff, and social workers. She came to understand that many social workers and mental health practitioners do not understand the needs of LGBTQ people.

Messinger shared two stories to show the lack of understanding often received by this population. When Messinger was trying to get pregnant, she went to have a medical procedure related to fertility. The doctor asked if she might be pregnant. Messinger then reported the conversation the following way:

> Him: (Laughing, but serious) Now that means no unprotected sex!
>
> Me: Well, I am a lesbian, so I could have sex all day, and I wouldn't get pregnant.
>
> Him: (shocked) But I thought you were trying to get pregnant?!
>
> Me: I am. I am using insemination, but that hasn't worked, so that is why I need the procedure.
>
> Him: (still confused) Oh. Well, we just haven't had *one of you* before.
>
> Me: (Pause) Well, you probably have, because the doctor who referred me works with many lesbians with fertility issues, but they just probably didn't say anything.
>
> Him: (looking at the nurse and rolling his eyes) Well, I guess it takes all kinds. (L. Messinger, personal communication, September 12, 2017)

Messinger said the lack of support at that vulnerable moment was very difficult for her. Her partner, Boo, also shared a story regarding the lack of understanding, this time from a mental health provider. Boo came out to her parents as a teenager in the 1970s in the South. Her parents were Southern Christians and very concerned about the possibility that she was gay, so they sent her to a Christian counselor. The counselor saw her for weeks, built rapport with her, and then tried to talk to her about belief in her homosexual identity, as it was called in the 1970s in the South. He told her, "If you keep with this (homosexual identity), you will never become anything!" Boo was devastated that this trusted person would tell her she was doomed to live a terrible life, and never returned to his office. Boo was lucky to have had supportive and loving parents who instilled in her such a strong sense of self that she could reject the counselor's hateful message. Messinger noted that even for a therapist to refuse to see a LGBTQ client can be very damaging and rejecting to the person (L. Messinger, personal communication, September 12, 2017).

Fortunately for Messinger and Boo, they found support in other people and eventually found each other. They now live in North Carolina (although Messinger is taking a 1-year fellowship in Richmond, Virginia, in 2017/18), with their 70-pound pointer mix dog, Jack. Messinger works in the university administration at the University of North Carolina Wilmington, overseeing community engagement activities throughout the university. When she teaches classes, she usually teaches policy, diversity, qualitative research, and community and organizational practice. She has also taught electives on working with the LGBTQ population and human sexuality. She continues to do a great deal of research on the experiences of the LGBTQ population. In 2006, she edited a book with Deana Morrow on working with the LGBTQ population (Morrow & Messinger, 2006), as well as editing a case study workbook. Messinger has also been an advocate on LGBTQ issues, serving on governing boards for Equality Alabama and Kansas Equity Coalition and the American Civil Liberties Union (ACLU) of North Carolina.

Messinger's advice to students is that it is extremely important for all students (including LGBTQ students) to educate themselves about working with LGBTQ populations. You cannot simply decide that you will not work with this population if you are not comfortable with them, because you will encounter them everywhere, in every realm of social work practice. Be intentional about your relationships with the people in your life who identify as LGBTQ, learn about them and their experiences, and bring that learning into your practice. She says that it is also important to remember that people have multiple identities such as ethnicity, income level, religious identity, and many others (intersectional identities). All of these pieces contribute to how people live, what they value, and what they need in practice. She suggests to "always follow that old social work aphorism of starting where the client is and being culturally humble, but undergird that with research on best practices and population history and culture." Every LGBTQ individual you meet will come from a different background and have unique experiences, so you need to keep all these pieces in mind for your practice, just as you would with any other client. Also, never forget that no matter what kind of practice you do— casework, counseling, community organizing, or policy advocacy—social workers must always advocate for social justice within their settings and in their larger communities.

ETHICS: DR. FREDERIC REAMER

Few social workers will dispute the idea that ethics is central to the social work identity and profession. We have a recently updated guide in the 2017 version of the National Association of Social Workers (NASW) *Code of Ethics*, which gives social workers information on our core mission and values. It also gives us guidelines for practice to provide safety for both the client and practitioner. The NASW *Code of Ethics* (NASW, 2017a) should be one of the first things that you as a social work student read in your education. You can download it from the NASW website for free. The field of ethics has been around for thousands of years—think of Aristotle and Socrates (F. Reamer, personal communication, August 6, 2017). The solidification of ethics for social work developing into a practical, well-understood concept has taken some time. In the 1920s an experimental draft of a code of ethics was written and attributed to Mary Richmond (Reamer, 2016). The first document attempting to develop ethical practice was published in 1947 by the Delegate Conference of the American Association of Social Workers (Reamer, 2014a). The NASW formulated their first version of the *Code of Ethics* in 1960 (NASW, 2015). The most current version was written in 1996 and updated in 2008 and 2017. In addition, there is a new set of standards for guiding technology in social work practice endorsed by several social work organizations, including the NASW and Council on Social Work Education (CSWE; NASW, 2017b). The current *Code of Ethics* and supporting material such as the technology standards are essential to ensure that all social workers have a common basis of understanding regarding our values and the ways we express them.

Ethics were not always regarded in the same light as they are today. Reamer (2014a) discusses the five stages of ethics in the evolution of social work. He starts with the Morality Period, when the social worker was more concerned with the morality of the client than the practitioner. Early social welfare was often concerned with the idea that individuals or families were in need of assistance because they were somehow morally corrupt (Jansson, 2012). For example, the family with no income needed food because the father was a "drunk" who could not work. You can see some examples of this in the earlier chapters of this book. The Great Depression helped shift the thinking away from the Morality Period, as large numbers of people became unemployed and the problem began to be seen as a systems issue. The second stage, the Values Period, followed this as the shift away from the client's morality and to a clarification of the values of social workers became a focus of the 1940s through the 1970s (Reamer, 2014a). In the 1970s, the shift toward applying the ethical constructs brought social work into the Ethical Theory and Decision-Making Period. The rise in scandals and malpractice litigation likely contributed to this shift, and led into the next phase: the Ethical Standards and Risk Management Period of the 1990s. The existing NASW *Code of Ethics* was produced in this state. Finally, social work has moved into the Digital Period, along with the rest of the world. As more social workers utilize technology in practice, such as using televideo therapy sessions for practice and email for communication, we need to continue to develop our methods to protect client privacy and confidentiality. Complex issues around boundaries in social media, informed consent when working with clients who are not met in person, and the documentation and storage of client information in the digital age continue (Reamer, personal communication, July 17, 2017). Social work is giving more attention to this area by providing updated standards, such as the Standards for Technology in Social Work Practice that was updated in 2017 (NASW, 2017b). It is important to note, however, that while we have guidelines, our ability to make ethical decisions is not tied to just these formal guidelines (Reamer, 2013). Social workers need to have additional resources, training, the support of supervisors and other workers, and their own values to assist their way through making ethical decisions when faced with a dilemma.

Our current understanding of ethics is vastly different than in the beginning stages of social work, when the morality of the client was a primary concern. The ethical ways to best work with our clients, with our colleagues, and with our responsibilities to the profession are now a much bigger concern. In this litigious environment where a social worker may be sued for making a mistake, having a protocol for behaviors has become perhaps even more important. We need to know how to best serve our clients while providing appropriate documentation (Reamer, 2005), confidentiality (Millstein, 2000), mandated reporting (Reamer, 2006), and ensuring appropriate boundaries (O'Leary, Tsui, & Ruch, 2013; Pugh, 2007). Macro level workers should be aware of best practices and how they fit in with social justice issues, whether or not to comply with agency policies that the workers consider not ethical, and how to deal with situations relating to whistle- blowers from organizations where there is unethical conduct (F. Reamer, personal communication, August 6, 2017). There are now standards for how to deal with other professionals if they are impaired in their ability to practice due to substance use, family issues, or anything else that may prevent them from fully functioning in their role as a social worker (Reamer, 2014b). Ethics encourages social workers to increase their cultural sensitivity and to work toward social justice (Guttmann, 2006). We understand that even with guidelines, in reality practice can be messy. Social workers are taught about ethical dilemmas and how to attempt to resolve them (Guttmann, 2006; Reamer, 1990). Ethics in social work can be taught as an entire course, so it is beyond our scope to discuss all the implications here. However, ethics is such a cornerstone of social work practice that it was deemed important to include in this text as a key area of focus for the 21st century.

Dr. Frederic Reamer is one of the central figures in ethics research and application for social work practice. He has researched and written extensively in the field for 40 years. Reamer was the chair of the task force that wrote the current version of the NASW *Code of Ethics* (NASW, 2008). He is currently the chair of the NASW Technology Standards Task Force, and has served on the *Code of Ethics* Revisions Task Force for some time (NASW Foundation, n.d.-b). Some of his books include: *The Social Work Ethics Casebook: Cases and Commentary* (2009), *Boundary Issues and Dual Relationships in the Human Services* (2012), and *Social* Work Values and Ethics (Reamer, 2006). In addition, Reamer is one of the editors of the *Encyclopedia of Social Work*. He speaks on ethical issues to the media, including as a commentator on National Public Radio (NPR; NASW Foundation, n.d.-b). He has been an advisor to the governor of Rhode Island and served on the State of Rhode Island Parole Board (NASW

Foundation, n.d.-a). He has received numerous awards for his contributions, including the Distinguished Contributions to Social Work Education award from CSWE in 1995 and the Excellence in Ethics award from the NASW in 2015.

Reamer was born in Baltimore, Maryland, on June 13, 1953. His mother moved to Baltimore after meeting his father, who was a pilot for the U.S. Air Force. When his mother died from a brain tumor when Reamer was only 6 years old, he had many people supporting him and showing the family kindness, including family friends and Reamer's first-grade teacher, Laura Warren. Reamer remembers a time shortly after his mother's death that influenced him to go into criminal justice. He remembers:

> My father took my brother (age 9) and me (age 6) to the local public library branch in Baltimore. I was just learning to read. While my brother accompanied a librarian to select books to borrow, I wandered the aisle glancing at book spines and jackets. I came across a book whose cover included the photo of a prison inmate in his cell. I was mesmerized and leafed through the book's pages and photos. For months, whenever we visited the library, I went straight for that book, took it off the shelf, sat on the floor, and stared at the photos. I recall wondering what it was that these inmates did that led them to prison, what prison life was like, and so on. That was the beginning of my lifelong interest in criminal justice and criminology. . . . I have never lost that fascination or curiosity about what leads people to commit crimes and how we, as a society, ought to respond. (F. Reamer, personal communication, July 17, 2017)

Early impressions can make an enormous impact on an individual. In this case, an experience at the age of 6 became the basis for a lifelong interest.

Reamer attended Baltimore Polytechnic Institute in his high school years, and was involved in sports such as soccer and baseball. He was also active in learning mechanical drawing and drafting, which helped shape his interest in maths, science, and engineering, leading into his later teaching emphasis on research methods and data analysis. He worked part-time at his father's law firm during high school, spending some of his time going into prisons to obtain signatures for legal documents from the inmates (F. Reamer, personal communication, July 17, 2017). When Reamer began college at the University of Maryland—College Park, these experiences led him to study the field of criminal justice. Reamer realized that a graduate degree would be necessary to work as a professional in the field and attended the University of Chicago, obtaining his master's degree in 1975. He moved directly into his PhD program, beginning in the department called the Committee on Human Development. However, he soon became frustrated with the abstract and theoretical nature of that department, and wanted something that would focus more on the practical application of the theories. He discovered the School of Social Service Administration, and after reading the course descriptions had an "Aha!" moment. He quickly found his home in the social work profession (F. Reamer, personal communication, July 17, 2017).

Reamer's new home in the social work program soon gave birth to the ideas that shaped his career in ethics. Reamer states that his interest in ethics began when he was a doctoral student, finding ethical issues relating to inmates' rights such as privacy and confidentiality. He states, "I can pinpoint, almost to the day, when my interest in the daunting ethical issues in the social work profession began, and it was when I was a doctoral student at 969 East 60th Street. I was focusing on the criminal justice system, and I thought, 'There must be a lot of complicated ethical issues in this type of social work.' It was like a light-bulb went off" (University of Chicago, 2005). He attended a lecture on bioethics, and thought that similar connections could be made between ethics and social work. However, very little was being published on social work ethics at the time (F. Reamer, personal communication, July 17, 2017). Forty years of practice and research in the area of ethics came out of that time.

Once he graduated with his PhD in 1978, Reamer moved into practice and teaching, first at the University of Chicago and eventually at his longtime home at Rhode Island College. He currently enjoys teaching research and data analysis courses, and, of course, ethics. Reamer states that he believes the skills learned in research and statistics help with understanding logic, which is essential to social work, and that the concepts in research can sharpen one's thinking as a social worker (F. Reamer, personal communication, July 17, 2017). Reamer also continued in the field, doing social work primarily in the criminal justice arena. He was involved in group work with prison inmates, working in the forensic unit at the psychiatric hospital with clients who had been found not guilty for criminal offenses due to mental illness, on the Rhode Island Parole Board, and as the director of the National Juvenile Justice Assessment Center. Reamer states that working in prisons has had a profound impact on his values and thinking. These experiences have caused him to "think long and hard about what is most important in life, the value of personal freedom, the purposes of punishment and rehabilitation, the possibility of redemption, capital punishment, and justice. These are fundamentally important issues" (F. Reamer, personal communication, July 17, 2017). He continues, saying "I have spent years talking with crime victims and inmates about how one poor decision, one bad moment can turn life upside down in a flash. As a result, I take little for granted and do my best to be mindful" (F. Reamer, personal communication, July 17, 2017). Working with people who have lost their freedom due to one decision can make one much more reflective on the decisions they make in life.

These early postdoctoral years shaped Reamer's life in additional ways. While nearing the end of his doctoral studies, another student, Deborah Siegel, was referred to him as she needed a statistics consultant for her own research. As Reamer states, "the rest is history" (F. Reamer, personal communication, July 17, 2017). They both now teach at Rhode Island College in the School of Social Work. They eventually had two daughters. Their eldest daughter, Emma, also majored in criminal justice, first working with high-risk teens and then shifting into loss prevention with a national retail corporation. Leah majored in biology and has worked as a clinical researcher at a medical center, focusing on physical trauma and wound care, and is entering graduate school for public health.

Throughout Reamer's 40 years in social work, he has written 21 books and more than 140 journal articles and book chapters. He has served as a social worker in both correctional and mental health settings, as well as on the Rhode Island Parole Board. He has taught at several universities, but made Rhode Island College his home in 1988 and has been a part of the faculty ever since. He lectures around the world, including in countries such as India, South Korea, Sweden, Italy, and Germany. In addition to these more typical social work activities, Reamer encourages social work students to be open to life's surprises. He says that he was invited to be a commentator on NPR on his work in prisons in 2003. This led him into a radio career (on top of the rest of his work!), hosting a weekly NPR program called *This I Believe–New England* since 2007. He says that "Life is full of surprises, and, sometimes, delightful challenges" (F. Reamer, personal communication, July 17, 2017). Radio shows are certainly a different form of social work, but a wonderful opportunity to educate the public on issues relevant to the field.

When asked what advice he would give to social work students, Reamer says his best advice is to "appreciate the complexity of social work ethics and avoid the temptation to think that reviewing the NASW *Code of Ethics* is sufficient. Fully understanding the NASW *Code of Ethics* is essential, but is only a beginning" (F. Reamer, personal communication, July 17, 2017). He suggests that in order to practice in an ethical manner, students need to take time to explore many ethical concepts in depth. These include concepts such as: (a) the nature of core social work values; (b) the nature of ethical dilemmas when social workers must manage conflicting duties and obligations, conflicts of interest, termination of services against clients' wishes, or the use of remote or distance services; and (c) managing ethics-related risks to protect both the client and the professional (F. Reamer, personal communication, July 17, 2017). As we can see through Reamer's long career and multitude of publications focused on social work ethics, this is a highly complex area. As a social work student, you cannot devote too much time to learning and understanding social work ethics. Almost everything is related to ethics, including the way resources are distributed in our current economic and political system. Green social work attempts to tackle ethical issues in another way.

GREEN SOCIAL WORK: DR. LENA DOMINELLI

There is no question that the distribution of resources around the world is unequal. Those in wealthier countries utilize a disproportionate amount of resources. Within those wealthier countries, a small number of citizens hold even greater wealth while there are those who continue to live without food or shelter. Social and economic issues are closely linked (Mayadas & Elliott, 1997), as are economic and environmental issues. The difference between considering simply the impact of social justice (looking at the social and economic inequities present) and environmental justice is the focus on social injustices that arise out of environmental issues and concerns (Miller, Hayward, & Shaw, 2012). Social workers with an environmental focus say that the poorest of these populations are the ones that are hit the hardest when there is an environmental disaster (Gray & Coates, 2012). In the Global South, it is the poorest who are left with no options but to overfarm land or cut down forests, leading to the degradation of the soil (Gray & Coates, 2012). People living in poverty, particularly people of color, are more likely to live near health hazards such as waste dumps or manufacturing plants (NASW, 2003). When there is a war or internal conflict in a country, people in poverty are often the most impacted, as they have fewer choices or methods of escape or control.

As social workers must always be concerned with the most vulnerable, the impact of the environment on those in poverty should be a factor that we consider. We must then also be concerned with the state of the environment worldwide. A greater attention to what is called environmental social work is called for. The NASW (2006) notes that "all forms of social work practice are effected by environmental degradation" (p. 139). The shift on social work's focus on the Person in Environment to include the actual ecology of the physical space around the person is a critical component (NASW, 2006). When we consider this environmental justice perspective, both humans and the natural world are seen together as part of the universal whole (Miller et al., 2012). As both the frequency and complexity of environmental crises escalate (Dominelli, 2012), we need increased attention to the area of environmental justice for both human beings and the entire natural habitat.

Dominelli (2014) extends the definition of environmental justice to include the well-being of the earth itself. She states that environmental injustice is "society's failure to ensure the equitable distribution of the Earth's resource in meeting human needs, simultaneously providing for the well-being of people and planet earth today and in the future" (p. 339). The inclusion of the physical planet and looking toward the wellness and care of humans in the future creates the focus on a sustainable, healthy environment. Dominelli defines green social work as "that part of practice that intervenes to protect the environment and enhance people's well-being by integrating the interdependence between people and their socio-cultural, economic and physical environments, and among peoples within an egalitarian framework that addresses prevailing structural inequalities and unequal distribution of power and resources" (Dominelli, 2012). In order to create a system that allows for the long-term support of the planet and all of the current and future people in a more equal power structure, changes will need to be made to our way of life. Our systems related to technology, industry, and large businesses will need to be adjusted. Western cultures in particular need to refocus their attention on the natural environment, as many non-Western traditions have already integrated this thinking (Ramsay & Boddy, 2017).

Social work as a profession of change agents is well positioned to increase environmental justice. Our systems training and interdisciplinary methods may be key in developing methods to facilitate the work needed to make sustainable changes (Schmitz, Matyók, Sloan, & James, 2012). Social workers are very familiar with two of the contributors to environmental problems, poverty and violence (Schmitz et al., 2012). Our work in areas such as economic development and conflict resolution can contribute to lessening these problems. Skills in team building, negotiation, community development, multilevel assessments, education, and in holistic interventions may help build communities that practice social justice in areas that impact the environment (Ramsay & Boddy, 2017). Additionally, the macro training that includes policy and advocacy will be highly necessary for change. Social workers will need to be active in their roles in forming policy and bringing attention to these issues in the media to make more preventative changes, instead of simply dealing with the aftermath of an environmental crisis (Dominelli, 2012). Unfortunately, some have noted that social workers have not been as involved in the fight for environmental improvements as they should be. It is possible that the social work focus on the individual and clinical realms may overshadow the necessity for work in this area. There does seem to be a shift toward a stronger environmental focus in recent years, especially in publications and in the student body (Ramsay & Boddy, 2017). Hopefully a renewed interest in this area by the younger generation of social workers will create a movement toward environmental justice.

One of the leaders in the area of environmental or green social work is Dr. Lena Dominelli. Dominelli is currently a professor of applied social sciences at Durham University in the United Kingdom. She is an educator, practitioner, and researcher. She works to help remove social inequalities and injustices and assists communities to change the social and physical environments (Durham University, n.d.). Much of her research and writing focuses on how social work can participate in worldwide environmental change, including *Anti-Racist Social Work* (Dominelli, 2008), *Social Work in a Globalizing World* (Dominelli, 2010), and *Green Social Work: From Environmental Crises to Environmental Justice* (Dominelli, 2012). She has served in offices such as president of the

International Association of Schools of Social Work (IASSW) from 1996 to 2004 and is currently the Head of IASSW's Committee on Disaster Interventions, Climate Change and Sustainability. She has won several awards for her work, including a medal from the French Senate, and honorary doctorate from the University of KwaZulu Natal in South Africa, and an honorary professorship from the East China University of Science and Technology in 2010 (Durham University, n.d.).

When talking about what social workers can bring to the environmental movement, Dominelli stated in an interview that "We certainly bring the negotiation of what happens to daily life, and people's daily life experiences and routines, so we are embedded in that and can bring that to the table. But we also do a lot of research. Some of it is blue skies research where we theorize new ways of approaching the problems that we have. We are good coordinators and communicators, so we can actually help translate the science into something that people can understand" (Dominelli, 2015).

When traveling for a conference in 2013, Dominelli stated that in this location "there is an interest in linking the structural issues, the big social problems, with the personal ones, and I like that. That fits in with my model of social work, as well, that I try to propagate in U.K." (Dominelli, 2013). This model is green social work. Green social work is a newer term, and an area that Dominelli invented. She says that this form of social work is "multidisciplinary, so I work with physical scientists and the social sciences, social workers, and community development workers. And we try to look at the person in the environment in a different way, in that we actually ask ourselves 'Why do we have so many social problems?' Is it because of people being not very good, lacking in capacity, or is it because of the systems we've set up? So, we look at the two together. And what we've been finding is that actually, it's got a lot to do with the systems, and so we're looking at how can we improve the quality of life for everyone without destroying the earth and its resources, and the environment that nurtures us all" (see the full YouTube video at https://www.youtube.com/watch?v=rHABLdCVR8A for the interview). Part of this work is looking at disasters such as earthquakes and floods and how this impacts both the earth and the people in it, and how we can try to look at new models of social development to create self-sustaining jobs as well as greater ecological systems. Promoting renewable energy and reducing the need to use fossil fuels are areas to work on regarding these changes (Dominelli, 2012).

TRAUMA IN SOCIAL WORK: DR. ELLEN DEVOE

The field of trauma work within social work has been exploding in the past few decades. More and more practitioners are working with clients who have trauma backgrounds. We are beginning to understand how important trauma can be in the development of children, as well as the long-term impact on adults. The Adverse Childhood Experiences study looked at the number of traumatic events an individual had as a child and the health impacts as adults. This groundbreaking study clearly linked trauma to numerous physical health problems in adults, including heart disease, cancer, and early death (Felitti et al., 1998). We are also able to physically see the impacts of trauma on the brain due to improved technology. We know that trauma changes the way our brain functions, including an increase in the stress hormone activity and changes in the system that allow us to filter important information from irrelevant information (van der Kolk, 2014). The understanding that a large percentage of the population has experienced at least one trauma has also brought this area into social work's focus. While the *Diagnostic and Statistical Manual of Mental Disorders* (5th ed.; *DSM-5*; American Psychiatric Association, 2013) lists a lifetime rate of Posttraumatic Stress Disorder (PTSD) at around 9% of the population (American Psychiatric Association, 2013), social workers and other mental health workers in the field know that the impacts of trauma go far beyond this diagnosis alone.

Having a greater understanding of the high rates of trauma and the long-term impacts has led social work to become more involved in trauma-related treatment and prevention. Evidence-based practices specific to working with individuals who have experienced trauma are expanding. Van der Kolk (2014) discusses three primary approaches to trauma treatment: the more traditional top-down talk therapy methods, medication to treat symptoms, and bottom-up approaches that work with the physical body and its experiences. Many students (and perhaps some practitioners) are relatively unfamiliar with the last category. There are many examples of evidence-based treatment and new areas being developed and researched to see if they can assist in healing from trauma. Emerson (2015) discusses using yoga to help trauma survivors reconnect with their body. Shapiro formulated a process called eye movement desensitization and reprocessing (EMDR) as a method for working through trauma (Shapiro & Forrest, 2004). Research has been completed in other areas that show promise for trauma healing, such as dance movement (Levine

& Land, 2016), theater (van der Kolk, 2014), and neurofeedback (van der Kolk, 2014). As we learn more about trauma and how to assist people with trauma backgrounds, hopefully we will improve our ability to assist these individuals through a variety of treatment formats.

Dr. Ellen DeVoe is an excellent example of a social work leader in the trauma field. She has worked with and written about her research in multiple trauma-related areas. She began working with traumatized children in a group home before even beginning her social work degree and has since published in areas relating to violence exposure in children, domestic violence, sexual abuse, and the impact of the September 11 attacks. Due to her work in the trauma field, Dr. DeVoe was awarded the Teaching Excellence honor from Boston University's School of Social Work in 2008. She was also listed as one of the 30 most influential social workers alive today by Social Work Degree Guide (Rufener, 2014). She is currently an associate professor at Boston University and heads the doctoral program for social work and sociology. Dr. DeVoe also founded the Trauma Certificate Program offered by that school to help students become more educated in trauma work (Boston University, 2017). She has recently been working on the CSWE task force to increase education around trauma in the social work curriculum (E. DeVoe, personal communication, September 8, 2017).

DeVoe was born in Indianapolis in 1964. She speaks of her early interest in trauma work as possibly coming from her family history. When she was 5 years old, her father, John Devoe, died. Her mother, Jane, remarried a widower who had five children of his own. Being in a mixed household of eight children who all lost a parent at a young age was a formative experience. DeVoe speaks of the family as being raised with an eye toward service and giving back. Her second father, Alan, was active in the civil rights movement, as well as being interested in and writing about the Civil War and Robert E. Lee (E. DeVoe, personal communication, September 8, 2017). She enjoyed playing sports in high school, especially basketball, and continued this through college.

DeVoe, like many in social work, says she did not know what social work was until college! She studied history and women's studies at Princeton University. She says that learning about women's studies while playing sports in the early years of Title IX was eye-opening, and gave her a good foundation for social work. Even in women's studies, much of the thinking and teaching was very male-dominated (E. DeVoe, personal communication, September 8, 2017). After completing her degree, her first job was in a group home for children who had been temporarily removed from their parents. Both her educational background and her work in this position led her to decide to return to school for her master's in social work. DeVoe and a friend decided to move to Colorado to go back to school—partially so she would be able to live in a place where she could learn how to ski!

DeVoe felt like she had a good foundation for social work and loved her program at the University of Denver. She worked with the public schools, particularly with kids from different ethnic backgrounds, and loved working with kindergarten and first-grade children. PTSD was viewed very differently during this time, especially in children. After graduation, she took a fellowship working with children with developmental disabilities, and tried to stay away from full-time trauma due to its intensity. However, she realized how much trauma and violence were a part of so many children's lives. DeVoe ended up staying in the trauma field, although she did not think she would be able to carry out clinical work with trauma-related issues in children. DeVoe did clinical work with children in Michigan for about 7 or 8 years before she returned to school for a joint social work and psychology PhD program at the University of Michigan. She says that although the program was challenging, her self-care plan of playing ultimate frisbee got her through the program (E. DeVoe, personal communication, September 8, 2017).

DeVoe did not particularly plan on becoming a professor while she was in the program, and did not end up teaching until near the end of her program. She says that when she started, she was terrified, but loved it. She gives a lot of credit to the incredible mentors she had while she was in school. These experiences led her toward teaching, which is also a way she feels she can have an impact on more people. Teaching trauma-related issues is easy to do wrong, and DeVoe's experience allows her to educate an entire group of up-and-coming social workers on how to practice well in this area. While teaching classes on trauma and clinical practice at Boston University, she also continues to consult and research in trauma-related areas. Although DeVoe's scholarly work is listed as "Effects of Violence Exposure on Children, Domestic Violence, Sexual Abuse, Research on Interventions With Children and Families to Address Violence, and September 11th" (Boston University, 2017), she has contributed to even more areas in her actual work. DeVoe states that one of her favorite projects was working on a violence prevention project in the Bronx (E. DeVoe, personal communication, September 8, 2017). DeVoe has also been surprised at how much impact her studies on the September

11 attacks have had on her, and how she has ended up with more of a military and global focus after this event. Some of her more recent research has been with the military, such as a study on how to better assist returning veterans in reengaging with their children at home (DeVoe, Paris, Emmert-Aronson, Ross, & Acker, 2017; Ross & DeVoe, 2014).

DeVoe says that the most helpful advice she received from a mentor is that you, the individual, need to have your own life first, before you as the social worker. She stays busy with three children. DeVoe and her partner Don have two teenage boys and a 12-year-old daughter. The family enjoys outdoor activities together, and they all enjoy sports. DeVoe says that her first priority is being a mom (E. DeVoe, personal communication, September 8, 2017). One of DeVoe's favorite activities is mountain biking, although she does not have the opportunity to do this as much on the East Coast. The family travels to the mountains each summer to engage in nature. At home, DeVoe also enjoys nature through gardening. DeVoe suggests that social work students should be aware of how important self-awareness is. She also suggests that for clinical work, students do not always need to be so overly focused on having the client tell them his or her whole trauma story, and that trauma-informed care utilizing other interventions (such as sports and physical activity as interventions) and looking at structural violence is highly important. It is also helpful to be aware of how quickly our understanding of trauma and the brain is changing, and that our field will need to stay aware of these changes (E. DeVoe, personal communication, September 8, 2017).

NEUROSCIENCE: DR. JILL LITTRELL

Social work has always drawn from other disciplines to better inform our practice. Due to advances in technology, the field of neuroscience has grown tremendously in recent decades. Farmer defines neuroscience very simply as "the science of the brain or the science(s) of the nervous system(s)" (Farmer, 2009, p. 1). We now understand that the brain can be changed at the level of the neurons because of social and psychological factors (Montgomery, 2013) including the environment a child is brought up in and the levels of social support the individual receives throughout life. We know that the mind and body are very strongly connected. The changes in the brain due to social factors impact the body, including our physical health (Littrell, 2008). Knowledge of these systems and how much they impact our clients is so important that Farmer calls neuroscience the "missing link" for the field of mental health and social work (Farmer, 2009).

The brain is involved in shaping our behavior, thoughts, and emotions (Farmer, 2009). Trauma can have a particular impact on the body, brain, and our ability to function and have relationships with other people. Smaller amounts of stress or trauma may or may not change the brain, but moderate or significant amounts can impact memory by damaging the neurons (Applegate & Shapiro, 2005). Van der Kolk (2014) shares this in a very clear statement:

> If an organism is stuck in survival mode, its energies are focused on fighting off unseen enemies, which leaves no room for nurture, care, and love. For us humans, it means that as long as the mind is defending itself against invisible assaults, our closest bonds are threatened, along with our ability to imagine, plan, play, learn, and pay attention to other people's needs. (p. 76)

If the brain is stuck in survival mode, it is functioning on a level where we often cannot recognize what is actually happening around us. In addition, the body will actually store the traumatic memories as sensations in the body, not as linear memories (van der Kolk, 2014). The autonomic nervous system (ANS) in a healthy human is balanced to allow unconscious activities such as breathing to work together with conscious decisions like making a plan. When it has been disrupted, we begin to see the symptoms of what we have termed various mental health diagnoses in the *DSM-5*. Research is now showing us that for many of our common diagnoses, such as depression and anxiety, it is the combination of the genetic or biological factors and the environmental factors that ends up causing the symptoms that are developed (Littrell, 2015; Miehls, 2011). If a genetic or biological factor such as a particular gene that predisposes one to depression is present, and then a stressful situation is introduced into the environment, the diagnosis is more likely to become a reality for an individual (Littrell, 2015).

Although it is beyond the scope of this book to offer students a crash course in neuroscience, we do suggest that clients are able to rewire their brain to improve many of their areas of difficulty. We now know that the brain can reshape itself to be able to respond to new situations, and that this can happen not just in childhood, but throughout an adult's life. This ability to change is called plasticity (Miehls, 2011). This can be important for treatment. As Farmer states, "psychotherapy can change the brain, just as the brain can set the parameters of psychotherapy" (Farmer, 2009, p. 103). Both traditional talk therapy and somatic therapies such as yoga therapy and neurofeedback can bring about this change (Emerson, 2015; Montgomery, 2013; van der Kolk, 2014). Making physical life changes such as diet, exercise, and yoga can change the brain to lessen inflammation and bring about positive changes in mood and other disorders (J. Littrell, personal communication, July 27, 2017). We can also use the technology of neuroscience to improve the effectiveness of varying interventions or even select an intervention that better fits the individual. For example, new brain-imaging technology can be used to measure neural outcomes. The strength of the brain circuitry in the prefrontal cortex can show variation in how effective an intervention such as cognitive behavioral therapy could be for an adolescent in a drug prevention program (Matto & Strolin-Goltzman, 2010). Using this technology can allow us to develop specific treatment plans that will target the areas of brain circuitry that have a deficit or are overly utilized.

There are not many social workers who have ventured fully into the area of neuroscience. Dr. Jill Littrell is one of a handful who has. Dr. Littrell started her career in social work, although she was always very interested in science. After earning her PhD, she went back to school for a graduate degree in biology. She recently published the book *Neuroscience for Psychologists and Other Mental Health Professionals: Promoting Well-Being and Treating Mental Illness* (Littrell, 2015). Rather than focusing on neuroscience alone, the book covers the influence and interplay of the immune system on the brain and the larger nervous system. According to Littrell (personal communication), the broader story of how the immune system influences mood and behavior is very relevant for conditions such as psychosis, major depression, anxiety, and PTSD, where focusing on neuroscience alone yields a limited perspective. For devising interventions that social workers can provide, knowing the mechanism through which the immune system impacts mood and behavior along with how social workers can assist clients to optimize their immune function promises to yield more effective treatments.

Littrell was born in 1948. She grew up in Omaha, Nebraska, a very conservative part of the country. She states that they did not even have the *New York Times* there growing up! Her father, James, ran a heating and air conditioning business. Littrell says that one of the lessons she learned from her father was kindness (J. Littrell, personal communication, July

27, 2017). She has two brothers and a sister. As a child she was a book-worm, and liked everything except gym class.

Littrell says that in order to understand who she is, one should know how the times that she grew up in shaped her. She lived through the same years as the Clintons—she is from the same era. College was all about the civil rights movement, the women's movement, and the war in Vietnam. She thinks that is the reason why she is a social worker now, and that she was very much captured by the events of those times. One of her first jobs was cleaning rooms in a hotel, but after that in college she got a job at the state hospital. During that time she worked 40 hours a week in the hospital and was very involved with the patients, working a great deal with the adolescents. She says this was in the heyday of behavioral modifications such as running token economies, and that it was a lot of fun! She was also involved in demonstrations against the war and other forms of activism during college. She thinks this was a time when there was a lot of concern for civil rights, and this was very impor-tant for her and her friends.

In 1970, Littrell went to the University of Wisconsin at Madison for graduate school. The state hospital paid for her to attend to get her master's in social work. There continued to be a focus on demonstrations and civil rights, as this was a very active time period with a great deal of activism (which she contrasts with the time period now). She was inter-ested in neuroscience by this time, and as an elective took a course in physiological psychology (J. Littrell, personal communication, July 27, 2017). After completing her degree she returned to the state hospital, which primarily focused on clients with a diagnosis of schizophrenia. Littrell thinks it is really interesting how different the diagnoses are in the hospitals today versus in the 1960s and 1970s. At the time, you did not see depression or bipolar disorder. She says she only saw three peo-ple with bipolar disorder during the 7 years she worked at the state hos-pital, but now everyone gets these diagnoses due to the changes in the criteria in the *DSM*. She also ran a group home for delinquent kids in Omaha for a year before she moved to Phoenix, Arizona, after a divorce (J. Littrell, personal communication, July 27, 2017).

Littrell worked with Child Protective Services, both in ongoing care and investigation, when she first moved to Phoenix. She eventually returned to graduate school so that she could work on her PhD in clinical psychology at Arizona State University. Her dissertation mentor was Robert Cialdini, a major expert on persuasion and a best-selling author (J. Littrell, personal communication, July 27, 2017). She learned a lot about neurotransmitters, the use of medications, and the overall area of neuroscience in this program. She worked in the Drug and Alcohol department in the Veterans Administration and then at Cigna Health Plan working with addictions. She went on to publish two books on alcoholism based on these experiences. After leaving this position she did some private practice work as well as teaching part-time at Arizona State University, where she says she taught almost everything. She also took some classes in chemistry and immunology to learn more in the area of psychoneural immunology. Littrell was then offered a teaching position at Georgia State, and since her husband had retired, they were able to move to Georgia. She says Atlanta is a great place to learn about various areas of neuroscience due to some of the scientists who were working in the field and the free seminars she was able to attend to learn more about the field. After receiving tenure at Georgia State she applied to graduate school for a master's degree in biology—molecular genetics and biochemistry. She continued her research in areas relating to neuroscience, which she said she was and is able to do because the field is exploding (J. Littrell, personal communication, July 27, 2017). She hopes the world, including both mainstream medicine and social work, will catch up to the revolution in neuroscience, epigenetics, and psychoneuroimmunology, which includes the related area of the gut microbiome!

Littrell has now been married to her husband Gus for 40 years. She met him when he was her statistics teacher! Having a husband with that background was very helpful for research, especially quantitative analysis. After having written several books on using the statistical software SPSS, he now writes fiction books (J. Littrell, personal communication, July 27, 2017). They do not have kids, but Littrell is very involved with her brother Jordan's children, including helping them with their homework. Jordan works with the Centers for Disease Control and Prevention (CDC) and was in charge of the Ebola crisis, going to West Africa during the event. She says her brother, who is 16 years younger, is gay, which also had an influence on her. She states that she also continues to be a social activist, and spent time working on Hillary Clinton's campaign for the 2016 presidential election. Corruption in many areas—including finance, psychiatry, and medicine—continues to be very distressing and needs to be a focus for change. She helps out with an immunology lab of Yuan Liu, who is at Georgia State, and her husband, Ke Zen, who is in China, proofreading papers on topics that she might not have known about otherwise. She also enjoys yoga.

When asked what advice she would give social work students regarding neuroscience, Littrell thinks it is important because it provides a rationale for why diet, exercise, and yoga are important. She says that the drugs work less well than these other interventions, but she does not think anyone will be convinced of this unless they know the whole story. She says selective serotonin reuptake inhibitors (SSRIs) are a good example, as they are used to decrease depression. However, serotonin works on six different circuits in the brain, and one of them increases depression. Because of this, doctors do not really know how the drug will impact the person, and he or she can become suicidal instead of decreasing depression. Unfortunately, she knows multiple real-life examples of times this was the impact on the individual's brain, and some of the individuals did commit suicide after taking SSRIs. Taking a diet and exercise approach could avoid these negative impacts. Addictions are another area where information on neuroscience has something to contribute. After learning how drugs capture the brain's motivational system, students may appreciate that addiction is not about using drugs to feel good. (It is the wanting system, not the liking system.) The addicted person uses drugs because he or she has to. New parents get up in the middle of the night because they are hardwired to do so. If new parents acted on the principle of pleasure being required for inducing behavior, the human species would not have survived. The same system that compels new parents to get up in the middle of the night to feed their infant is the system that gets captured by addicting drugs. That is why addictions are so scary. The survival system, which is in all of us, gets diverted into serving a distorted purpose (Littrell, personal communication).

You will become a better social worker if you have an understanding of neuroscience, in particular the way the brain works and how interventions can impact or change the brain. Students should take some time during this or other classes, or outside of the educational system, to learn more about the interconnection between the brain and the body. As science and medicine continue to develop, we will have more information on how to work with clients who have been physically altered by their life situations. This is an exciting time to be a social worker!

LESSONS LEARNED

Our last CSWE competency is perhaps the widest known and most easily identifiable in social work practice. Competency 6 holds at its center the core of the work that we as social workers are engaged in. Although the work may look different now than in the earliest chapters of this book, engaging with people in a way that attempts to help them find solutions to their own issues has always been our calling. Both micro and macro works attempt to do this in their own unique ways. Read through the following competency and discuss how the individuals in this chapter express this competency. It reads:

Competency 6: Engage With Individuals, Families, Organizations, and Communities

Social workers understand that engagement is an ongoing component of the dynamic and interactive process of social work practice with, and on behalf of, diverse individuals, families, groups, organizations, and communities. Social workers value the importance of human relationships. Social workers understand theories of human behavior and the social environment, and critically evaluate and apply this knowledge to facilitate engagement with clients and constituencies, including individuals, families, groups, organizations, and communities. Social workers understand strategies to engage diverse clients and constituencies to advance practice effectiveness. Social workers understand how their personal experiences and affective reactions may impact their ability to effectively engage with diverse clients and constituencies. Social workers value principles of relationship building and interprofessional collaboration to facilitate engagement with clients, constituencies, and other professionals as appropriate. Social workers:

- Apply knowledge of human behavior and the social environment, Person in Environment, and other multidisciplinary theoretical frameworks to engage with clients and constituencies

- Use empathy, reflection, and interpersonal skills to effectively engage diverse clients and constituencies (CSWE, 2015, pp. 8–9)

Now that you have read this chapter and reviewed several individuals who have engaged in social work practice, discuss how you see each of them in this competency. Many of these people have moved into macro areas of practice. How does this competency apply in these areas?

CLASSROOM ACTIVITIES

1. Consider your experience in working with people who identify as part of the LGBTQ population. Do you think they are treated equally in comparison with other nonmajority groups? How is this population treated on your own campus? If you have an LGBTQ office or support center, consider going there and speaking with the staff and students to learn more.

2. Read through the NASW *Code of Ethics and Standards for Technology in Social Work Practice*. If you have already read them, do so again! What do you think are the key components of each? What might be the most difficult areas to achieve competency in? What areas of these are you not as familiar with as you should be?

3. How do you think the environment could impact your clients now and in the future? What do you think you as an individual could or should do about this? Are there inequities in the way the environment is utilized in our society?

4. Trauma undoubtedly impacts the individual who has experienced it. Learn about the Adverse Childhood Experiences study. Discuss the mental and physical health implications of this in class.

5. Take some time to research the brain. Consider making a brain model. What are the main components? What social work interventions might impact different parts of the brain? Discuss how neuroscience will be important for the future of social work.

REFERENCES

American Psychiatric Association. (2013). *Diagnostic and statistical manual of mental disorders* (5th ed.). Arlington, VA: American Psychiatric Publishing.

Applegate, J., & Shapiro, J. (2005). *Neurobiology for clinical social work: Theory and practice*. New York, NY: W. W. Norton.

Boston University. (2017). Ellen DeVoe, Professor. Retrieved from https://www .bu.edu/ssw/profile/ellen-devoe

Carlton-LaNey, I. (1997). Social workers as advocates for elders. In M. Reisch & E. Gambrill (Eds.), *Social work in the 21st century* (pp. 285–295). Thousand Oaks, CA: Pine Forge Press.

Council on Social Work Education. (2015). *2015 Educational policy and accreditation standards for baccalaureate and master's social work programs.* Alexandria, VA: Author.

Cummins, L., Byers, K., & Pedrick, L. (2011). *Policy practice or social workers: New strategies for a new era.* New York, NY: Allyn & Bacon.

DeVoe, E., Paris, R., Emmert-Aronson, B., Ross, A., & Acker, M. (2017). A randomized clinical trial of postdeployment parenting intervention for service members and their families with very young children. *Psychological Trauma: Theory, Research, Practice, and Policy, 9*(1), 25–34.

Dominelli, L. (2008). *Anti-racist social work* (3rd ed). New York, NY: Palgrave Macmillan.

Dominelli, L. (2010). *Social Work in a Globalizing World.* Boston, MA: Polity Press.

Dominelli, L. (2012). *Green social work: From environmental crises to environmental justice.* Malden, MA: Polity Press.

Dominelli, L. (2013). Professor Lena Dominelli: "I invented green social work" [Video file]. Retrieved from https://www.youtube.com/watch?v=rHABLdCVR8A

Dominelli, L. (2014). Promoting environmental justice through green social work practice: A key challenge for practitioners and educators. *International Social Work, 57*(4), 338–345. doi:10.1177/0020872814524968

Dominelli, L. (2015). Lena Dominelli, Durham University [Video file]. Retrieved from https://www.youtube.com/watch?v=_2h7cBKtECQ

Dominelli, L. (2017). Social Work challenges in the second decade of the 21st century. *Affilia, 32*(1), 105–107. doi:10.1177/0886109916681390.

Durham University. (n.d.). SASS staff: Professor Lena Dominelli. Retrieved from https://www.dur.ac.uk/sass/staff/profile/?id=3635

Emerson, D. (2015). *Trauma—Sensitive yoga in therapy: Bringing the body into treatment.* New York, NY: W. W. Norton.

Farmer, R. (2009). *Neuroscience and social work practice: The missing link.* Washington, DC: Sage.

Felitti, V., Anda, R., Nordenberg, D., Williamson, D., Spitz, A., Edwards, V., . . . Marks, J. (1998). Relationship of childhood abuse and household dysfunction to many of the leading causes of death in adults: The Adverse Childhood Experiences (ACES) study. *American Journal of Preventative Medicine, 14*(4), 245–258. doi:10.1016/ S0749-3797(98)00017-8

Ginsberg, L. (2005). The future of social work as a profession. *Advances in Social Work, 6*(1), 7–16. Retrieved from http://journals.iupui.edu/index.php/advancesin socialwork/article/view/71/62

Gray, M., & Coates, J. (2012). Environmental ethics for social work: Social work's responsibility to the non-human world. *International Journal of Social Welfare, 21*, 239–247. doi:10.1111/j.1468-2397.2011.00852.x

Guttmann, D. (2006). *Ethics in social work: A context of caring*. Binghamton, NY: The Haworth Press.

Jansson, B. (2012). *The reluctant welfare state: Engaging history to advance social work practice in contemporary society* (7th ed.). Belmont, CA: Cengage.

Levine, B., & Land, H. (2016). A meta- synthesis of qualitative findings about dance/movement therapy for individuals with trauma. *Qualitative Health Research, 26*(3), 330–344. doi:10.1177/1049732315589920

Littrell, J. (2008). The mind-body connection. *Social Work in Healthcare, 46*(4), 17–37. doi:10.1300/J010v46n04_02

Littrell, J. (2015). *Neuroscience for psychologists and other mental health professionals: Promoting well-being and treating mental illness*. New York, NY: Springer Publishing.

Matto, H., & Strolin-Goltzman, J. (2010). Integrating social neuroscience and social work: Innovations for advancing practice-based research. *Social Work, 55*(2), 147–156. doi:10.1093/sw/55.2.147

Mayadas, N., & Elliott, D. (1997). Lessons from international social work: Policy and practices. In M. Reisch & E. Gambrill (Eds.), *Social work in the 21st century* (pp. 175–185). Thousand Oaks, CA: Pine Forge Press.

Miehls, D. (2011). Neurobiology and clinical social work. In J. Brandell (Ed.), *Theory and practice in clinical social work* (2nd ed., pp. 81–98). Washington, DC: Sage.

Miller, S., Hayward, R., & Shaw, T. (2012). Environmental shifts for social work: A principles approach. *International Journal of Social Welfare, 21*, 270–277. doi:10.1111/j.1468-2397.2011.00848.x

Millstein, K. (2000). Confidentiality in direct social-work practice: Inevitable challenges and ethical dilemmas. *Families in Society, 81*(3), 270–282. doi:10.1606/1044-3894.1018

Montgomery, A. (2013). Toward the integration of neuroscience and clinical social work. *Journal of Social Work Practice, 27*(3), 333–339. doi:10.1080/02650533.2013.818947

Morrow, D., & Messinger, L. (Eds.). (2006). *Sexual orientation & gender expression in social work practice: Working with gay, lesbian, bisexual, & transgender people*. New York, NY: Columbia University Press.

National Association of Social Workers. (2006). Envionrmental Policy. Washington, D.C.: Author. Retrieved from https://www.socialworkers.org/assets/secured/documents/da/da2008/referred/Envir_mentalPolicy.pdf

National Association of Social Workers. (2015). Celebrating 55 years of the NASW *code of ethics*. Washington, DC: Author.

National Association of Social Workers. (2017a). *Code of ethics*. Retrieved from https://www.socialworkers.org/About/Ethics/Code-of-Ethics/Code-of-Ethics -English

National Association of Social Workers. (2017b). *NASW, ASWB, CSWE, & CSWA standards for technology in social work practice*. Washington, DC: Author.

National Association of Social Workers Foundation. (n.d.-a). *Frederic G. Reamer: International Rhoda G. Sarnat Award*. Washington, DC: Authors. Retrieved from http://www.naswfoundation.org/recognition/FredericReamerSarnat.asp

National Association of Social Workers Foundation. (n.d.-b). *NASW social work pioneers: Frederic Reamer*. Washington, DC: Authors. Retrieved from http://www.naswfoundation.org/pioneers/r/reamer_rick.html

O'Leary, P., Tsui, M., & Ruch, G. (2013). The boundaries of the social work relationship revisited: Towards a connective, inclusive, and dynamic conceptualization. *British Journal of Social Work, 43*, 135–153. doi:10.1093/bjsw/bcr181

Pugh, R. (2007). Dual relationships: Personal and professional boundaries in rural social work. *British Journal of Social Work, 37*, 1405–1423. doi:10.1093/bjsw/bcl088

Ramsay, S., & Boddy, J. (2017). Environmental social work: A concept analysis. *British Journal of Social Work, 47*, 68–86. doi:10.1093/bjsw/bcw078

Reamer, F. (1990). *Ethical dilemmas in social service* (2nd ed.). New York, NY: Columbia University Press.

Reamer, F. (1997). Ethical issues for social work practice. In M. Reisch & E. Gambrill (Eds.), *Social work in the 21st century* (pp. 340–349). Thousand Oaks, CA: Pine Forge Press.

Reamer, F. (2005). Documentation in social work: Evolving ethical and risk-management standards. *Social Work, 50*(4), 325–334. doi:10.1093/sw/50.4.325

Reamer, F. (2006). *Social work values and ethics* (3rd ed.). New York, NY: Columbia University Press.

Reamer, F. (2009). *The social work ethics casebook: Cases and commentary*. Washington, DC: NASW Press.

Reamer, F. (2012). *Boundary issues and dual relationships in the human services*. New York, NY: Columbia University Press.

Reamer, F. (2013). *Social work values and ethics* (4th ed.). New York, NY: Columbia University Press.

Reamer, F. (2014a). The evolution of social work ethics: Bearing witness. *Advances in Social Work, 15*(1), 163–181.

Reamer, F. (2014b). *Impaired social workers/professionals*. In *Encyclopedia of Social Work*. New York, NY: National Association of Social Workers and Oxford University Press. Retrieved from http://socialwork.oxfordre.com

Reamer, F. (2016). *The NASW code of ethics*. In *Encyclopedia of Social Work*. New York, NY: National Association of Social Workers and Oxford University Press. Retrieved from http://socialwork.oxfordre.com

Ross, A., & DeVoe, E. (2014). Engaging military parents in a home-based reintegration program: A consideration of strategies. *Health & Social Work, 39*(1), 47–54. doi:10.1093/hsw/hlu001

Rufener, B. (2014). *The 30 most influential social workers alive today*. Retrieved from http://www.socialworkdegreeguide.com/30-most-influential-social-workers-alive-today

Schmitz, C., Matyók, T., Sloan, L., & James, C. (2012). The relationship between social work and environmental sustainability: Implications for interdisciplinary practice. *International Journal of Social Welfare, 21,* 278–286. doi:10.1111/j.1468-2397.2011.00855.x

Shapiro, F., & Forrest, M. S. (2004). *Eye movement desensitization & reprocessing: The breakthrough "eye movement" therapy for overcoming anxiety, stress, and trauma.* New York, NY: Basic Books.

University of Chicago. (2005). Frederic Reamer, PhD '78: 2005 recipient of the Edith Abbott Award. From News and Notes. Retrieved from http://www.ssa.uchicago.edu/frederic-reamer

University of North Carolina Wilmington. (2015). We are UNCW: Telling our story, one Seahawk at a time. Retrieved from http://uncw.edu/profiles/messinger_lori.html

van der Kolk, B. (2014). *The body keeps the score: Brain, mind, and body in the healing of trauma.* New York, NY: Viking Press.

Index